THE COMPANY OF VIOLENT MEN

ADVANCE PRAISE FOR THE BOOK

'*The Company of Violent Men,* originally conceived as a journalism thesis in America, evolved into a compelling demonstration of exemplary journalistic practice and storytelling—a heart-pounding journey through the shadowy world of terrorists and Maoists on the Indian subcontinent. A "tranquil evening" in Dhaka shattered by an unexpected "bloodbath" ignites a relentless quest for answers that reads like a thriller. With each page, you'll find yourself deeper in a web of intrigue, danger and revelation, as Roy's fierce dedication to uncovering the truth keeps you reading'—John B. Judis, journalist and author

'A fascinating and free-flowing mix of reportage, memoir and meditations on investigative journalism, *The Company of Violent Men* is a gritty and granular exploration of faith, extremism and primordial loyalties. What sets this book apart is a singular and fiercely independent voice that privileges observation above everything else—Roy's refreshing approach is not weighed down by preconception, not tethered to political prejudice and not hewn, as many such works are today, from a predictable and deadening ideological bloc'—Mukund Padmanabhan, former editor, *The Hindu*

'Roy is that fearless journalist who risks not only interviewing the "violent men" (and women) of the title but telling the nuanced political and personal stories that drive militancy in South Asia as they are. If you've longed for a book explaining terrorism and conflict that goes beyond simplistic tropes of "good vs evil", start here'—Shannon Tiezzi, editor-in-chief, thediplomat.com

THE COMPANY OF VIOLENT MEN

Stories from the Bloody Fault Lines of the Subcontinent

SIDDHARTHYA ROY

EBURY PRESS
An imprint of Penguin Random House

EBURY PRESS

Ebury Press is an imprint of the Penguin Random House group of companies whose addresses can be found at global.penguinrandomhouse.com

Published by Penguin Random House India Pvt. Ltd
4th Floor, Capital Tower 1, MG Road,
Gurugram 122 002, Haryana, India

Penguin Random House India

First published in Ebury Press by Penguin Random House India 2024

10 9 8 7 6 5 4 3 2 1

ISBN 9780670095131

Typeset in Sabon by MAP Systems, Bengaluru, India
Printed at Thomson Press India Ltd, New Delhi

www.penguin.co.in

To Brother Mohib.
You stared in the face of a depraved genocide and faced the cowards' bullets and yet defiantly dreamt of fathering peace.

Contents

Preface

'Yes. Educate, Organize, Agitate is what I said. But I never said it would be easy,' Babasaheb said to me, sitting in the corner of the Lehman Library at Columbia University.

I was pretty miffed with him that night. Especially given how the slanting beam from the ceiling light gave him a one-sided smirk.

A snowstorm had frozen New York City that night and my journalism programme director had frozen half my thesis grant. She told the grant-giving committee that she didn't 'believe' I'd do a good job. And my thesis adviser meekly submitted to the director's diktat, choosing his job security over defending me and my proposal.

But I had gone to Bangladesh nevertheless. On borrowed money.

As a result, now I was down to my last few dollars. Cold, hungry and sitting around in heated libraries working on my report and looking around. Looking around for some better-off student or teacher who might leave an unfinished coffee or some uneaten scraps in a salad bowl.

And here he was, my Baba, the man who had shown me the way into journalism, playing riddles.

'You're too lost in the reeds of Bangladesh's swamps [to tell a newsworthy story],' was my adviser's remark, curt and short, on seeing the first draft. As a politics teacher, he wanted a tight, stiff shot of terrorists versus the State. The kind I was being trained to write. Instead, I'd brought in a long drink of the muddied political waters of the Padma.

To be fair, he wasn't alone. American news has neither the patience nor the need to listen to so much nuance about a country they can barely place on the map. And I was given a very small grant and an even smaller brief. Fly to Dhaka. Investigate what happened at the Holey Artisan Bakery. Profile the Islamic State terrorists involved. And return.

Instead, I'd reported way more than Holey Artisan and written way beyond the patience of American news headlines.

'So what do you think I should do, eh?' I asked Baba.

'I don't know. Write a blog, maybe? Someone somewhere will read it, I'm sure,' he replied.

'And what about all the money I spent reporting? I'm already eating supermarket leftovers and drinking free samples of soup to keep the damned cold and hunger out of me!' I protested.

Baba didn't respond. He was, after all, just a bust, and this conversation was one of the many imagined ones I often had with him.

Thankfully, I didn't have to blog it out. I didn't even have a blog.

Anthony Bourdain and his team at Roads & Kingdoms published material which had been rejected by the adviser and the director as an article called 'Cricket in the Caliphate'. They even made it the featured piece in their newsletter.

The article was very well received; it got me a job and a grant from the Pulitzer Center and, ironically enough, went on the Journalism School's website as a featured student work.

A longer version of that article is where this book starts; it goes on to other, though very similar, things.

Since this book is a bit like a memoir, I must give a little background on how I came to be the kind of journalist I am.

I went to Columbia in the middle of my journalism career to get a very expensive stamped paper that said I was a legitimate journalist. I did this on the advice of some veterans of Indian journalism—well-meaning editors with whom I had worked. The advice was given when I asked them how I could lose the 'new entrant' tag, despite five years of work, and be accepted into the ranks of 'real' journalists.

Now, I come from the generation that was in primary school when the world's first direct-to-TV war happened. Iraq One under George Bush in 1990. Then came Iraq Two and Afghanistan under his son, George W. Bush. And from that point on, neither America's wars nor their casting of war news to screens near us has stopped.

Regimes have changed, nation states have altered both in geographies and in relevance, the Internet has gone from challenging the system to enforcing it and the dream of a global village has turned into the nightmare of a murderous lynch mob of village idiots. But those war reporters who made their way into our living rooms have stayed.

The bulletproof vest-wearing, mic-holding white men and women on the warfront, parleying with their sharp-suited studio colleagues who appeared in our living rooms in the 1990s never left. They have remained the stereotype of what a 'real' journalist looks like. And I tried to become that stereotype.

I've kind of failed at that. And not merely for the lack of a bulletproof vest.

Despite having earned my living solely as a professional journalist for the past decade and a half, and that too primarily for American publications reporting politics and conflict, I am, at best, an itinerant journalist—an outsider to the ranks of real journalists. This is partly because of who I am but mostly because of how the business of news is conducted.

After all these years of being in and out of newsrooms, I see two things quite clearly on both sides of the editorial desk.

One is that when it comes to the business of news, neither are news corporations pious purveyors of absolute truths nor should the job of keeping a journal be called an *ism*.

And two, the understanding and telling of truths takes time. Something 24x7 news cycles—both mainstream and social—don't have.

What news consumers consume are headlines and sound bites. Daily news serves nothing more. It's all just a never-ending series of big breaking stories about new wars, bombs and acts of political violence. And even then, the stories are woven along predetermined partisan lines catered to fit ever shrinking attention spans.

Then again, being a reporter has let me travel to places far beyond tourist maps and travel advisories and into conflict zones I'd never have managed to reach if not for a piece of plastic that had a photo of me and PRESS printed on it in large letters.

I've walked into the lives and minds of people very different from myself and seen glimpses of things hardly different from me. People connected to some recognizable and violent newsworthy event in the recent past. Some are victims, others are perpetrators, but most are people between these extremes. And their stories had no place in the reports I was writing.

That's why this book.

To tell the story of what I heard after the news crews left. To share what I saw when I looked beyond the burqa and the beard, beyond the olive-green of one fighter and the camo fatigue of the other, and to talk to the humans who wear these facades.

What this book does is put together my reported notes that didn't make it to the final edits of the articles I wrote.

Spanning five years—2016 to 2023—the events and interactions in this book are spread out across Germany,

India and Bangladesh. Though I did go to other countries in search of violent men, spent time in their company and recorded their stories, I have little to tell from them beyond what I've reported.

About the name of this book, *The Company of Violent Men* wasn't the first choice. For the longest time in my head, it was called 'The Rejects'—meaning that which was rejected from my stories at the edit table. But by the time I finished the draft, I realized I was giving in to vanity by calling them *my stories*.

Sure, I tell the stories from my point of view, and there are snippets of my life in them. But the lives and actions of these men and women I talk about would've taken the same trajectory even if I hadn't reported about them. My own story, however, is now indelibly coloured by theirs.

In this book, you'll meet some militants and refugees, clandestine agents and insurgents, reporters and wheeler-dealers—some extraordinary and some very ordinary individuals caught in circumstances that news headlines, including those of my own stories, have flattened into convenient tropes of good and evil and us and them.

Among other things, this book is an attempt to un-trope them. Bring them back to life as real, living, breathing humans. Engaged as they are in the making, containing or narrating of large-scale, world-changing and violent activities, they are humans nevertheless.

These violent men and women I speak of, some of them fight for faith, others fight for power. Many fight just to belong. But peel away the burqa or the badge, scratch the skin of a military officer or a mercenary, and the fears and failings that lie beneath are not so foreign from yours or mine.

This book hasn't been written to either exonerate the perpetrators or gloss over the injustices done to the victims by giving their characters larger canvases—but to highlight the basic human fragility we share with them.

A word of caution to the reader: These are unfiltered dispatches. Unlike my news reports, I've held nothing back except for the names of men whose lives may be endangered by the writing of this book and women who are victims of sexual assault.

Not everything is pretty or polite.

Moreover, if you have chosen an ideological side for yourself in any one of the conflicts I've referenced, you might not find me saying things you'd want to hear. These dispatches simply share what I witnessed first-hand through my imperfect eyes. Eyes seeking not so much to judge but to understand.

I offer nothing but my version of the stories. I offer no guarantees that my version will agree with yours and will take no umbrage at others giving their versions. But I do hope these stories make you see beyond the extremes that news wants you to see. The way I saw these people when breaking bread with them, sharing a cigarette or simply walking alongside without the constraints of the interviewer–interviewee protocol.

In short, this is my attempt to put on record the sense of lives lived under extremes—to see past stereotypes for better or worse. We are all, I still daresay, fellow voyagers on the same turbulent waters, just trying to stay afloat. That is the simple truth this book tries to share.

So, to end where I started, I say: Yes, I was lost in the reeds of Bangladesh in 2016 and 2017. And I have continued, very often and very willingly, being lost in the reeds of other places. In this book, I collect some of those rejected reeds, weave a basket out of them and put in some untold stories I've been meaning to tell for a while.

A Gonzo in the Fog

'Beautiful.'

The word just slipped out—I hadn't meant to say it. I felt embarrassed having said it. That fog smothered wetland and the stories of the place Afzal had been telling me, the word should've been deathly, not beautiful.

It was quarter past sunrise time and the compass in my phone said I was facing East. But there, at the edge of that vast wetland—which Afzal and his people call the *beel*—there was no sun I could see in the sky. I saw no sky either. The silver-grey slush of cold mud flowed into a vast, shallow sea of still, turbid waters. And the waters merged into the fog-shrouded skies. The world was a cold, wet continuum in greyscale.

A little embarrassed, I turned my head to check Afzal's reaction. But my swarthy, stick-thin guide showed no signs of having heard me. Like me, he too was staring into the haze. Little puffs of steam escaped through the scarf covering his nose and mouth, before curling up around his ears and head.

'The beel is as dangerous as it is beautiful,' Afzal muttered, after a long time.

The next moment, he stood up and walked to the edge where the last bits of hard earth ended, and the slush of sinking mud began and, sweeping his rough, cracked finger across an imagined horizon, said, 'They'd come from there. First the pirates, later the dacoits and then the Maoists. They would run amok in the village—looting homes and beating people. They didn't really have much to loot, so they'd make off with the paddy harvest or maybe someone's chickens and goats. When the police came, they'd disappear into the beel. It's always been like that.'

'Did Bangla Bhai hide in the beel, too?' I asked.

'He didn't have to hide from anyone—least of all the police. Come on. The visitors will be assembling soon.'

Pulling his headscarf tighter and back up to his nose, without waiting for me, Afzal began walking back to the village with long, flamingo-like strides on the porridge-like earth. I scrambled in pursuit before my guide disappeared into the greyness.

I'd read of these floodplains—the beels—and their stories. Tagore waxed eloquent about them in his *Glimpses of Bengal*, writing to his muse from a boat that floated around Bengal through his vast family estate. In fact, until I read Tagore, I thought the oft used khaal-beel was just a repetitive compound. Khaal-beels flood when the rains come in. Khaal was a stream or canal, I knew. And beel, I assumed, meant the same thing.

But Tagore told me, no—beels are shallow flooded fields.

I'd read ghost stories, too. About fish-loving phantoms who thronged these wetlands, annoying and scaring lost humans for kicks, if not devouring them.

There, that cold January morning, it was stories of some demons that had brought me to the edge of the vast beel in Bagmara village of Rajshahi in Bangladesh. Only, the villains in this story weren't imagined creatures of lore and myth but real humans who had killed and tortured far more men and women than ghosts ever have.

My journey didn't begin in Bagmara, though. It had begun five months ago in Dhaka at the Holey Artisan Bakery. The bakery was the site of a terrible hostage crisis and night-long carnage where diners and staff were slaughtered one by one, until the paramilitary came in the next morning and killed the hostage takers.

Like the German Bakery in Pune and Café Leopold in Mumbai, the Holey Artisan Bakery in Dhaka seems—now in hindsight—like an obvious place for attention seeking Islamists to attack.

Nestled in the heart of the diplomatic enclave, beside the long, green Gulshan Lake that flows like a river through the heart of Bangladesh's capital, Holey had sat like an Elysium of quiet and verdant opulence in a city overridden with the pandemonium of dusty poverty. It served Western fare at big-ticket prices. A meal there cost what the majority of Dhaka's residents earned in a week. And thereby, it became a haunt for the city's crème de la crème—diplomats, NGO honchos, mandarins of the charitable–industrial complex of the West and such others who needed a break from the poverty they worked tirelessly to alleviate.

Islamists called it a 'den of vice' and planned their assault.

What had begun as an idyllic dinner on the balmy evening of 1 July 2016 ended in a bloodbath in the wee hours of the following day, leaving twenty-two people dead.

Even before the smoke and dust had settled, the Islamic State claimed responsibility via their online mouthpiece, the Amaq. Releasing pictures of six young men in their twenties posing with the Islamic State's black flag, the emir—meaning commander or ruler—for the Bengal region, Shayk Abu Ibrahim Al Hanif, hailed them as martyrs to the holy cause of building the Caliphate.

From 2 July onwards, headlines around the world shrieked. American and Bangladeshi news companies made common cause and called the Holey Artisan attack Bangladesh's 9/11. Pundits spouted wisdom on prime time and the Internet explained, with a coroner's precision, what had happened and why. Heads of states sent in their solidarity messages, and Islamophobes rent the cyber realm with cries of 'Enough is enough!'

In Bangladesh itself, mainstream Islamist parties gave mealy-mouthed responses, and the ruling Sheikh Hasina government swore vengeance. She doubled down on her recent decision to reopen the war crimes tribunal and put to death Islamists who had supported Pakistan in the 1971 Liberation War.

Before the week had ended, everyone outside Dhaka and those not personally affected by the incident had forgotten about it.

As horrible as the carnage had been, it was, after all, just another terrorist attack in a world that was burning every day, every moment. An attack on a touristy landmark by a global jihadist organization, hysterical headlines, expressions of condemnation by the West, subsequent curbs on democracy and civil rights: it was all the same. These were things everyone had grown accustomed to since the real 9/11, George W. Bush's War on Terror and his fatwa stating either you were with the American State or you were a terrorist.

For me, though, the Holey attack was different. In a selfish sort of way.

I was then, at the ripe age of thirty-five, returning to college at Columbia University's Journalism School in New York City.

Having given up my day job of being a coder, I'd become a struggling journalist some five-odd years before, and my disapproving family a year before I left for New York. And there I was gearing up to buy myself a stamp of approval from the best journalism school brand on earth.

This would, I imagined, be my ticket to joining the hallowed ranks of foreign correspondents who put on bulletproof vests and hard helmets and gave briefs to cameras as bullets and bombs streaked in the background.

When Holey Artisan happened, it was still all about the Middle East in New York's posh foreign journalist cliques.

Every newsroom and leading journalist had someone who knew Arabic, and analyses of why X had happened in Karbala or Y in Kandahar were churned out almost before the Xs and Ys had happened. Bush's pre-emptive war had birthed and embedded pre-emptive war analysis in its wide eagle wings. But neither were Bangla speakers in demand nor did Bangladesh exist on their political map. Arabic, not Bangla, was still the lingua franca for professional jihad watchers.

The Islamic State opening a new theatre in a country, not in the Middle East, was a shocker for these pundits. Nobody from the multitudes of American non-Muslim experts of Islamic politics and history had any inkling that a Holey Artisan-like episode was even possible.

But that was hardly surprising to a Bengali like me.

During my many conversations about armed and extreme Islamism, I saw how Americans had completely forgotten the role their country played in arming Bangladesh's occupier, Pakistan, when the former sought freedom from the latter. How, using the fig leaf of international cooperation and global security, they had directly sponsored the killing of millions of Bengalis. And thereafter, under the guise of supporting Islamic cultural studies, how the American State had doled out aid to pro-Pakistan, fundamentalist clerics in Bangladesh, thereby ensuring extremist political Islam never died.

Present-day Americans have no memory of the fissures their country had left behind after the 1971 Liberation War. A war in which the seculars won but the fundamentalists didn't lose. They knew nothing of how Bangladesh had exported cheap ideological labour for their previous Afghan war when they were arming the Afghan mujahideen against the Soviets.

But I came from a family that had not only known but lived, died and suffered under this history. I had grown up hearing stories of the men of my family being lined up in front of firing squads and the women being raped by the

Pakistan Army. *And* that all of this was done by Islamists armed with American dollars and guns. I had read books and newspaper archives that held up in gory detail what had befallen Bangladesh and the Bengali language in the name of Muslim identity and Islamic jihad.

So, on 1 August 2016, armed with my mother tongue, the aforementioned personal history and some Python scripts that scraped the Internet for chatter around relevant keywords, I began my own personal investigation into Holey Artisan—what happened before and what was happening after.

It must be made clear that though I am of Bengali descent, I have grown up in Pune, amidst Marathis. While fluent in Bengali, I had never really spoken the language to anyone outside my immediate family. The Western part of Bengal, on the Indian side, where my parents were born, was a place I was unwillingly dragged to every summer for vacations. The East, in what used to be Pakistan, was a place I knew of through books and stories. Through school and college, comrades and crushes, I never became very Bengali or any less Marathi.

But there in New York, in the days spent sitting in a building they had named after Joseph Pulitzer, grouping, sorting and reading the patterns of data my scripts had scraped, with nights in the Bengali section of the library they called the Butler Library. Poring over newspaper archives from the Liberation War, conducting my own personal investigation, I became obsessed with being Bengali—with becoming a narrator of how Holey Artisan very much was, but also wasn't merely, a subset of West vs Islamic State.

I was convinced I was seeing patterns others had missed. Convinced that of all people, it was I who would explain why Tamem Chowdhary, the leader of the Islamic State in Bengal, did what he did. Like me, he too was a Bengali child of the Liberation War, only one generation down. He too had grown up in Canada—a land no less foreign than Maharashtra, where

Bengaliness and the history of the Liberation War were alive inside the walls of a nuclear family. Like me, he too had his side chosen by the stories of his family. His side was the Islamic version of Bangladesh, and mine was the Bengali version.

The only insignificant difference was that his side had barely lost in 1971, while mine had not really won.

The very first piece of homework I submitted to my J-School professor Alexander Stille—an assignment called 'Profiling a Nation State'—took Holey Artisan as the cue for talking about the birth of Bangladesh and the evolution of its national identity. Bangladesh, I asserted, was one of the first and few post-1960s countries that reaffirmed the root word of *nation* as *nativity* by choosing its linguistic identity over its religious one. The master's thesis proposal I gave to the course director, Tali Woodward, was a re-investigation of Holey Artisan, picking up the pieces from where the headlines had given up.

And that's when reality hit.

The problem with the reports we are dying to write is akin to the descriptions of lovers our heart yearns for. From being mesmerizing silhouettes in the moonlight of our imaginations, they often turn to unremarkable cut-outs in the daylight of reality.

While Stille had been on the kinder side of ho-hum about my assignment, Woodward straight out blocked half my thesis money even after the decision-making committee on grants had sanctioned the funds. She said she didn't think I had a story worth telling.

Of course, Woodward's open dislike for me had much to do with this blockage. For one, I'd refused to be an unquestioning pro-Hillary, anti-Trump junkie in the run-up to the 2016 American elections. Then there was my pesky eagerness to point out American imperialism's role in birthing the very demons they claimed to be fighting from Iraq to

Syria. Worst of all, I had a habit of saying that the alleged Russian interference in American domestic politics, which they kept asking everyone to join in outraging against, was exactly what America had been openly and proudly doing for decades.

Woodward, as head of the MA programme, was busy crafting a pro-Hillary coterie. And she didn't like dissent. Not one bit. So yes, I was asking for it.

But I'd been a professional journalist for five years before Woodward had any say in what I wrote. And I knew her point about me not having a story to tell—or at least a story that befits a news report—had some merit.

Nobody can stop one from making a personal blog post filled with rants fuelled by nothing but their obsession, passion and emotion. But an editor who runs a news outlet has both a right and a duty to ask for the facts and quotes and a well-formed story with characters, quotes and solid reporting.

I did have something to start with, though. The three-odd months of my investigation—September, October and November of 2016—generated a lot of scraped data and historical references. But I needed to get to Dhaka. No amount of data would replace actual ground reporting. With my thesis grant blocked, I was running short on the ticket and stay costs.

So I borrowed from friends and family, promising to return their dues once the story was written. By then, I'd hustled for many years and was confident I'd have enough content to sell and pay them back.

But then other hurdles popped up.

In the first week of December, I started working on a long list of people I was going to interview. Direct participants in the terror vs counter-terror ops, ideological participants, those in circles of power and influence who had insights beyond the reach of a Google search. Most importantly, those in politics who were likely to either benefit or be adversely affected by everything that had happened post-Holey Artisan.

By the time I landed in Dhaka in the last week of December, the list had come down from well over forty to under twenty. Those in government gave nothing more than canned responses, and those in politics doled out partisan rhetoric. Besides, a lot of rejections happened because I didn't have an email address that ended in the name of a famous news corporation. I was, at best, a freelancing low life whose portfolio of work was attached at the end of the email body and, at worst, a bloke punching way above his weight from a student email ID.

Some journalism clubs offered me paid accreditation to overcome this hurdle. But I couldn't part with the twenty dollars these clubs were asking for. I chose food over the accredited vanity.

What I had working for me was leads that were exclusive to me, generated through my open-source investigations. Leads which even the *New York Times*, *Washington Posts*, and *Al Jazeeras* of the world didn't have. Since there was no way to be an accredited journalist,

I would follow those leads and be a gonzo reporter.

The Secret Garden

'Mr Roy, you've booked for two days. Is that how long you will be staying?' the greying White landlady of the room I'd rented on Lichu Bagan Road asked. Without waiting for an answer, she added, 'No discounts on extensions will be given. No guests. No drinking or smoking. Breakfast will be two slices of bread with butter, one egg and a cup of tea or coffee if you want Western, or *parota–torkari* from the eatery downstairs if you want Bengali. Rest of the meals, you have to eat out or order in from the two eateries downstairs. And you are to use only the common toilet.'

Her tone suited her persona. The aged spinster had set up a Christian congregation in the heartlands of Bangladesh; she also ran an orphanage. She had spent many years taking in poor kids and feeding them two square meals a day with a side of Bible and baptism.

Just like a member of the orphaned flock she tended, I nodded dutifully and accepted everything the austere Christian evangelist said. After all, no matter what the condition of the place or the conditions laid down, Lichu Bagan Road is where I would have to stay. Sure, it wasn't the Taj Mahal Hotel. But with a bed and a washroom, the place perfectly suited my needs and the depth of my wallet.

The happy happenstance was the lifting of the ecclesiastic dourness within an hour of my checking in. After she read out the house rules, my landlady said she was leaving town until the turn of the year for her annual religious retreat in the countryside. She left one of the grown-up orphans she'd brought in from her menagerie to run the place in her absence.

'Allwyn,' the dark, shy young man smiled and said his name after Madame High Priest left to save some more souls and tend to her flock.

I extended my hand and introduced myself in Bangla, '*Ami Siddhartho . . . Siddhartho Raay.*' 'Erm . . . so Allwyn, I'm really craving some good coffee and a smoke,' I said. 'Will you show me around? We could go to a good coffee shop and get some real coffee instead of the boring Nescafé.'

Allwyn grinned and, with barely a moment's pause, said, 'Let me change my shirt.'

'Google Maps doesn't work here, *bhaiya,*' Allwyn said when he saw me looking at my phone as we walked. 'Besides, I know this place better than Google!'

We were making our way through one of the many unkempt alleys that lined the potholed main Lichu Bagan Road.

'But you won't always be around, no?' I replied, grinning and putting my phone in my pocket. 'What will I do when you aren't with me and I have to find the coffee shop?'

Lichu Bagan Road does no justice to its English translation, Lychee Garden. Far from being a sylvan street that runs by an orchard of lychees, the area is a messy middle- and working-class neighbourhood typical to nations in the subcontinent I call home. It is so nondescript, several well off residents of Dhaka I met over the next few days were perplexed as to where this place was—they'd never heard of it. A gent even joked about how I had clearly found myself a rather 'secret garden'.

What my landlady, sweet Allwyn and the Dhaka bourgeois didn't know was that, for me, Lichu Bagan did in fact hold a promising secret fruit I was after—a small under-construction, bare-bricked two-storeyed house converted to a mosque.

A location that had an Internet connection whose IP address had figured prominently in my investigations.

Back in 2016, it was still possible to figure out the location of a post on any of the popular social media platforms with just a few lines of Python. In countries like Bangladesh, where internet connections are very slow, people hardly ever use VPNs. This made geolocating and mapping of posts fairly accurate. This nameless unfinished mosque had appeared time and again on those maps.

The scraping scripts I had been running for several months were programmed to look for certain keywords in posts being made by anonymous handles raging against the Bangladeshi government's actions against Islamists. Using geolocation of those posts and some specially crafted links in comments I made on those posts, the scripts would mark points on a map where the keywords clustered and keep daily versions of a map for me to read.

Something about the mosque seemed to be attracting those who were convinced that Bangladeshi Prime Minister Sheikh Hasina was a satanic infidel incarnate and that bringing her government down was a holy task every true Muslim in the country needed to undertake without any delay.

'What are you here for, bhaiya?' Allwyn asked, sucking loudly at the last dribbles of his cold coffee at the crummy little coffee shop he'd chosen for us.

He had been constantly chattering since we'd stepped out, and I had all but tuned him out after a few minutes. I wasn't being rude to the boy. It's just that we had passed the mosque in question on our way, and I was trying to save its location. The poor mobile internet kept drifting my location marker all over the screen, and I was muttering swear words at it, trying to stabilize the drift.

'I'm writing a thesis for my college,' I replied, putting my phone away. For good this time.

'Report, you know . . . like homework?' I added, since Allwyn didn't register the word 'thesis'.

He grunted a 'hmm', indicating either that he understood or didn't care. Tossing the plastic cold coffee glass into the trash can with perfect aim, he changed the topic.

'Where will you be going from Dhaka?'

'Do you like cricket?'

'You know there's this really nice shop that sells export reject clothes . . .'

Allwyn kept talking on our way back as I made mental To-Do notes. I liked him. Besides his lovely smile, his friendliness and a younger-sibling vibe, he was safe company to keep. Despite his questions, he wasn't looking to get answers or learn anything about me—he was always giving information.

Days of Piety, Nights of Sin

I don't quite remember if it was on the first or the second day of my stay at the Lichu Bagan apartment that I woke up on a Friday morning to two voices singing in the streets below. Still not fully awake—'Allwyn *chaa* . . .' I called out and rushed to the tiny balcony to see whose grand, soulful voices they were.

'Do they come here often?' I asked Allwyn, who promptly brought me a cup of tea and an ashtray. I pointed at the two cripples dragging themselves in the dirt of the street below, singing to the city people to rise to the glory of Allah. One sang baritone, the other tenor. The two distinct pitches rose and fell in sync with each other like the big and small waves that lap at the Padma's shores. There on the dirty, potholed Lichu Bagan road, these men were a moving, vivid symphony that needed no instruments.

A small digression about this kind of music, poetry and political Islam is due here. Not something new or unknown by any means. Yet something that I've felt strongly since long before I became a journalist.

Whenever I've found myself in the rut of that tired old question about whether or not Islam is a religion of peace, I've chosen to stay quiet. For, since very early in my life, I've seen that in the cacophony of moderates and extremists, haters and apologists, nobody is willing to listen to me say, 'There *is* no religion of peace or violence. For that matter, there is hardly a religion of anything. It is entirely what a religionist brings to the table and dishes out in the name of his or her belief.'

People often conflate my journalism and scholarship of Islamist extremism as some personal Islamophobia.

A German reporter had once irritably told me, 'But you, of all people, know how much damage these Muslims cause! In your own country! Are you going to pretend that Islam isn't a problem?'

She didn't have much of a career in Germany and had found her fortune in India telling stories of this and that Hindu guru and godman. Her work found patronage from the Indian Hindu Right Wing, and she started getting long-stay visas for India to do her reporting where other critical voices were struggling to get theirs. Soon, what had started as her personal religious exploration with a side of flaky reporting turned into a celebration of political Hinduism and a shaming of political Islam.

When she met me and learnt about my work, she very enthusiastically and wrongly assumed that like her, I too was pro-Hindu and anti-Muslim.

'If you are parroting the lines you have learnt from Indian internet warriors, I'd say please look up real history books,' I'd replied, with little attempt to hide the irritation that had been building up after an hour of talking to her. 'There is no India without Islam, just like there isn't one without Hinduism, Buddhism, Sikhism, Jainism, atheism and every other major ism you can think of. Every bit of what we call India or Indian culture is seeped with these different colours. Political denial or partisan lies aren't going to rub those colours off.

'So don't ask me to be an absolutist and say Islam is good or bad. Tell me whose Islam we're talking about. If it's Osama Bin Laden's, then it's bad. If it's Ghalib's, bring it on! As for the destruction of people and culture and carrying out of genocides, you, as a German, should know it can be done with extreme efficiency without any Islam.'

The reference to Ghalib was lost on her. The reference to Nazis wasn't. She walked off paying for her beer, and not mine, even though she had asked me out that evening in Bonn.

So no, I do not have an answer to whether Islam is a religion of peace. However, what I've said many times to myself is, 'Islam most certainly is a religion of music.' At least here in the Indian subcontinent. And if I was ever willing to die for Islam and the greater glory of Allah, I'm quite certain it wouldn't be from the passions ignited by the fiery speeches of hate-filled mullahs. It would be for the songs of fakirs who taught me to love Him like the greatest love there can be.

'Come, come . . .' I rushed Allwyn. 'Let's go buy them some breakfast.'

Allwyn looked a little incredulous but played along. By now, he knew I wasn't the 'normal' type. Besides, with his landlady away for what she said was charity work and what I suspected was some New Year's Eve shindig she did with her lot, we had broken a lot of norms in that apartment.

'*Ekhon na korta*,' the baritone cripple refused my offer of chaa and breakfast while taking the taka I gave him. And explained the 'Not now, mister' stating it was Friday morning—their most important hour of collecting alms.

Friday is Bangladesh's official weekend. On this one day when quotidian drudgery takes a break, menfolk of Dhaka come out to buy their vegetables, fish and meat at the weekly morning markets. Clusters of chaa, cigarette and gossip form at the roadside stalls. Hearts get kinder, thoughts merrier and alms more generous. So yes, the men were right to stick to business that morning and not waste it having breakfast with me.

'But why don't you come to the mosque for jumma?' chimed in the tenor cripple.

'Which mosque?' I asked—my heartbeat picking up pace.

'Right that way.' He pointed in exactly the direction I had hoped he would. 'We'll be there. You'll meet many good Muslims like you!'

My voice climbed several notes of eagerness as I happily took up their offer, my hand yanking Allwyn's just in time to stop him from eagerly intervening and enlightening the singing cripples about my religious identity.

'Oh, so you are a Hindu!' Allwyn had remarked when we'd met for the first time. My name was enough for him to know. And then he'd added, 'I used to be a Muslim, you know. Meaning I was born to Muslim parents. But they died when I was four or five. My uncle kept me for a while but then gave me away to Madam's [the landlady's] orphanage. I became a Christian there.'

'Do you remember your parents?' I'd asked.

'Not really. I can't recall their faces very well.'

'What about your Muslim name? Do you have one?'

'That I do . . . but I don't care to use it any more. I like being Allwyn. I like being Christian. My uncle would beat me for every little thing. He was such a big man, and I was so small, yet he'd hit me with full strength. And my aunt wouldn't feed me. If I complained, she would give me a few blows and call me names.

'Once, just before Eid, I was upset and crying about not getting any new clothes while my uncle had bought many for his children. He got angry and hit me. He punched and slapped me so hard that I fell unconscious, and my ears started bleeding. I was taken to a clinic nearby where, seeing my condition, the doctor threatened to call the police on my uncle and aunt. That's when they gave me up for adoption at Madam's orphanage.

'So I don't care to be Muslim any more. It was Christians who brought me up and gave me a home after all.'

That was the last of our conversations about religious identity. Allwyn always had a lot of other things—food, mainly—to discuss. Even on that Friday morning when

I urgently stopped him from disclosing my religious identity to the cripples and hurriedly turned him around with a firm hand on his shoulder—food had come to the rescue.

'How about some *bhuna* (slow-cooked) spicy beef for lunch? Friday should be a good day, right?' I asked him. 'Let's quickly shower and head out for some clothes shopping and a good lunch afterwards. What say?'

On purpose, I reached the mosque well after the formal *jummah* congregation had given way to the informal *chaa* drinking clusters. I'd gone alone, sending Allwyn away post-lunch.

Prayers at small mosques are very close-knit community affairs. And this one was obviously going to be an even smaller congregation. So even without Allwyn's proclamations, and despite my beard styling and a few rote-learned phrases from the Koran, I'd be caught out as an impostor easily. Needless to say, losing my cover could not only end my investigations for good but could, in fact, end me.

At that time, Dhaka was simmering with Islamist vs secular sentiments. The memories of another Roy, who was beheaded in full public view, were still fresh. I had to tread cautiously.

'*Arey . . . ashen ashen*,' the cripples recognized me and welcomed me. 'Shadab *bhai* . . . meet . . .'

'*Ami* Yasin Ahmed Bappa,' I said, shaking hands with a stocky young man the cripples introduced me to. He had a skullcap and a full face of unruly beard and was clearly the alpha of the cluster. My name had been made up on the spot—Yasin and Ahmed are regular Muslim names and Bappa was my nickname on my mother's side.

'Just call me Bappa,' I said to Shadab Hossain, dialling up my New York twang.

For all the heady anti-West sloganeering Bangladesh's Islamists did, they were, in my experience, no different from the majority of Bangladeshi society in their thrall to all things White. Most would trade all their religious–political convictions for a visa before you could say jihad.

'Where are you from, Yasin?' Shadab asked in English, trying to match my accent but getting it horribly wrong and mangled.

'*Ami New York theke aschi* [From New York],' I replied, in Bangla.

'So what brings you to Dhaka?' By the grace of Allah, he took my cue and shifted to our mother tongue.

'I'm a student and writing a thesis on Bengali music and culture. I heard these two men singing in the morning and started talking to them.'

'What were you two singing?' he asked the two cripples with an imperious air and a smile curling on his lips. 'Your voices are now going from Lichu Bagan to New York, eh?'

Shadab laughed. Everyone else laughed along.

'Let's sit on the terrace and talk, shall we?' Shadab offered. My New York spiel had worked. His tone with me was very different from the one he took with his lackeys. He was the Big Boy among the Small Boys around him, but he was treating me like an equal.

We walked up a flight of stairs to the unpolished concrete terrace on the first floor of the mosque.

'Where are the mats?' Shadab barked at one of his emaciated lackeys. Even as the cripples slowly made their way up, two people rushed down and brought us woven straw mats to sit on.

'What do you do, Shadab Bhai?' I started my trademark innocuous questioning once we sat down.

'Tours and travels,' Shadab replied. 'Family business. We are the biggest Hajj and Umrah tour operators here. My grandfather started it. And now I'm the third generation.'

'Oh! How interesting! I've heard Hajj and Umrah travel packages are very good business.'

'Ah . . . brother . . . Hajj and Umrah aren't business . . . it's our duty . . . as Muslims!'

'Shadab bhai has sent all of us for free!' the emaciated lackey chimed in. 'Like his father, Shadab bhai is an angel for us poor people! Otherwise, a rickshaw puller like me would never be able to do the Umrah.'

'No, no . . . I didn't mean it that way . . .' I offered sheepishly.

'Ah . . .' Shadab shushed his peasant admirer with affected irritation. And continued, 'No, no, you see, Yasin bhai . . . we have a fleet of cars, autos and buses in Dhaka and Mirpur. We also do regular holiday packages. Both domestic and international. X Tours and Travels . . . my office is right there . . .' he pointed to a building across the street.

'But when my grandfather started this business, he made it clear that we will never charge a taka from any poor person. So we charge those who can pay, and take only a nominal amount from those who can't.'

'Correct me if I'm wrong, but doesn't the government have subsidized Hajj and Umrah travel packages? And isn't there some scheme by which it reimburses travel agencies for the costs?'

'Oh, please . . . they say these things but do nothing. If anything, this government would stop all Hajj and Umrah if it could!'

'Oh! When did they stop?'

'They haven't stopped . . . but the delays in reimbursements are getting longer. And it's not like the government packages are any better or cheaper. See, I don't want to talk politics, but I don't know how much you know about the present government. It's least interested in helping the people of the country. They just have one agenda—minority appeasement. Take from the Muslims of this country and gift it to the minorities! That's their agenda!'

'You mean Hindus?'

'Not just Hindus . . .' Shadab's voice spun down into a thin hum as he strung together carefully chosen words. 'See, I have no political agenda . . . but as one regular Muslim to another, I say that this government is against believers. Real believers,

I mean. The ones who care about being pious. So, it's obvious they don't want to spend money on things like Hajj and Umrah!'

For the next hour or so, Shadab held forth. I aided him by playing the dumb Americanized Bengali who just nodded, hemmed and widened his eyes with enlightenment every now and then. With frequent interventions of agreement and support from his lackeys, out came his family history and political plans for the future.

Shadab came from a family of activists who worked with Bangladesh's largest Islamist party, the Jamaat-e Islami. Originally from Sylhet, they held sizeable land in the days before the Liberation War of 1971. Sheikh Mujib's party had 'looted' their lands under the guise of liberation and they were forced to relocate to Dhaka. The mosque we were sitting in and the few houses they owned next to the mosque were built on land they had bought for cheap back in time.

Given the organizers and mass leaders that Shadab claimed his grandfather and father were, they ensured electoral victories for the big names of Jamaat-e Islami. Shadab dropped some really big names when telling this part of his family history.

Despite his opening phrase about not being political, in the flow of conversation, he eventually revealed that he was preparing to run for office in the local elections when the Shahbag Square movement had happened.

'Mass movement, my foot!' Shadab angrily (and literally) spat out. 'That bunch of godless ruffians and characterless women were running amok, and Sheikh Hasina exploited it to the hilt. They derecognized the Jamaat-e Islami as a political party, despite it being the third largest one in this country, and several of our leaders were put to death under a political witch-hunt this Hasina calls the War Crimes Tribunal.'

'But inshallah, we will resist,' Shadab said, in a voice that had become fervent and preacher-meets-politician at that point. 'Sheikh Hasina has forgotten that our belief withstood the might of the Indian Army. The Hindu army butchered us and ruined our mothers and daughters . . . and yet we weren't finished. Those who side with and befriend and make room in their lives for the un-Islamic are children of Iblis. And that's what this Hasina is doing!'

Shadab had paraphrased a quote I had heard very recently.

'Joshimuddin Rahmani?' I asked, hearing the quote.

'You know Joshimuddin Rahmani?' Shadab grinned and looked around at his lackeys for a resonance of his new-found appreciation for the dumb American Bengali.

'Yes, I have followed his sermons often—he's very well regarded in the US.'

I wasn't entirely lying.

I had heard many hours of Joshimuddin Rahmani's sermons, which were quite popular among the Bangladeshi Muslim diaspora in the US. And while most of Shadab's bluster was uninteresting to me, my ears had pricked up at the quote.

Muhammad Joshimuddin Rahmani was an Islamist preacher and the leader of the jihadist outfit Ansaruallah Bangla Team. He had seen a meteoric rise with his fiery sermons—or *waaz*, as they were called around here—going viral on social media. His calls for practising remorseless jihad in public and brutal austerity and morality in private had become the rallying point for hundreds of radical young Bengali Muslim men and women the world over. And until his abrupt arrest in 2013 and the crackdown on his outfit, he was fast becoming the Bengali equivalent of Anwar al-Awlaki—the American scholar and preacher who had become the voice of Al Qaeda.

In fact, the Holey Artisan attackers who I had come to investigate were all ardent followers of Rahmani. Akayed Ullah, the New York bus terminus's bungling bomber, and Shagor, an engineering student and wannabe Hizb-ut Tahrir terrorist from Mirpur who I investigated a year later, were similar fans of Rahmani.

'See!' Shadab said, turning to his lackeys and grinning with unreasonable pride. 'Don't I keep telling you? It's our brothers who have left this country and stayed away from this mess who are still walking the right path!'

'*Haw haw* [yes, yes]', the lackeys chimed in.

'Brother . . .' Shadab continued with renewed vigour. 'Let me tell you something—my brother Aftab runs an IT company. We have made it our mission to spread the word of Huzoor Joshimuddin to every corner of the world.'

'*Haw haw,*' the lackeys cawed in agreement again.

The rascals had gone into an open-eyed slumber while Shadab was holding forth. Clearly, what Shadab had been telling me was a practised routine. Two of the lackeys had turned to more interesting things like picking at the frayed ends of the mats we were sitting on, while the tenor cripple was doing the same with his nose—just with more intensity.

Shadab hadn't noticed or had chosen to ignore the boredom of his lackeys because he had found a fresh new audience in me.

Apropos nothing, the rickshaw puller lackey proposed, 'Shadab bhai . . . how about some *chaa-biskoot*?' A proposal to which, yet again, the lackeys resonated with agreement.

'Damn!' I cursed in my head. Just when the foreplay had ended and the real dirty talk could've begun, these idiots wanted a tea break!

But I couldn't sound very eager to continue the conversation, so I indifferently suggested, 'Why don't we go down to a shop and get some tea? I would like a smoke with that.'

'You can smoke here,' the rickshaw puller said.

'Here?' I asked, surprised. 'No. I can't smoke on the balcony of a mosque,' I clarified. And I meant it.

'You are right, Yasin bhai. Absolutely right. Let's all go down.' Shadab said gravely, and we went down for a tea and smoke break.

The conversation broke into small talk thereafter. I knew I'd have to try again in a day or two—somehow engineer a chance to run into Shadab and meet his brother, Aftab. I retired to my room, still upset at Kalu [the rickshaw puller] and company's ill-timed tea break, and began plotting passable and innocent excuses to visit Shadab.

Little did I know that Kalu would become the excuse that very evening—only a few hours from the tea break.

At around 7 or 8 p.m., my brain fried with worry about returning to New York empty-handed, I told Allwyn I needed a drink.

'You will have to buy it,' Allwyn said. 'You can because you have a foreign passport.'

In accordance with Islamic laws, Bangladesh is a dry country. But like all 'dry' places across South Asia, alcohol is quite readily available should one be ready to shell out an amount significantly higher than the label price. Every State machinery that implements prohibition also makes sure to leave several gaping holes through which the merriment and bribes flow unfettered.

In Bangladesh, this happens in three ways.

One is illegal bars that pay the cops and local administration off. These are cheap and dirty places that serve bottom shelf liquor brought in from Nepal and India. Two, five-star hotels which serve top-shelf everything in posh settings, but you pay with a kidney and two bits of your liver even before it's affected by alcohol damage. The rule is they're supposed to serve only foreign citizens, but in reality, the only question asked when serving is whether the customer would like his or her drink neat, on the rocks, or with water and soda—not passport copies. The third is a few specific shops that sell bottles to foreign passport holders.

'No, I don't want to drink at home . . . I really need to step out,' I told Allwyn. 'Don't you know any local places we can walk to?'

'Local places . . .?' Allwyn pondered for a moment. 'There is one nearby. But you won't like it, bhaiya. It's . . . you know . . . not standard at all.'

'As long as I can get a drink there, it's standard enough. Let's go, please.'

I've always flaunted my street cred, setting it many notches above what it actually is. Bourgeois me? Hell, no! Bring on the plebian, subaltern, proletarian, and such other things are all sentiments I've said aloud to people. But as I walked into the drinking hole Allwyn had taken me to, every hidden bourgeois bone in me revolted and retched at the stench of the 'non-standard bar'.

Like the mosque, this too was an unfinished construction. Hidden away behind a fish and meat market, it was a barely lit room, no more than six by eight feet, six-odd small square tables, rancid liquor in glasses and an equal amount spilled on the floor. Four or five men stood behind a jail-like grilled counter and gave out little bottles in exchange for cash. A tray of glasses and water jugs stood next to the counter; patrons were expected to serve themselves.

Farts, burps, sweat and the stench from the day's wet market mixed with the fumes of liquors unknown to me. I swooned.

The bar had shocked me and I had shocked the bar back. Every single man in that establishment gave me a once-over—not saying I don't belong there, but silently asking, 'Why would you come in here?'

'Bhaiya, cash,' Allwyn said in my ear. I handed him some notes and shrugged a 'Whatever' when he asked what I wanted.

While Allwyn headed to the bar to order, I muttered to myself, 'You are going through with this, you entitled piece of shit. You want to be gonzo? *This* is gonzo.'

Allwyn came back with a small bottle of clear liquid in one hand and a beer can that looked like a Foster's. A man with a rag and glasses came along with him and barked at two very drunk men at a table. They muttered curses at the cleaner but gave up their table for us.

Alcohol is undoubtedly horrible for the body and mind. I'd never recommend it to anyone. But if, like me, your heart is troubled by the thought of the idyll of a classless society being way beyond the visible horizon, I would say alcohol is the next best thing to the Revolution.

The company of drunks, more often than not, is one of equals. Ethyl alcohol coursing through the veins doesn't care about your caste, class or identity. In addition to vision, judgement and prudence, it blurs social divides too. A drunk Lord is as crass as the lowest of his peasants and every swooning janitor is as authoritative as a judge.

This company of drunks was no different.

The awkwardness that had set in the room when I walked into the bar had dissipated by the time I clinked my can with Allwyn's glass. The 'non-standard bar' had gone back to its standard humming buzz interspresed with sprodaic bursts of laughter, epiphanic and boisterous observations about life and swear words.

'Oh!' I exclaimed, taking my first swig. This was my first encounter with Bangladesh's homegrown beer brand, Hunter. The makers of Hunter had really put in an effort to make the can look just like a Foster's. It tasted much better than Foster's though—which, I daresay, doesn't take much effort. But for a country that outlaws alcohol, the brewers of this broth had done well enough for the price point.

It must've been half an hour since we walked in when Kalu—the rickshaw puller—appeared on the scene.

Both Allwyn and I were two rounds in and I had almost forgotten about work. Allwyn's chatter was fun, and the smells had stopped bothering me as much as they had when I first set foot in the bar. Even though I refused to eat any of the shredded salad and soggy peanuts he'd ordered, I did take a piece of the diced boiled eggs sprinkled with salt and red chilli powder.

'What are you drinking?' I asked Allwyn.

'*Bhodka.*'

'Let me have a try.' I set my third Parliament cigarette down, reached over and took a sip from his glass.

This was no vodka. It was some scouring paint thinner.

'That's hard!' I said, laughing and washing the bitter effervescence down with a gulp of Hunter beer. And that's when I heard, 'Arey . . . Yasin bhai!'

Kalu was standing by my table with a loony grin. I was stunned, unsure of what to say, and Allwyn looked from my face to Kalu's.

'Oh . . . Kalu bhai . . .' I said, with a forced smile and eagerness, as if I'd met an old friend. Inside though, the mild high of Hunter beer was vanishing and I was sinking into a feeling of being the hunted.

The grin on Kalu's face said, 'So you too are a sinner after sundown, eh? Pious American–Bengali who refused a smoke on the mosque's balcony!'

Fuck! After this, there was no way I'd be able to go back to Shadab, Aftab or their mosque and IT company. The best I could hope for was that I'd leave Lichu Bagan in a day or two and lament that my exclusive lead had turned dead.

I exchanged some banal pleasantries with Kalu—Bengali versions of the American non-committal 'We should hang out some time,' and left soon after.

I don't know if the paint thinner had dulled him or if he was catching on, but Allwyn was remarkably silent on the way back. He had neither made any attempt to clarify to Kalu that my name wasn't Yasin, nor asked why I was Yasin and Siddhartho at the same time. But he didn't bring me my ashtray the next morning, nor did he smile when he set down my breakfast.

'Shit happens,' I told myself and left the apartment by nine in the morning. I had three people to interview that day. Explaining myself to Allwyn wasn't anywhere near being a priority.

Around four that evening, in the middle of my second interview—the first time I met Sharmee Hossain, who would become instrumental to my reporting—I got a call from Allwyn.

'Someone named Shadab bhai is here to see you,' he said, handing the phone to a familiar voice.

'I'll be back by around 7 or 8 p.m.,' I informed Shadab and asked, 'Anything urgent?'

'We'll meet and talk when you're back. I've taken your number from Allwyn here. I'll call you around then.'

My tummy growled with anxiety. Had Allwyn shared my real name with Shadab? Had he given him copies of my ID that I'd submitted when checking in?

But I had a job to do. I couldn't keep worrying.

And maybe Allwyn hadn't said anything. So, Shadab would only know what he did from Kalu. Which was that I drink—that's all. As if there were no Joshimuddin Rahmani-following Muslims who drank—or did much worse. Besides, if push came to shove, I'd go to the police. If that didn't work, I'd reach out to the embassy or some lawyers. Given the current political situation in Bangladesh, Shadab had a lot more to hide than I did.

Besides what was I going to do? Not go back to the Lichu Bagan apartment? My laptop, camera and passport were all there. And by giving me advance warning, Shadab had only made me better prepared than I would've been if he'd come unannounced.

The rationalization didn't entirely quell the discomfort roiling in my tummy. The feeling only grew as I made my way back to Lichu Bagan and walked up the stairs.

Allwyn wasn't home when I got there. I used the spare key he'd given to let myself in. He arrived after I'd finished a shower and had sat down to upload my interview notes to Google Drive and keep a copy in my encrypted USB stick.

Around 7.30 p.m., the doorbell rang. It was, as expected, Shadab.

I went to the living room expecting the Lichu Bagan strongman to sport a grim visage. But lo and behold, he had a grand smile on him!

He was dressed in jeans and a T-shirt two sizes too small, looking like Johnny Bravo. He had lost the skullcap too and the only thing 'Islamic' about his visage was the facial hair—overgrown and unruly as before. With him was a man dressed in a tucked-in white shirt and khakis who appeared to be in his early twenties—a thinner and younger version of Shadab.

'Yasin bhai . . . this is Aftab,' Shadab said, in his usual loud voice.

Phew! Allwyn hadn't given away my real name. 'Aftab is my younger brother—the one who runs the IT company.'

This most certainly wasn't the meeting I was expecting. Where I had thought my lead had dried up, the lead had walked right into my apartment!

'*Chaa*?' I asked and, without waiting for them to answer, told Allwyn to bring us some.

'I wanted you to meet Aftab,' Shadab came straight to the point. 'He has been . . . *oy* . . . Aftab, why don't you tell Yasin Bhai yourself?'

'So I did my computer science from East West University. And instead of taking a job, I offered to help Abbu (father) set up his website . . . for the travel business you know. I built the website, added a payment gateway and then did social media as well.'

Aftab rambled on, detailing everything he had done. Since I understood these things, I asked him a question or two every few minutes. Questions like what backend was he using, where was he hosting the site, was he using Tweetdeck or something similar to automate his social media posts, and so on.

In around twenty minutes, I had every bit of information I would want if I ever desired to snoop remotely around his set-up. What I didn't know was whether his setup also doubled up as infrastructure for propagating jihad.

'Have you considered training people?' I asked. 'As an entrepreneur, isn't it difficult to get the right talent?'

Aftab's face lit up at this question.

'Oh, bhaiya . . . don't even get me started on that! It's very difficult to find good talent. If they know anything, they ask for so much money or simply take up work online! In fact, that's why Abbu said we should start a training academy . . .'

' . . . especially to train those from poor families, you know,' Shadab found his 'in' into the conversation. 'We can't just . . .'

At that point, Allwyn came to take away the empty cups and Shadab stopped for a moment. Then, completely changing the topic, he addressed Allwyn. 'Where have you been taking your sir? That bar is a rickshaw puller's place, you idiot. How can you take sir there?'

Lest the chiding get to Allwyn and he blurt unpalatable truths out, I interjected—'Not his fault'. 'Allwyn warned me not to go. It was I who insisted on going there. Staying in the West has put some vices in me, you know—I've not been a very good Muslim.' I added a self-deprecating statement to seal the charade.

'Oh, come on, Yasin bhai. A man needs his drink once in a while. In fact, let me take you to a nice place. A standard place. Best in Dhaka, I tell you!'

Of course, I agreed. Men talk when drunk. From what I'd seen and heard of these men thus far, they would talk even more when drunk.

They took me to a loud and garishly lit establishment. It was called Fire *and* Ice or Fire *on* Ice. By Dhaka's standards, the place had remarkably high prices and unremarkable food. But it had a large bar menu and an even larger collection of rich locals who were drowning their exasperations of having liberal, first world aspirations while living in a conservative third world country.

The two brothers spoke a lot. But nothing of any use to me.

Shadab got drunk sooner than Aftab and began to hold forth about how the Devil's party, the Bangladesh Awami League, had dashed his hopes of running for office from the Jamaat-e Islami and he had been forced to make arrangements with the lesser devils of the Bangladesh National Party.

The latter kept talking about his dream of moving to Silicon Valley and alternated between asking me for advice and dropping names of people who had founded this and that start-up.

I tottered home that night empty-handed. These men weren't terrorist material. Sure, they were running a bunch of social media handles trying to milk the anti-Sheikh Hasina, pro-Islamist sentiments, but that was about it. They weren't planning anything beyond trolling.

My lead had died.

Reaching the Lichu Bagan apartment, I found the front door locked from the inside. The deal was that any resident could enter and leave at any hour using a set of keys. I'd forgotten to carry mine. I called Allwyn angrily, asking him why he'd locked the door and insisting that he open the door immediately.

'The door is open, bhaiya,' he said, groggy in sleep.

'No, it isn't!' I spat back.

'I'm standing at the door. Where are you?' I heard his voice—through the phone and down the stairwell from a floor above.

I'd been knocking on the wrong door in the middle of the night.

Cricket in the Caliphate

I met Sharmee Hossain, a linguist trained at Rutgers, over a cup of coffee not far from the Holey Artisan Bakery, on the very first day I landed in Dhaka. She was a professor at the North South University, where one of the hostage takers had been a student.

Sharmee said she didn't know the student personally nor did she know anyone else who did. As is the case with all self-radicalized actors, nobody usually does until the act actually happens. More importantly, Sharmee had this conspicuous insularity to the Holey Artisan attack. An attitude that said, 'Sure it was a thing—but it was not the biggest or most surprising thing that had happened or was happening.'

But meeting her was great.

For one, though not an active participant, Sharmee was close to the young leaders of the Shahbag movement and had a dispassionate ringside view of the many debates and tumults Bangladesh's youngsters were going through. In fact, she introduced me to a whole bunch of young Bangladeshi student leaders who had broken the political taboo of not speaking about the unfinished war crimes trials that was set up right after Bangladesh's Liberation War.

Starting off on Facebook groups, these young Bangladeshi men and women started pointing fingers at those who had sided with Pakistan during Operation Searchlight in 1971. They started talking about how the co-conspirators and allies, who had the blood of over three million Bengalis on their hands and had displaced another ten million, had not only gone unpunished, but had reinvented themselves as businessmen, media honchos and politicians of the Jamaat-e Islami and were still going strong.

The resentment had flowed from the virtual world and into Dhaka's streets and gathered around Shahbag Square. Soon splits along political–ideological and partisan lines akin to the time before the Liberation War surfaced.

Islamists on one end, seculars on the other, with all manner of partisan interests in the middle, political tents were pitched. And though the seculars had the clear upper hand this time, Holey Artisan happened.

Tamem Chowdhary and the young boys of his nascent cell of Bangladesh's Islamic State hit back and declared, 'We Islamists exist!'

Sharmee took me to Bagmara—her ancestral home in Rajshahi district—which became instrumental in my reporting.

'You won't find your answers here,' she said, sipping her tea, after almost an hour of talking. 'Come with me to Bagmara. I'm organizing cricket matches there.'

'Why Bagmara specifically?'

'Firstly, because that's where Jamat-ul Mujahideen's Bangla Bhai had set up his first base. And secondly, because it's a microcosm of this entire youth, politics and violence phenomenon, you know.'

I read up about Bagmara that night. Five days from the conversation, I was on an early morning train with Sharmee.

We ate a breakfast of diced potatoes cooked in a thick, yellow soup of split peas and greasy parathas. We drank two rounds of chaa, warming our hands on the earthen cups. Nearly an hour after the scheduled departure time, the train blew its horn and lurched to life, leaving behind the refuse strewn rail yard of Dhaka station and it made its way northwest through the slowly thinning morning fog.

Sharmee nodded off soon after the train started and I pulled out a collection of essays written by her father—independent Bangladesh's first minister for education and press aka propaganda, Sardar Amjad Hossain. *Bangladeshe Joy Porajoyer Rajniti*, it was called, meaning the Politics of Victories and Defeat.

Sharmee's famed father had been a journalist before joining the Liberation War under Bangladesh's founding father, Sheikh Mujibur Rahman. The book detailed a time when nationalists had won against the occupying Pakistani army, only to have the guns they had given to the people to fight with turned back at them. The war for liberty and dignity had degenerated into internecine fighting and the fractious unity of the Mukti Bahini (Liberation Army formed under Sheikh Mujibur Rahman) had splintered along ideological, partisan and fiefdom-driven lines.

'The problem is that the guns never went away,' a villager later told me, his right arm hanging dead. He was among the scores of 'visitors' who came to tell me stories after my early morning visit to the beel. Holding up their broken bodies as proof of how the Caliphate was anything but the utopia that the extremists promised, they told me stories of their lives under it.

During the Liberation War of 1971, most Bengalis joined to fight off the Pakistani establishment. Despite their own harsh differences, West Pakistan's Parliament, under civilian leader Zulfikar Ali Bhutto, had joined hands with arch-rival and military chief General Agha Muhammad Yahya Khan to deny East Pakistani leader Sheikh Mujibur Rahman his prime ministership, even though Sheikh Mujib had won the elections decisively. When Mujib cried foul at being denied his position, they launched an attack that sought to obliterate the Bengali identity, starting with the language.

With help from India, the Bengali nationalists won and the pro-Pakistan Islamists lost. But once that was accomplished, there was little agreement on what their new nation would look like.

Ideas ranged from a Soviet-inspired, one-party state under Sheikh Mujib's Awami League (of which Amjad Hossain was a member) with Bengali-ness as the national identity to a militaristic one under General Zia-ur Rahman, with less Bengali-ness and more Muslim-ness.

The guns—which the Indian Army had given to the liberation warriors to battle their long-time enemy, Pakistan—were kept by the different parties to be used against each other.

But I'm getting ahead of myself; back to the train.

I don't recall how much time had passed since we left Dhaka, but the rusty beast we were riding was hurtling past the Teesta River, and I was reading about Sardar Amjad Hossain and slaughtered tradesmen and revolution when his daughter woke up.

Seeing the open book in my hand, she said, in a low sleep smothered voice, 'By the time I grew up, Baba was too big a man to be a regular father. A regular father to regular kids, you know? When school was off, my siblings and I would mostly go to Bagmara with my mother and my siblings. We did regular things that regular families do.'

'And I remember a much happier Bagmara than I see now,' she continued. 'We were all Muslims; we still are. But the political 'ism' wasn't around. Far from being locked inside a burqa, women had a very strong voice. They used to play sports too.'

Although Sharmee steered clear of participating in politics directly, unlike her father, she still felt a strong responsibility towards her community. In fact, this particular trip was meant to organize cricket matches in the town. Though the games were hardly a cure for her town's ills and the young men's radicalization, it was a start. At least that's what Sharmee had reasoned.

In the immediate aftermath of the 1971 Liberation War, with Sheikh Mujib becoming the executive head and taking on the monicker of 'Father of the Nation', Bangladesh had more or less set its course towards becoming a secular, progressive nation.

Bagmara, led by his lieutenant and comrade, Amjad Hossain, was no exception. Hossain had taken it upon himself to make Bagmara a model of the new Bangladeshi modernist and progressive idyll.

His project was short-lived, though.

The pro-Bengali Awami League had won, but the opposition pro-Islam, pro-Pakistan lot hadn't really lost. The largest Islamist party, the Jamaat-e Islami, had a considerable share of the votes. And there was General Ziaur Rahman and his centre-right Bangladesh Nationalist Party, which said that it wanted a free Bangladesh but one with Islam as the overarching identity, rather than the Bengali language. Sheikh Mujib's own party and coterie broke down into many factions, and he was gunned down by those who had once been close to him.

Politics and political alliances in Dhaka changed rapidly. Amjad Hossain ended up losing the backing of the Awami League and joined the centre–right militarist Jatiya Party, floated by former Chief of Army Staff General Hussain Mohammad Ershad. It was a party that would in time betray the promise of democracy and install its own junta.

Hossain got death threats from armed Left-wing groups, Islamists and even former colleagues from the Awami League. He moved away to the safety of Dhaka city and, in 2004, Bagmara slid from being the dream project of secular progressivism to the seat of the first-ever caliphate declared by an Al-Qaeda-affiliate terrorist group in South Asia.

Siddique-ul Islam, the man who set up the caliphate, had been a member of the student wing of Bangladesh's largest mainstream Islamist party, the Jamaat-e Islami. Irked by the Jamaat-e Islami's decision to become inclusive and admit women as party members, he broke away from them. He brought together some other zealots like himself and formed an armed militant group. He named the group, Jamaat-ul-Mujahideen Bangladesh, and himself *Bangla Bhai*—Bengal's Big Brother.

I was in Bagmara in 2016, nine years after Bangla Bhai had been killed, trying to piece together a story from the ruins of his Caliphate.

'Look at this poor devil,' Amjad—my second local guide in Bagmara, besides Afzal who had taken me to the beel—said, pointing to his bedridden neighbour. Amjad was taking me around, showing me spots, introducing me to people who had tales to tell from the time when Bagmara was under the iron fist of Siddique-ul Islam.

'The man can't even shit and piss. Tell him, Musa. Tell him how they beat you.'

There on a charpoy, in a three-by-five feet room in a mud house adjoining a cowshed, lay Musa—an emaciated, mangled relic of a human being.

Musa couldn't really talk. All he could do was gurgle and squeak while froth collected at the edges of his misshapen mouth. But he started his narrative with gusto through agitated gurgles, frothing, as his hollowed-out eyes grew big and small. His wife, who had been standing behind the threshold to the cowshed, pulled the *ghomta* of her saree lower, came in and rolled up his mud-stained dhoti.

There were his broken legs. They were ghastly twisted twig-thin limbs with dried-up gashes of rolled back flesh. Bones threatened to tear through the scrawny, dark, warty skin.

I've been taught to be unemotional. Emotional reporting is bad reporting. But seeing this living corpse of a human, my temples throbbed, as I tried to hold back tears. Until I couldn't. A couple of drops rolled down defiantly.

Musa's wife burst out in sobs. His gurgles screamed of anger and hopelessness. Amjad, my rough and tough guide, who wouldn't shy away from shooting someone dead should the need arise, rained slaps on his own forehead and cursed in childlike helplessness.

My 'reporting expedition' had just brought alive every injustice done to Musa, his wife and Amjad. Injustices that would never be undone. Never avenged.

Born to a family of farmhands, Musa owned no land, heads of cattle or granaries. He eked out a living tilling in the fields of others. This also meant he was useless to Bangla Bhai, whose goons were collecting taxes from the villagers. So, the big, brave, fat Bangla Bhai used Musa in the only useful way possible.

He beat the man nearly to death and made a mighty show of his power.

'He was always a dimwit,' Amjad said, recounting Musa's story. 'He knew nothing of who had taken control and how the laws had changed. One afternoon, walking past Bangla Bhai and his men, he lit a beedi. They took it as insolence and punished him by hanging him upside down from a mango tree. They beat him with rods and staves till his spine broke and the flesh on his legs hung off the bone.

'When they were hanging him up, Musa kept shouting and asking what he was being punished for. Even when the first blows rained down on him, and we [the villagers] were made to watch, he still thought it was a matter of mistaken identity. But then, as the blows came in hard and fast, he just bleated like a goat being slaughtered.'

Just as we stepped out of his dingy home, Musa hailed us back by rattling his makeshift bell—a spoon in a steel bowl—and gurgling something frantically to his wife.

'Please tell the people outside to help us with medical expenses,' she translated his gurgles. I nodded.

When Bangla Bhai first came to Bagmara in 2004, his mujahideen force was a ragtag joke. The 'warriors' moved around in tuk-tuks and had only one gun. The rest of their armoury was just choppers, rusted rods and bamboo poles.

But against an unarmed peasantry, with some very well-calculated blindness on the part of the then ruling Bangladesh National Party thrown in, Bangla Bhai became a mighty jihadi. Nothing and nobody could stand in his way when he and his cohorts took over the surrounding region and imposed a religious curfew.

All non-religious social gatherings, including meeting for singing, plays and sports, were banned. Heavy taxes were exacted from the villagers. Those too poor to pay in cash had to part with their grains and fowl. Women were put under strict dress codes and forbidden from stepping out without male supervision. Young girls were banned from going to the madrasa.

In fact, Bangla Bhai hated education so much, he turned the local school into a prison and torture centre.

Anyone who dared step out of line was brought to weekly kangaroo courts, presided over by Bangla Bhai, and severe punishments—from beating with rods to summary executions—were meted out.

'They said I was a Maoist,' a man with a dead, paralysed hand said. 'Me a Maoist? I was under threat from them for being pro-Amjad Hossain! Bangla Bhai took me in and asked me to pay a fine for my crimes against Islam. The sum they demanded of me wouldn't come together even if I had sold everything I owned, including myself, my wife and my child. So, they hung me from the tree and gave me a battering. One guy would beat me, tire out, and another would take over. I was lucky that I passed out; they thought I was dead and dumped me in a ditch. I woke up and crawled home at night and hid there for months. All the others they took in that day never came back.'

The news that a reporter was in the village, asking about Bangla Bhai's time spread very fast and over a dozen people gathered in Sharmee's outhouse to talk to me.

'He claimed there were new rules now,' one among those gathered said. "We're going to follow the Sharia," he declared. But all the time that he was here, not once, not even once, did anyone see him praying.'

The group echoed in agreement.

'We're all Muslims. We and our forefathers have been Muslims since forever. So at first we didn't even know what Bangla Bhai meant when he said that from now on, everyone would live like good Muslims,' someone else said.

'The thing is, Saeed bhai,' the man with the paralysed hand took over, 'Bangla Bhai didn't really have any rules. He didn't know any Islam. Even our local, semi-educated qazis and mullahs knew more Quran and Hadith than him. He just made things up as he went along. Even the name of his party. One day they said they're Al . . . Al . . . what was it?'

'Al-Qaeda,' I completed.

'Yes, yes . . . Qaeda, qaeda. Then he said he had fought in the Afghan war against Soviets and he was Taliban. He just said whatever he liked.'

'He had only one rule, sir . . .' another man added. 'Beat us poor people up and take our money and food.'

'Bangla Bhai was allowed to do what he did because he was doing the government's dirty job by hunting down the Maoists,' Sharmee had explained on the train ride. 'They didn't expect him to turn around and challenge Dhaka.'

She was right. My research had shown the same. The Purbo Banglar Communist Party (Communist Party of East Bengal) was an armed group that operated out of Rajshahi. They had thrown a direct challenge to the incumbent Prime Minister Khaleda Zia. Khaleda Zia's centre-right

Bangladesh National Party had formed an alliance with the Islamist Jamaat-e Islami and was on a mission to Islamize the country.

It was a continuation of the unfinished work begun by her late husband, Bangladeshi military dictator General Ziaur Rahman, that of reversing the Bengali first identity of Sheikh Mujibur Rahman and the Liberation War to one that was Muslim first and Bengali second.

Given the constraints of running a parliamentary set-up with courts and laws, the Khaleda Zia-led Bangladesh National Party government unleashed Bangla Bhai and other Islamists upon their political opponents as a Track Two technique. This is common to politics all over the world. States create and unleash a monster, let it run amok, and then clamp down on the civil rights of regular citizens, citing the monster.

Clearly, Bangla Bhai had been given complete impunity as long as he stayed within the confines of Rajshahi. That understanding continued until 2005. In August 2005, his team coordinated bombings in roughly 500 locations around Bangladesh. In November, he killed two sitting judges and attempted a suicide attack.

Thanks to the shabby state of Bangla Bhai's ragtag team, the bombings caused relatively little damage, and the suicide missions were duds, compared to the ones done by the battle-hardened fighters of the real Al-Qaeda in Afghanistan. But Bangla Bhai had made his intentions and ambitions clear.

The mandarins of Dhaka finally stirred.

Past declarations of him being elusive, impossible to tame, dreaded and superbly trained notwithstanding, the day Dhaka decided he needed to be caught, it was done in no time.

The day the Rapid Action Battalion—the principal paramilitary unit of the Bangladeshi army—zeroed in on him, the 'big brother' who likened himself to Afghanistan's Mullah

Omar was hiding in a pathetic tin shed in Mymensingh, far from his Caliphate. He surrendered with barely a whimper or a shot fired.

Bangla Bhai was captured and hanged in 2007, along with six other members of his group.

By the time I set foot in Bagmara, nine years later in 2016, to piece together his story, all I got was the trail of broken bodies that his Caliphate had left in its wake.

***

'Won't you come in and have tea?' young Najma and her elderly mother asked me. I had just met them and though Najma spoke well, at first she refused to give an interview or be recorded.

'Fine, I won't record you or quote you if you don't want me to. But at least help me understand what happened,' I said, and Najma softened. She invited me to have tea to make amends for starting off with an outright refusal.

'Not now,' I said with cautious politeness. 'I need to finish my work. But once I do, I'll come and have tea. Only if you promise to feed me snacks with it though.'

Najma's ancestral home had been taken over by Bangla Bhai as his headquarters. Taking all the best rooms, he had relegated her large undivided family to the storerooms and the kitchen.

'Of course, I remember all that happened when Bangla Bhai was here,' Najma said, which surprised me, given her youthful appearance.

'Bhai? When did that rascal become your bhai?' her mother interjected. The woman's age had broken her back and she was bent over and walked with the support of a bamboo stick. But age hadn't taken away the sharpness of her tongue.

'If I'd birthed such a baby, I'd kill it in the crib,' the woman said with disgust, and pretended to spit.

Life had been hell for women in particular during Bangla Bhai's reign. One of the first things Bangla Bhai had done was issue a dress code for his subjects. Men had to keep a beard, and women were to stay in a full burqa beyond the threshold of their homes. The womenfolk couldn't be seen on the streets without an escort who was either a brother, son or husband.

A cluster of women had begun clustering around Najma and her mother. They were filling water at the communal tap outside Najma's house. And though they'd giggled at me and my camera when they first saw me, they'd refused to talk when I asked for bites. Hearing Najma's mother's bold words, they began speaking.

'How does one work in the fields with a full burqa in this hot and sweaty country?' one woman asked me.

'They wouldn't let us step out without male supervision. When the man is in the fields, how does a woman carry his lunch to him?' one woman asked.

'We had this neighbour—a Hindu woman,' another one narrated. 'She was riding pillion on her husband's motorbike on this very road where we are standing and talking. Bangla Bhai's boys beat the couple to a pulp because the wind blowing against her saree had revealed a patch of her midriff.'

Next to the house stood the infamous mango orchard where Bangla Bhai held his kangaroo courts. 'The cries, brother, the cries . . . we can still hear them,' one of the women said, pointing out a particularly old, gnarly and sturdy one. This was the one from which alleged sinners were hung upside down and beaten while others watched. Not watching was a punishable crime, too. I pictured the corpulent Bangla Bhai sitting at the far end, relishing the pain of stick-thin Musa being bludgeoned.

For a while, we all just stood there saying nothing. Almost as if, unspoken, we'd all agreed to observe a minute of silence to apologize on behalf of humanity to all those who had been beaten, broken and killed by one of the most violent men in the history of Bangladesh.

'Things are better now,' another woman said, breaking the silence. 'We can bathe in the ponds again. During his time, Bangla Bhai had mandated full hijab for women at all times outside their homes. Getting into the water in public was out of the question. Full hijab, full day's work and no bathing in ponds in summer? I hope that rascal is born a woman in his next life to feel what we felt.'

Eventually, bored of Najma's familial mud house, Bangla Bhai moved to the largest concrete structure in the village—the Hamirkutsa Government High School.

'We were on a short break,' the school's assistant headmaster told me over tea with some other teachers. 'When we returned on a Monday, we found half the school taken over by them. Then they began using it as their command office and torture centre.'

Conveniently for Bangla Bhai, the school too had a sturdy mango tree in the courtyard.

The children had gone into a fit of collective fear the first time they'd heard the howls of a prisoner being broken. A stampede ensued, and some of the kids had tried to jump off the second-floor balcony.

'Later that week, we all went to Bangla Bhai and requested him not to do any of these activities [beating and torture] during the day. And he kindly agreed.'

Exams were excused that year.

***

Sharmee and I sat in the small courtyard after dinner on the first night in Bagmara. Unlike us, the two migratory city birds, villagers sleep early. The cold night was so quiet, I could hear dew dripping onto the tin roof. Quiet enough to hear the cat purring as she rubbed her arched back against Rabeya, the housekeeper. Rabeya was the same age as us and more of a pal than an employee for Sharmee.

She spoke very little, smiled a lot and cooked like a dream. If not for the accident of birth that had tied her to this village, she would have made it big in the city.

She had survived the Caliphate and two terrible husbands but said little about either her political or private past. When I'd pressed her to tell me what she saw of Bangla Bhai's time, all she said was, 'You know, men do what men do.'

'Bangladesh is just waiting for a dictator,' Sharmee Hossain said. She was now thinking aloud.

'It's not victimhood that's driving the young men to terrorism,' Sharmee had said to me back in Dhaka, explaining the phenomenon of wealthy young men from her university being members of the Holey Artisan attack team. 'It's the macho persona that attracts them.'

This has been a recurring theme in Bangladeshi political life. Overwhelmingly a Muslim country, Islam isn't under any threat whatsoever. And yet, every now and then, someone comes up with a militant group that blows things up citing the urgency of saving their fragile faith. Faith is but a euphemism for fiefdom and the fragility isn't that of Islam but of their own egos, which need to boss over others to be stroked.

Pockmarked with coups, wanton partisan violence and religious politicization, Bangladesh has taken a tortured path to democracy. Much has been gained in public health, education, food security and the like. But the polity is weak and beholden to partisan agendas and the powerful few. Individuals with sufficient money, muscle or political influence can do almost as they please with little fear of the law.

'It's almost like this country is waiting for a *byata* [tough guy] leader. And the day that happens, we'll forget all of this democracy and representation and dive headlong into a dictatorship.' Sharmee said.

This sentiment had been echoed by the villagers too.

Although everyone said things were much better now that Bangla Bhai was dead and his Caliphate dismantled, the peace was, at best, an unquiet one, amid the terrors of what threatened to rise back from the dead.

'Bangla Bhai was captured and killed, Saeed bhai,' Amjad told me on the motorcycle ride back from Hamirkutsa School, 'but the ones who sided with him back then—the Jamaat guys for example—they're still around. In fact, right after the Jamaat-e Islami was derecognized, they wiggled their way into the Awami League. The leaders sitting in Dhaka have no idea of the ground reality. For them, it's just "get the guy who can bring in the votes".'

'These kids need better idols,' Sharmee said. Rabeya had gone to bed and we sat in the guest room now, me smoking my last cigarette for the night. 'They need activities they can spend their energies on. And I'd rather make that cricket instead of jihad.'

Through her elder brother, a TV producer, Sharmee was trying to rope in some cricketing stars to add glamour to the event, funded primarily by the two siblings. These annual games gave the young men of Bagmara an opportunity to compete and come together as a team, far from the influence of moralizing fundamentalist Islamists.

During our time in Bagmara, many people came to see Sharmee. She met them in a small outhouse that held a larger-than-life portrait of her father. As she doled out money, tea and a patient ear to her visitors, she shunned all talk of politics and running for office.

Late one afternoon, the cricket team boys came in. Smiling, reedy young boys, full of beans and chatter.

There was to be an inter-village tournament. If there was enough money, they'd rent floodlights and, like the stars of the Bangladeshi cricket team, play a 'day and night match.' If not, it would be Twenty20—a fun-filled, shorter version of the game. At any rate, they needed bats, balls and a roller to even out the hard, lumpy ground adjoining the village.

'During the rains, Bagmara looks like an island,' Afzal had told me on our way to the beel. 'The waters come up to the edge of the village, and waves lap against it.'

Rimmed by tall palms, this part of the village stood several feet above the fields that led to the beel. In the fullness of winter when I was there, the waters of the beel had receded many miles. But the exposed earth, with its gradient of hardness that went from solid and lumpy to soft slush, attested to Afzal's description.

It's difficult, well-nigh impossible, to cultivate the beel-adjacent areas even when there's no water. But the villagers had worked hard to do as best as they could and a paddy crop had been harvested on a slim band of land. The onion crop was just about ready, and the first verdant rows of potato plants had sprouted. A clutch of other vegetables, including snake gourds, bitter melons, chillies and pumpkins, grew as well. Not enough to sell, but great for the savoury, five-spiced vegetable melanges the villagers made for lunch.

The ones who made the most of the dry beel land were the aforementioned cricketers. Each afternoon, riotous noises erupted in the fields as the sports stars of the Bagmara Cricket Club honed their skills.

Sharmee, Rabeya, Afzal and I went to see them on my last day in Bagmara.

Three bamboo sticks driven into the ground made for the wicket at the striker's end, where the batsman stands. The non-striker's end was a misshapen stone with some sweaters covering it. One lanky young man was running down the pitch and delivering a wayward ball, while another, equally lanky, chap was taking blind swings with a worn-out bat at every delivery that came his way. A set of barefoot outfielders ran all over, caring nothing for their feet that bled from the sharp straw stumps left behind from the paddy harvest.

Anger, untamed aggression, jubilation, despair and curses were flying fast. The fine English definition of cricket being a gentleman's game be damned—this was the sport at its finest!

There was action off the field as well. While the young men played, the girls watched from the village edge, and grown-ups let loose volleys of abuse every time the ball was hit into the crops.

The energy was contagious. Everyone got sucked in, including this not-very-sporty reporter.

'Go, bat. Let's see if you Indian men are any good,' Sharmee teased.

Challenged on both my masculinity and nationalism, I handed the camera to Afzal and valiantly jumped into the fray. In no time, I had made a complete fool of myself. I lasted only an over or two and got caught out by the wicket keeper trying to hit a square cut.

The uneven lumpy ground, the tennis ball, the chipped bat—this was just like my own school days, when I'd play in the gullies of my neighbourhood or at the ground adjoining the Dalit ghetto where my friends lived. Just like my lot when we were their age, these kids were merciless on the ground. The team I was playing against howled and hooted like a bunch of raucous baboons when I got caught out.

But once the match was over, high fives, hugs and selfies flowed. Unkept promises were made of seeing each other again. I proudly posted our twilight-tinged group photo to Facebook.

Later that night, I was treated to a feast. Rabeya had cooked up a storm for our last meal. The first course was of large, juicy vines of *pui shaak* (Malabar spinach) that grew on a bamboo machaan at the edge of the big pond next to Sharmee's house. The greens had been slow cooked with fish head. Unannounced, Sharmee's neighbours had brought in dishes they'd cooked for the 'guest' from abroad. By the time I reached the pièce de résistance of the dinner, goose cooked in a mildly spiced curry of grated coconut, I was gasping for breath and my heart was calling for a spare belly.

The overeating and loud protests against third helpings notwithstanding, my gut shamelessly made way for dessert—rashogollah from Afzal's brother-in-law's shop.

We left an hour or so after dinner. I hugged Afzal and Amjad and fist-bumped Rabeya. Another series of unkept promises to meet again were made. And Sharmee and I drove off into the cold, fog laden night with what remains one of the best stories of my life.

'Sid,' Sharmee said in the car, on our way back to Dhaka. We were, by then, safely outside Bagmara, and she had reverted to using my real name. Throughout my time in her village, on her instructions, I'd identified as Saeed and had worn a beard in the Muslim style.

After all, they hadn't all gone away, as Amjad had warned.

'I want these cricket matches to happen regularly. But I don't know where the funds will come from. Do you think if people read your story, they'll help me?'

The headlights were fighting a losing battle against the darkness and heavy fog that had blanketed the unlit roads and the fields beyond. Visibility had gone down to under ten feet. In the car's silent, pensive confines, I think I saw Sharmee and her cricket matches more clearly.

Were the cricket matches she and her brother funded just some charity work? Or was it that in going back to Bagmara, in continuing his work for the town, she was taking on the mantle of her dead father? Or was it just an abortive attempt at channelling the men and their violent energies to fight with balls and bats, instead of guns and bombs?

As for her question about people helping her with the cricket matches, I didn't know the answer. So, as I'd done to Musa, the man with the dead hand, and innumerable others who mistakenly pinned their hopes on me, thinking that telling reporters their stories would better their lives, I mumbled some words and nodded.

Shaa, Shuari and a Hot Meal of Rice

I had run into Shaheen three days before the end of my stay in Kutupalong—the largest camp in the cluster of Rohingya refugee camps in Cox's Bazar, Bangladesh. And the 'running into' was hardly metaphorical. The nine-year-old girl almost got crushed under the wheels of my car.

The morning had begun earlier than usual, and the previous night had ended late. I'd slipped into an exhausted slumber within a minute or two of leaving the hotel.

'Sir . . . sir . . . wake up . . . they need IDs . . .' I woke up to Abu, softly nudging me.

Abu—my young, saturnine driver turned ad hoc translator and guide—had let me sleep until we were at the main gate.

'They' were the black fatigue clad paramilitary personnel of the Rapid Action Battalion hovering around the gate, asking visitors who they were, why they were visiting and how long they would stay for the day.

With the ID check done and having returned the ever-so-slight but friendly nod from the officer who'd seen me almost every day, I was fumbling to get my camera assembled and the mic attached on my phone. There was no time to waste.

And right then, it happened.

Abu slammed the brakes, the car bumper hit the dirt road, and dust flew up. Lenses, battery and mic spilled onto the dashboard. Abu let out a string of Chittagonian swear words, mixed with him slamming the horn down, a clamour from bystanders and a burning pain in my left shoulder where the locked seat belt's edges cut into my skin through the shirt.

The reason for all this commotion was Shaheen.

Wearing a dress frayed at the edges, with lily-like flowers imprinted on it but faded beyond an identifiable colour, she stood well under four feet tall. Perfectly trimmed bangs of jet black hair threw her fair face and impish smile into relief.

Hugging a whole carp in a transparent cellophane bag to her chest, she had blindly run into the car's path, halted for a fraction of a moment, then bolted to the other side.

Abu opened the door and made a start for Shaheen, shouting at her for being a stupid, careless girl. But we managed to catch only a glimpse of her when she paused for another moment, looking back at the mess she'd caused, before disappearing into the maze of tarpaulin covered thatch houses.

It was all so quick. Neither Abu nor I could have possibly followed her. Besides, what would I do if I had caught up with her? Given a lesson in the virtues of road safety to a genocide survivor?

'Let it be,' I told Abu, reminding him we had more important things to do and didn't need a near-accident holding us back.

Abu parked his car under a tree not far from the chowk and, while he caught up on lost sleep, I walked into the camp with Ilyas—my Rohingya translator—west of the chowk, down the mud road that led to Mohibullah Mohammed's thatched home. Mohibullah was the chief organizer of the Arakan Rohingya Society for Peace and Human Rights, a spin-off from the Arakan Rohingya National Organization. He had taken on the monicker 'Peace Father' and become the most prominent face of repatriation demands inside the camp. He was one of the first people I'd interviewed.

Soon, the daily reporting routine took over—interviews with the refugees about life in the camps, profiling of lives before the genocide, scanning of documents that testified to how the social standing and education of regular self-respecting humans had been tossed into pyres lit by the Burmese military and so on and so forth.

This continued until around noon when the women sent their children to remind the menfolk that it was lunchtime and they were waiting.

'Come join us,' Mohibullah and his comrades said warmly.

As always, the Rohingyas invited me to share their meal of dal and rice, made from the meagre rations handed out by the aid agencies. As always, I politely refused.

'You carry on, I have some more work to finish. I'll see you post lunch.'

From the very early years of journalism, keeping an emotional distance from those we report about had been drilled in by seniors. It's a good rule to follow. Especially when building dikes against an enormity of proportions like the Rohingya genocide. Breaking bread with the subjects one is reporting on is antithetical to that keeping of distances.

Besides, I had very little time left in the camps and needed to use all the hours I had there to report as much as possible. Being friends or eating meals wasn't going to pay my bills.

In short, it was a day like the many others I'd spent in the camp, except for one thing—Shaheen.

'Can you find out where that girl from the morning lives?' I asked Abu, returning to the chowk. 'Don't say anything to her or her family. I'll finish my photographing and see you in an hour or so.'

'Sir . . . do you need me [to come along]?' Ilyas asked. He knew I'd say no. And I did.

'Take a break—I'll have Abu call you if I need you.'

A little over an hour and a half later, I circled back to the chowk. Abu hadn't arrived. And since my phone didn't work in the camp, I had no way to contact him.

I sat down on the edge of a bench outside the camp's 'restaurant' and lit my last cigarette. In the rush of the morning, I'd forgotten to restock.

The restaurant was just a larger version of the bamboo, mat and tarpaulin thatches that the Rohingyas live in. Unpolished wooden planks made for both long tables and seats.

The place served food to the manual labourers and security who worked in the camp. People like me—reporters, aid workers and similar hordes of distress tourists—didn't go there. So I caused a small commotion by sitting down.

The bespectacled man who ran the cash counter barked at the last of the lunching labourers to make room for 'Sir', and the dishwasher came running with a rag to wipe a table for me. I motioned and grunted, indicating I wasn't going to order and was just resting my tired legs for a bit, and they needn't bother.

Half an hour or so later, with Abu still nowhere in sight and me having run out of my regular cigarettes, I bought a packet of the local brand a guy on the other side of the road was selling. The hard smoke went down like a beast clawing against the insides of my throat, and I asked for tea to soothe the pain.

By then, the lunch crowd was petering out, and the mud roads were emptying. Siesta time had set in.

The starch drained from rice pots and the leftovers of dal and potatoes in the dirty plates piled up next to the eatery had begun to rot. The stench had started roiling up in the afternoon heat.

Hot with the April sun, the wind raised little dust devils on the mud road. As the fine silt washed over me, the cashier tied currency notes in bundles with rubber bands, the dishwasher snoozed on an unoccupied bench, and the cook ground an uncovered aluminium pot full of raw lentil paste in a grimy blender. The lentil paste, mixed with salt, garlic paste, fennel seeds and chopped onions, would be transformed into deep-fried pakoras served with tea and muri (rice pops) seasoned with mustard oil and green chillies for the evening tiffin.

I saw all these things, but my mind kept returning to Shaheen.

As the episode of the morning played out in my mind's eye in slow, halting motion, I saw the little girl again. The hair, the dress, the carp. The running, stopping, running again. The little pause, the smile and the bolting off after.

Her face was clear in my head, looking back at me with a sweet, innocent smile. One I never will or ever want to forget. In fact, five years later, as I write these lines, I'm smiling back at her.

Through that smile, she had apologized for being careless and for the mess she'd caused the adults and their serious business with her silly antics. But she'd been so full of joy, there was very little of her already little self that she could have spared for any other emotion. And the carp had something to do with that joy.

'Another tea, sir?' the cashier asked, breaking my stupor.

'Sure,' I said. I didn't say no to another round of tea very often. Besides, I was occupying space at his place of business, so I might as well bill a few takas.

The sun was hovering barely a few feet above the edge of the camp by then. Rising from their siestas, the Rohingyas had started milling around the chowk. A crowd was gathering around the cigarette wallah who'd sold me the horrible tasting cigarettes. He, too, set a tea kettle on the boil on a kerosene stove.

Vegetable vendors had come in and set their stuff on rags laid out on the ground. I'd seen these evening markets before. Bottle gourd vines, water spinach, green chillies, onions and potatoes—only the basic cheap stuff the Rohingya could afford.

'Stop inviting sir to eat with us,' Ilyas had ribbed Mohibullah some days back. 'What will you feed him? All we eat every day is that damned rice and dal.'

'Siddharth bhai is one of us, no?' Rohim—a member of Mohibullah's team—had retorted. 'He loves his tobacco and tea just like a Rohingya. And Rohingyas eat rice no matter which meal it is!'

'Speak for yourself,' Ilyas cackled and, holding Rohim's tummy in a pinch, added, 'The rice is all settling here for you! Eat some dal too—you'll get some protein, you oaf.'

Proteins, other than what was in their watery lentils, were hard to come by. Neither was there much of a supply of meat and fish; nor did the Rohingya have the money to buy them regularly. Vegetables were the aforementioned vines and leaves, with only an occasional addition of a gourd here or a tuber there.

The only edibles in abundance in the camp were betel leaves and areca nuts.

Bangladesh, in general, and Cox's Bazar, in particular, grows a lot of these. In fact, the entire marine road going from the city to the camps is lined with betel farms and houses shrouded in groves of areca palms that sway in the sea breeze.

Local Bengali villagers come into the camps every evening with sackfuls of the lush green, pungent paan and the woody, bitter brown nuts the Rohingya call *shuari*. As the produce is local, the freshness is unsurpassed and the prices are low. Needless to say, the Rohingya make the most of this, and business is brisk. Men and women alike, it's hard to find a Rohingya whose face isn't stuffed at all times with the blood-red mush of paan-shuari-tobacco.

The Rohingya make a big fuss going to these evening markets.

There is an entire ritual—the putting on of clean clothes, the connoisseur-like checking of quality, the seeking of assurances from vendors that these won't be as bad as the last lot, and the vendors, in turn, doling out hyperboles like: 'If you get anything better than this at this price in this market—I swear on my dead father and Allah—I'll stop this business tomorrow!'

A joyous farce enacted every day for a few hours, these evenings let the Rohingyas live the mores of what quotidian life was in a land they, not long ago, called home. It is a time where, under the shroud of growing twilight, they can hide from the stark reality that life is nothing like it used to be or will ever be again.

'You know what a Rohingya really wants?' Korim, Mohibullah's lieutenant, asked me one day, grinning and baring his red-stained teeth.

It was another afternoon, and we'd had a long day of intense conversations about what the Rohingyas' demands were. Mohibullah had painstakingly taken me through the many treaties and agreements with the military junta, the other groups of non-Burmese Arakanese ethnicities who'd rebelled against Rangoon, the joining of forces with Bogyoke Aung San and, subsequently, his daughter Aung San Suu Kyi to demand democracy, establishing the many times the Rohingya had asked for and been granted autonomy and the right to self-determination.

The conversations had tired us all out, and we were taking a break with lemon tea—*shaa*, as they call it. The tea had very little sugar because very little was given to them. The salinity of the hard, brackish groundwater the Rohingyas drank and cooked in gave the tea a strange taste. The men had set forth some betel leaves, too, but I'd only taken some bits of the areca nut from the mixture.

'What a Rohingya really wants . . .' Korim continued, '. . . is to have his shaa, *shuari* and a hot meal of rice. In peace!'

It was almost sundown, and I was still waiting at the restaurant when a little boy, younger than Shaheen, walked across the chowk, dangling a live chicken upside down by one leg. At least one Rohingya family was going to have a non-basic dinner tonight. I took a photo of him from behind. He turned at the sound of the click, grinned, silly and shy, and promptly ran home just as Shaheen had done.

The cook brought me another tea and a plate of pakoras with it.

'No, no . . . no pakoras,' I said.

'No money, sir . . . just for tasting,' the cashier grinned and said from behind his counter. On cue, the cook grinned as well.

'Thank you,' I said and put one in my mouth. After a convincing number of chews, I lied, 'Very nice!'

The lentil was gluey and undercooked on the inside, and the outside had been fried to a rock. Coarse salt had been used instead of the powdered kind, and it sat in clumps of bitter salinity arriving unannounced in sudden shocks inside an otherwise insipid cud. Moreover, the oil used was as thick as engine grease and burnt beyond fitness for human consumption from repeated use.

But to make my lie convincing and honour the shopkeepers' kind gesture, I managed a few more bites and made expressions of satiety and hummed appreciation.

'Sir . . .' Abu had returned. Without saying anything more, he gave me and the pakora plate a look that said, 'Really?'

Refusing my enthusiastic offer to partake of the dal pakoras and handing me a bottle of water, he said, 'I found the girl.'

After five-odd minutes and some untraceable turns in the camp's maze, I reached the thatch house Shaheen called home.

Her mother—who appeared to be in her early thirties, with a face whose beauty hadn't yet been beaten out by the hard camp life—clasped her hands at her chest and let out a string of Rohingya as soon as she saw me.

'She's saying she's very sorry for what her daughter did,' Abu translated as the woman spoke. Abu wasn't as good as Ilyas, but would do for now.

'It's okay, it's okay,' I tried calming the woman down. But she went on with her loud apologies. Hearing the commotion, her neighbours came out. This was becoming a scene I didn't want to be in.

'Where's your daughter?' I asked. Fishing out a clutch of sweets from my bag, I said, 'Here . . . these are for her. Tell her I'm sorry about this morning. We are sorry. For scaring her.'

Abu looked me in the face, reluctant to translate. But then did as he was asked.

In my line of work, where cigarettes don't work, sugar does the trick with strangers who need disarming. Toffees and lozenges are always to be found in my bag.

In fact, from the second day that I set foot in the Rohingya camp, Mohibullah's daughter, Afnan, had made me triple my daily stock. Mohibullah, in addition to introducing many of his fellow activists, scholars and contacts in other parts of the world, had introduced me to his daughter Afnan—his ninth-born.

Not that he had planned to. But when Afnan just strolled into our meeting and sat down in the middle, he had no option but to.

Afnan had Down's Syndrome and couldn't speak. But we took to each other from the very first time we met. Well, to be honest, she took to my camera more than me.

Afnan had not only unabashedly walked into a meeting of august adults, but she also sat down right in the middle, paying no heed to her father's requests that she leave. Neither I nor any other adult in the group minded Afnan's presence, so Mohibullah gave up trying to get her to leave and resumed his conversations with me.

Barely a minute or two into the conversation, Afnan started poking her father in the leg. After ignoring her for a bit, 'What?' he asked, exasperated.

She pointed at my camera and, grinning, looked from her father's face to mine.

'No!' her father refused sternly. But the very moment we started talking, she resumed her poke-n-point routine. All the while smiling her potently disarming smile.

'You want a photo?' I spoke to her directly—miming the taking of a photo to bridge the language gap.

The offer turned the smile into an incredibly silly grin, and her cheeks blushed hard enough to look like a crimson burn. She shook her head, saying, 'No . . . it's okay,' but a moment later put on a pair of dark glasses and posed.

The adults gathered, abandoning talks of genocide and world politics, burst out laughing.

Of course, I took her photo. And to seal our nascent friendship, I fished out a few mints from my bag and gave them to the girl. She put one in her mouth and the rest inside her T-shirt, where they settled like little pebbles around her tummy at the place where she had tucked her top into her fraying skirt.

To this day, I don't know how, but even though Afnan never left the room, the news of this exchange of mints spread through the ether. Within a few minutes of the act, half a dozen of Afnan's friends appeared one after another.

From the next day, I became the guy who brought sweets and let kids take photos with his camera. A reputation I made sure never got dented till the last day by tripling my sugary stocks.

The offering of sweets convinced Shaheen's mother I wasn't there to admonish her or her daughter, and she calmed down. Her face went from pained apologies to a smile and, looking into the darkness of their damp thatch, she called out to her daughter by name.

After two and a half calls, the face I'd seen in the morning peeked out from behind a braided palm leaves partition. Then, on seeing the sweets, the smile from the morning appeared too. And she stepped out.

'She's always loved eating fish,' Shaheen's mother said. We were seated on a plastic mat with UNHCR woven into it. 'She's been begging me to buy her some fish for months. Today's the first time we're making it in the camp.'

They hailed from Maungdaw Township—close to the Bangla–Myanmar border. The family of four was well-to-do by Arakanese standards.

'He (Shaheen's father) was the only son, and we had a good farming business,' the woman narrated. 'I am a graduate, and after marriage, I'd completed my training as a beautician. My husband rented me a shop, and I started a ladies' parlour. It was all going well. Shaheen was born in 2011, and then my son in 2014. And now I've been in the camp since 2016. I was in another camp earlier but moved to Kutupalong in 2017.'

'Where are your husband and son?' I asked. It was a question that will haunt me for a long time to come.

'They didn't make it,' she said. Looking down at her knees, she went quiet. Shaheen sat still, hiding behind her mother.

'The Tatmadaw killed them,' Shaheen's mother said after a long pause, continuing to look down, sitting still as a statue. Shaheen noiselessly picked at a frayed fibre in the UNHCR mat. Teardrops fell on the woman's knees, and a patch of wetness gathered on her saree. Then came the sobs and larger teardrops fell on the plastic mat. In the quietude of the evening, they sounded like the wayward raindrops that precede a storm.

'Those men were so violent and so heartless. Like monsters!' the woman said of the Tatmadaw. 'I'd gone to see some relatives in another village with Shaheen. Her father had stayed back with our son. When I came back,

I was told they'd locked our house from the outside with my husband and son inside and then set fire to it. We hid in the fields until nightfall. Only after the platoon left did we realize others had been hiding in the fields. We took nothing. Nothing was left to take. I didn't even dig through the ashes to find my dead husband and son. I just held my daughter's hand and left.'

Quiet descended in the thatch again. Nothing I had ever read in school or learned on the field had prepared me for asking any follow-up questions or saying anything that made any sense any more. We all sat in silence for I don't know how long.

'We should leave, sir . . . the gates will close,' Abu said in a near whisper, breaking the silence.

'No, no . . . don't leave . . . one minute,' the woman rubbed her eyes clear and, bringing a big, beautiful smile to her face, asked us to wait and rushed into the space behind the partition.

She returned with two plates of rice and fish curry and set them in front of us.

'Please don't say no . . . this is the first time we've made fish. I don't have a real kitchen and none of the spices I need so it's not very good, I know. But please eat a bit.'

I convinced her to take back one plate, and Abu and I shared the other.

The curry was little more than a thin broth of salt and a lot of red chilli powder. But the carp was fresh and lent some umami substance to the curry.

'I've started doing some salon work for the women here now,' she said, beaming as we ate. 'Basic things like haircuts, threading and such. Whatever I can manage within these circumstances. And every taka earned is something, right? A madam in the school (run by an aid agency) has said she'll get me some more stuff like wax strips, scissors and combs.

If I manage to save up, I'll get a hairdryer too. I should be able to do better with that.'

'But all my income will probably end up in feeding Shaheen fish curry!' she laughed. Abu and I laughed with her. Shaheen grinned and once again hid behind her mother's back.

***

The next day—my last in the camps and the last but one in Cox's Bazar—Ilyas met me as usual.

'Did you go to meet Shaheen's mother yesterday evening?' he asked.

Ilyas—the lanky father of two lovely little girls, the second one being born of premature labour when he and his wife were trying to run away from the Tatmadaw—was a street-smart guy with a network of informants in the camp that made him invaluable to reporters like me. So it was no surprise he knew about my evening visit to Shaheen and her mother. He possibly even knew that I'd eaten fish curry and rice at their place and given sweets to Shaheen.

But he had a rotten mouth—and not just literally from the tooth and gum decay that came with his betel, areca and tobacco addiction. He was given to vile gossiping and name-calling behind people's backs.

'*Rubah,* sir . . . these are all rubah . . . not safe after evening,' he had said the first time he took me around the camp. It had taken me some time to understand that he was calling the villagers around the camp 'robbers', claiming they stole things from the refugee camps.

From that point on, I realized that for every one piece of helpful information Ilyas had, he had ten criticisms of everyone around—even Mohibullah.

'Shameless he is . . . producing so many babies.' He had said when I asked him about Mohibullah's family.

'He's a complete lout—numskull,' he said of Korim.

'That fat woman doesn't pay well. She doesn't even look like a woman!' he'd cackled about a Reuter's reporter.

'Yes, I did,' I said, replying to Ilyas's question asking if I'd met Shaheen's mother. 'Why do you ask?'

'You didn't call me before going there? You should have. Not good woman, sir . . . liar also.'

I looked at him questioningly.

'I know her well, sir,' he continued. 'She from Maungdaw, like me.'

Lowering his voice and bringing his foul smelling mouth close to my face, he said, 'She's a whore sir. Whore. That's why the money to be so pretty and do make-up, sir.'

'My biggest fear is about what we will become here in the camp,' Mohibullah had told me one day when we were simply talking and not doing any interviews. 'Refugees don't remain human, you know. Without basic human dignity and without a place to call home, they become animals after a point. Animals who'll do whatever just to survive. They'll fight and bicker over the smallest things.

'Already factions are forming inside the camp. Factions of people who don't like me because I talk of peace and want to go the democratic way. Many want to start an armed resistance, you know. They think guns, bombs and jihadist methods are the only way to hit back and assert power. They call me unmanly and spineless and are just waiting for a chance to pick a fight with me.'

Mohib's fears were proven right. On 29 September 2021, he was gunned down by members of the Arakan Rohingya Salvation Army, a jihadist outfit that swore allegiance to the Islamic State.

Ilyas called me after Mohib's killing.

'I'm scared, sir. I'm very scared. Please see if you can get me out,' he had pleaded.

The Hungry Ladies of Cox's Bazar

'Sir . . . ladies? You want ladies?' the cycle rickshaw puller turned his head and asked. The smell of his sweat and the rank breath of an empty stomach flowed with his hard Chittagonian dialect.

Having wound up my last day in the camps, I had decided to treat myself to a few drinks and headed to one of the star-rated hotels in the city—a place that served overpriced beer with a complimentary side of rudeness towards people who shared their skin tone.

Barely two small drinks later, I was craving some home-style fish curry and rice and had hailed the scraggy man's ride and told him to take me to a place where I could get that. I wasn't specific and, with the mild intoxication playing in my head, I didn't care to be.

He'd popped the question a minute or two into the ride.

'Sir' and 'ladies' was all I understood. But that was enough for me to understand what he was saying. This wasn't the first time I'd been offered sex in Cox's Bazar.

Far from it, in fact. Not a single evening had gone by without a toto (electric rickshaws that ply the city) driver who drove me to a bar for a post-work drink, or a waiter who served at my table while I ate dinner, offering me some more pleasures of the carnal kind.

It was an irritant initially, and I made an effort to say a loud and clear no. But over time, as one does with the all-pervasive stench of drying fish and the flies that roam the city's streets, I'd learned to ignore the solicitations.

Cheap hookers, meth pills and bad booze are what Cox's Bazar is all about after sundown. And men like these, who doubled up as pimps, were only trying to make a dollar or two from what's politely called the tourist trade.

And the State is an accomplice in Cox's Bazar's tourist trade. The social contract of don't see, don't tell is the proverbial win-win. In an Islamic country where alcohol is banned for citizens, Cox's Bazar's star-rated hotels don't do the mandatory foreign passport check. Yaba (meth) pills are as easier to get than good chewing gum. The cheap thrills rake in a lot of money for all involved, at whatever level of power and influence. Tucked away in the southern corner of the country, the sins don't affect the piety of the mainland.

A brown, Bengali-speaking single man with the local broth on his breath—I looked every bit like the Johns who came from Dhaka and Mymensingh for a day or two and did their bit for the local economy.

'What kind of women?' I asked.

'Good kind, sir . . . very good.'

'No. I meant, where are the women from?'

'All different kinds, sir. Bengali, Chakma. All kinds,' he replied. 'Chakmas give good service, sir . . . best,' he added, with an ugly grin, letting a fellow man know of his preference for the tribe from the hill tracts.

'Rohingya?' I asked.

'Ro . . . hing . . . ya?' he mused, searching his memory. 'Yes, yes! One place I know, sir,' and began pedalling with added purpose.

'But no Chakma?' he asked a moment later—the sweaty forehead wrinkled in a mix of curiosity and disappointment at my taste in women.

'No,' I shot back. 'Rohingya.'

With my limited knowledge of the city, I lost track of our route at the first right he took off the main road. By the time he'd taken a few more lefts and rights into ever-narrowing darkening lanes, I pulled the SIM out of my local phone and stored it in the watch pocket of my denim pants. I wasn't sure if I'd get mugged by roughnecks who guard such establishments. So at best they'd take my cheap phone and I'd be able to continue working with the same number. Besides, in all likelihood, Bangladeshi intelligence was tracking me and seeing my phone ping a location of the kind I was visiting would be the perfect way to discredit my work.

No words were spoken any more. The rickshaw puller halted at a medicine shop in what looked like a regular residential area. He didn't alight or say anything, only turning to look at me with a raised eyebrow.

It took me more than a few moments to realize that he was asking me to buy condoms. With a grunt that meant 'Oh . . . of course', I played along.

Just as I turned my back to him, he said, 'Sir—one request. Buy me a ladies' belt? My wife got a caesarian last week, and she needs a belt to keep her stitches together.'

'What?' I asked incredulously. His request sounded ridiculously out of sync with what we were out to do. 'I don't even know what that's called.'

'Just tell the shop . . . they'll know,' he said, matter-of-factly.

The servile, eager-to-please face had given way to a man who meant business. The power equation had changed. I, the well-off man, was the weaker one now. He, the man who knew the dark by-lanes, was now the stronger one.

I bought him a belt but asked for a packet of chewing gum, instead of condoms, and placed it in my pocket, before turning around.

The apartment wasn't far. A few more turns, and we were at a gate.

'Tell Maa I have a *babu*,' he told the watchman.

Babu—meaning an urbane gent in Bangla—is an old euphemism for John. I'd encountered the term many times in books and movies, and once when I interviewed an old, greying former prostitute on Mirza Ghalib Street in Kolkata for a column in *The Hindu*. But I'd never heard of a madam being referred to as Maa—the Bangla word for mother.

The madam didn't come out. Instead, the watchman returned and asked me to go to the first floor.

'How much?' I asked the rickshaw puller.

'Give me something for now . . . I'll wait here,' he replied. 'You'll return to the hotel, won't you?'

Dressed in a nightgown with a floral print, the madam, a heavyset woman who looked about as old as me, stood at the door on the first floor. Her right hand clutched a TV remote and the left propped up a maroon curtain at the doorway. She nodded and said, 'Come'. Her face was unsmiling and her voice non-threatening yet unsympathetic.

I'd never been inside a brothel before. Taught by what I'd seen in movies, I'd imagined the place to be swarming with lecherous men and loose women in a state of ugly orgy. But this was nothing like it.

A sofa set, a TV, a glass-top teapoy with a small rug under it, and a dinner table with a few bottles of alcohol and a vase with a plastic vine sat in the living room. The empty teacup on the tea table, a Hindi movie playing on cable TV and the slight depression in the single-seater sofa told me the Madam had been sipping tea and watching a movie until I came around.

Save for the harsh smell of strong, cheap perfume, which had mixed with air gone stale from tightly shut windows, this could've passed off for a regular Bengali household.

It wasn't a very busy night. Maybe because it was a weekday? I wondered.

Madam got straight to business. Speaking in Bangla with only the slightest hint of a Chittagonian accent, she said, 'Five hundred takas (five dollars) per hour or 2500 for the whole night. You have to pay in advance. We have drinks here, but you have to buy by the quarter'—and paused for a reply.

I was nervous and probably making it worse by trying to appear confident while avoiding her eyes.

'The watchman will get you food,' she continued and suddenly shouted to someone inside, 'OY . . . BRING ME THE MENU!'

'No . . . no, it's fine . . . I don't need drinks or food,' I said, coughing away phantom phlegm in my throat. A twenty-something young woman had brought in the menu—a fourfold home delivery leaflet from some restaurant nearby. Madam sent the woman back with a 'Keep it in room number two'.

At this point, three young women came and stood in the living room. They wore cheap make-up, faux gold jewellery and shiny cheap salwar kurtas, and reeked of the perfume that sat in every corner of this house.

I was supposed to choose.

'Where are they from?' Some strength had returned to my voice.

'Local girls,' Madame replied.

'Are they Rohingya?'

'Why?' Madame asked, her forehead wrinkling with doubt.

'I only want Rohingya.' I made it clear.

Madame paused, looking straight at me. And then replied, 'All three are Rohingya.'

I decided on the one who looked the oldest of the three. She wore a red and black dress with gold and silver sequins.

Ushering me into room number two, she asked me to sit on the bed, and went to get some water.

She returned with an empty whiskey bottle turned water bottle that she'd got from a fridge. After placing it and a glass on the small table next to the bed, she latched the door from the inside. Turning to me, she made a gesture with her thumb and forefinger and mouthed, 'Condom?'

I nodded and asked her to sit down.

'Wait, don't take off your clothes.' I spoke in a low voice. Fetching my ID from my wallet, I said, 'I just want to talk.'

She took the ID in her hand and pretended to read it.

'Do you speak Bangla?' I asked.

'Yes', she nodded.

'Listen, I'm a reporter. I just want to talk to you.'

She looked at me for a long moment and promptly ran out the door.

Fuck! I was in trouble. I should've taken the creepy fixer's offer and not tried this alone.

Two creepy fixers actually.

One was a pretty well known journalist who worked for the *Dhaka Tribune*, an English language daily in Dhaka. He had told me he could get me a Rohingya human trafficking story and interviews with trafficked women.

'I just paid for the night and got it done,' he had explained when I asked how he got access. 'You aren't shy about it, are you?' he'd asked, with a grin.

Yes, I was shy. But that's not the reason I hadn't taken up his offer. His question had made it clear that he had gotten the services he had paid for and was curious if I was interested in partaking in these pleasures. And no, I wasn't. The thought of ever having sex with a trafficked human was outright repulsive.

The other chap was this guy who had curated a whole Rohingya refugee tourism package—flight tickets, hotels, translators, interviewees, photographers, he had it all. He even had extras like one- or two-day getaways, wellness and spa packages.

Saving the world is a tough job. And given the burden the White men and women were carrying on their selfless shoulders in Cox's Bazar, I imagine they often experience back pain. But of course, they needed yoga, spa, massages and wellness resorts.

While half of the titans of the West's charitable–industrial complex were still busy hosting charity dinners in New York with baba ganoush on the menu as a show of solidarity for Syrians, the other half had descended in Cox's Bazar. So business for the tour operator gent was brisk, to put it modestly.

'We provide all services,' the man had said, when making his sales pitch to me over the phone when I was still in Dhaka. 'We'll arrange your tickets, stay, driver, translator, and take you to all the right people.'

Right people meant refugees who gave the best (or worst, if you will) stories. True as their stories were and gargantuan as the enormity heaped upon them was, the 'right people' had told and retold their tales so many times over, they'd nearly perfected the narrative to a script they'd repeat every time a camera or microphone came up.

'But sex stories are extra charge,' he'd told me, blunt and terse. I had called him from Dhaka based on the reference of a professor at Dhaka University.

A man who referred to investigating human trafficking as 'sex stories' wasn't really someone I wanted as my guide. Besides I couldn't afford and didn't need the extras he provided. Neither was I White nor was I saving the world. I'd just figure my way out with both my reporting and back pain issues on my own.

But yes, when the woman ran out the door, I regretted the decision to go solo.

Seconds later, Madame walked in with the girl. She looked very angry but calmly closed the door before talking to me.

'Reporter?' she asked. Her eyes went back and forth from my face to the ID. 'From Dhaka?'

I told her who I was and what I'd come for and hastily added, 'I won't take too much time and I'll pay the all-night rate. I just want to know a few things and won't identify anyone.'

If not my disarmingly nervous self, total beta man vibes, then the prospect of a full billing on a slow night calmed Madame down a bit. She took 1500 taka more than the all-night rate and sat down beside me and, looking straight at the girl, spoke in Rohingya.

I don't understand Rohingya. But one English word indicated what instructions she was giving to her girl.

'Detail,' she said—telling her not to give too many.

'No camera, no recording,' she told me in a no-nonsense tone. I held up my hands in acquiescence.

'Ask,' she told me. I had thought she would leave the girl and me alone to do the interview. But clearly, she was going to supervise it.

'A pen and paper, please?' I asked in return.

A look of incredulity passed over her face.

'For notes,' I clarified.

The girl fetched a pen and two blank sheets torn from a foolscap notebook. I picked up a dog-eared Bangla porn magazine lying on the table and, using it as a board, began noting her story for the next hour or so.

Inan—as we'll call the twenty-two-year-old woman—had come to Cox's Bazar a little over two years back, before the most violent phase of the genocide. She spoke a little Bengali—in all likelihood picked up from her work in the city. Madame filled in as translator where her vocabulary fell short.

'He was finalizing a deal to sell the shop (in Buthidaung town) and keep the money in the bank before leaving,' she said about her husband. 'We had decided to keep our house (in a suburb of Buthidaung) for when we return. So he stayed back while my four children and I left with my husband's cousin and his family. The cousin's brother had come a month or two before and had made arrangements for his family at the camp. Initially, I stayed with them, but then I got allotted my own camp.'

'My husband sent messages through some people who came from our area that he would take some more time than we'd thought earlier, but there was nothing to worry about. It's been fourteen months since I last heard from him.'

'The cousin is a good man, and he looked after us. But his wife's a bitch who didn't want me around. After moving out, I tried to do sewing work to make some money. But there just wasn't enough work. And the rations aren't enough for five people. So when Shakir Bhai (a Bangladeshi pimp who traffics in the camps) offered me a job in a shop in the city, I accepted immediately. Some women in the camp told me Shakir Bhai was lying and that he'd simply put me in sex work—'

'What do you mean lying?' Madame interjected. 'What were you doing before you came here? As if anyone has forced you to be here? Don't start off a drama just because you're talking to this guy!'

'No, no, that's not what I mean,' Inan pacified Madame. 'It is true. I honestly didn't care if I had to sleep with men for money. I told my cousin's wife to look after my kids while I was away. She refused at first. But then I offered her money and told her, "You're my only family; who else can I turn to?" She agreed.'

'How did you get out of the camp?' I asked.

Rohingyas are required to stay inside the refugee cluster, and the paramilitary mans all gates. If caught outside camp limits, Rohingyas face incarceration.

'Shakir Bhai arranged everything. He has very good relations with the *Majhi* (camp leader) and the police. Now I go to the camp for a week every month. I've never faced any trouble.'

As the conversation progressed, Madam agreed to let me speak to the other two girls as well.

They were even younger. Though they claimed to be eighteen and nineteen, the younger of the two looked no more than sixteen. Like Inan, they too hailed from Buthidaung. But they'd come more recently and spoke no Bangla. Inan translated for me.

The younger one was finishing high school in Myanmar when her family had been killed.

'I was at an aunt's for two days, when a man from our village came rushing to our place,' she narrated. 'He had gone to town for some work when he heard a platoon of the Tatmadaw was headed to a village nearby. Fearing the worst, he rode his motorcycle towards our village, planning to get his wife and two children out. But he was too late. The platoon had gone in and burnt both our village and the neighbouring one down to the ground. He came straight to my aunt's place and blurted it all out.'

The girl stopped talking and started sobbing.

The tears smudged her kohl and foundation and with them the pretence of being a street-smart hooker. She cried as any little girl would. The older girl hugged her, consoled her with soft admonitions, and wiped her teary snot with the edge of her dupatta.

Yet again, I understood nothing of what was said, but it sounded as if she was telling the crying girl not to be a baby.

The other girl had been luckier. Nobody in her immediate family had been killed, and they'd all crossed the border together. But the family was big, and her father was old. She tried to work at the camp with the aid agencies. But most of that work was labour-intensive and given to men. Sleeping with men for money was easier and paid better.

I asked if we could open the windows and if I could smoke.

'Too many mosquitoes in this room,' Madame said. 'Come to the living room.'

Madame and I sat down on the sofa, and she took a cigarette from me. The girls didn't smoke. They took the mint chewing gums I had bought at the medicine shop instead, and sat cross-legged on the floor.

'Why do you only have Rohingyas here?' I asked Madame. 'Why not Chakmas or others?'

'Take a guess, Mr Reporter,' Madame smiled for the first time. As did the girls.

I shrugged.

'Where do you think I'm from?' she teased me. 'Just because I'm fair-skinned and speak clear Bangla, people think I'm Bengali. But I'm Rohingya and I only have my people here. Besides, the Chakmas are unhygienic as hell. I had a few Chakma girls once. And Allah! Their food? They make all these stinking foods! They refused to eat what we do and made these curries with godawful smelling bamboo shoots. I threw them out.'

The Madam had come a long time ago—in 1992. Fed up of a childless marriage with a good-for-nothing husband, she had an affair with a Bangladeshi man who visited the camp regularly.

'I was young then. Couldn't tell love from lust. He promised me a job in the city and marriage. But then I ended up at a brothel. Those days were bad. They'd beat new girls a lot. We don't do that any more. I changed ownership twice before coming to work for our current *mallik* (owner). He's a good man. He had family here in Cox's Bazar, but then they all moved to Chittagong city. His father died, and he had to take over the family business there. He works in cargo handling at the port. He's a very good man. I run this place all by myself now. He never interferes. He doesn't drink or have any vices. He comes once a month and stays for a few days. He's a very good man, you know. Always cares for the girls. He's helped several girls to go to Malaysia, Pakistan and other foreign countries.'

'How do these girls manage to go outside the country?' I asked.

'He comes from a big family, you know,' Madame explained. 'He's got a lot of influence in Dhaka. So he arranges all the travel papers and all. First, we make local IDs for the girls and then arrange for weddings with men who live abroad. With that, the girls get passports and travel abroad. It's all legal.'

'After a few months, these girls will also get to travel abroad if they like,' she continued. 'See, as I said, the mallik is very good. There is no compulsion in our business. What is that horrible life living in the camps? Is it worth being stuck in that? And some of the regulars really love these girls. They have social problems and families, or else they would've been regular men—just like husbands. And mallik selects his team very carefully too. Never allows them to misbehave with the girls. Shakir, for example. Tell him no?'

The girls smiled and nodded their heads in agreement.

Shakir, the pimp—who I've never met in person—later became a source for my drug story investigations.

Hailing from a village near Bandarban—a reserve forest near the Bangla–Myanmar border—Shakir was employed as a petty labour contractor in the camps and worked for a gamut of international aid agencies. He was a contractor only by name and worked alongside the other labourers. The pay was small and the work excessive. So he had decided to become a mule for the Yaba (methamphetamine pills) that came in from Teknaf.

He'd receive the pills from fishermen working the Naaf River—the natural and political border between Bangladesh and Myanmar—and carry them by bus to Dhaka.

On one such trip to Dhaka, he was picked up by the police.

'I wasn't carrying any Yaba that day,' he told me over the phone some months after I first heard his name at Inan's place. 'I had gone to meet my uncle in the city. But someone had tipped the police off, and they caught me just as I was about to board. Since there were no drugs on me, they couldn't charge me with anything. But they were angry—really angry—about the wrong tip-off. And they took that anger out on me. They beat me with belts and sticks and kicked me with their boots until they were too exhausted to continue. I almost died. I lost so many teeth, you know?'

He stopped ferrying drugs after that episode and shifted to trafficking.

'I don't know what people have told you about me,' he continued. 'But I'm not some devil. I have a family, too. I do what everyone else does. Why don't you ask around and check if I've ever laid a hand on any of the girls? As if I force the girls to do anything? As if I'm the only one making money? Their own men, the military people, the police in the city, the politicians—everyone makes money. In fact, far more than I do. They [the Rohingya] love to play the victim. Who runs the Yaba business in Teknaf? Who does the deal with security? If the Rohingya men weren't actively doing all this, how would anyone get these girls out of the camps? Even the White people [aid workers] have girls sent to their resorts. Even media people like you. Ask anyone—it's all an open secret. Only poor people like me get fed to the police and are beaten and abused.

'And just so you know, all these girls started their business inside the camp itself. Only after they get into this line do I offer to take them to the city. They also want to increase their income and not limit their business to broke labourers and men from their own camps.

'These are the Rohingyas, sir—born criminals.'

I can't vouch for Shakir's version of the story or his character and ethics, but chunks of what he said were, in fact, open secrets.

Pills are ferried across the Naaf River and through Bandarban. The trade on this route grew so big and the number of drug coolies who crossed the densely forested borders grew to such large numbers that the Bangladeshi military had to carve out a unit and set up heavily armed checkpoints to guard the forest.

A few of the older refugee families—the ones who came in the 1990s and are based in one of the oldest camps at Teknaf—have made good money in the drug trade. Women who've lost their husbands, fathers, and any recourse to a dignified income, have gotten together and set up whorehouses in a place where no real houses exist. And they've done so with the full knowledge and participation of the leaders of the camps, the security and anyone with any power or influence.

Besides, it's a standard practice for the drug gangs to let some of their people get caught by the police every once in a while. That way, the State is seen as doing its job, without actually upsetting the narco-economy. According to some estimates, the narco-economy is only second to the shipping and maritime industry in southern Bangladesh.

I couldn't find any independent confirmation of the aid industry honchos getting hookers to service them. But their dollar salaries afford them lavish lives that are both an eyesore in contrast to the standard of living of those they serve or work with and an income generator like none other for the local population.

'They changed the face of this place and the transport and hotel business,' Abu, my driver, told me. 'I had a small car. But the Whites didn't want them. They wanted four-wheel drives and SUVs. Besides, they paid very well and had long agreements. So, I took a loan and got one. Now I have four vehicles in my name, and my elder brother has three! Even the hotel and resort guys are minting money with all these foreigners. Soon, they won't even need to depend on Bangladeshi tourists any more.'

'How much do you make?' I'd asked Inan and the brothel girls at the very end. They'd hesitated and looked at Madame for approval.

'It depends on how many [men] they can take,' Madame had answered on their behalf. 'And I told you the rate.'

'But how much do *they* make per client?' I pressed.

'See, the mallik takes 70 per cent of the billing and pays salaries to his people, does maintenance for this house, and whatever other expenses he has. The government and police need to be paid too. And every time a new girl comes, the security at the camps, their families and the maajhi and his men take money.'

'So if a client pays 500 takas, the girl gets just a hundred and fifty from it?' I asked.

'Yes, thereabouts,' Madame confirmed. She hastily added, 'But they have no other living expenses. And they have a week off when they're ill (having their periods). So they basically work only three weeks a month. Besides, some clients give tips, which they can keep.'

'They don't get paid during the week off, do they?'

'How can they be paid when they aren't taking any clients? Look at the markets. Food isn't cheap, is it? Our place always has good food. Whatever they feel like eating, they do. Tell him, girls.'

The girls smiled, nodded and hemmed in agreement.

'What do you usually eat?' I asked.

'Breakfast we make ourselves,' Inan said. 'But lunch, dinner and evening tiffin are sent by the caterer (a local shop that runs a tiffin service). We have rice, dal, vegetables and fish curry for lunch. For dinner, we usually have parotas and chicken or beef.'

'But I eat rice for dinner, too,' the nineteen-year-old chimed in, grinning. The chewing gum tucked between her lower jaw and left cheek peeked out. 'Without a hot meal of rice, I can't get any sleep. And she (poking the youngest one in the arm)—she demands ice cream every day all through the summer!'

The youngest girl giggled, hands cupped over her mouth.

While I didn't doubt their honesty, I did notice the needle marks on all their arms, including the youngest girl. They were, in all likelihood, still sticking to what their madame had instructed at the beginning of the interview. From their stories about what they liked consuming, they'd left a 'detail' about opioids out.

I put another 500 takas on the table saying, 'Ice cream money,' and smiled and stood up.

They all stood near the door with the maroon curtain and waved goodbye, wishing me 'Allah Haafiz'.

The rickshaw puller had kept his word and was there, waiting for me and chatting excitedly with the watchman. The watchman gave me a gratuitous gum exposing grin and a cartoonish salute, indicating it was tipping time.

'Hotel, sir?' the rickshaw puller asked, pedalling out of the maze of lanes.

He was grinning strangely. As had been the case with innumerable toto drivers, he'd made good use of the 100-taka advance and helped himself to some Yaba while I was upstairs.

'Turn right at Dolphin Circle and stop on the left—in front of the fish and rice place,' I said. 'You can get yourself some dinner, too.'

'No, sir . . .' he said—still grinning. 'I'll head home, shower and have rice. Dinner has to be hot rice at home!'

Lies, Damned Lies and Mint Tea

Unadulterated truth is rare in the shadowy and deceptive world of intelligence and counterintelligence. It's a realm dominated by liars and charlatans, each playing their own game of deceit and manipulation. As a reporter in this murky field, I've encountered many of these deceivers.

Most of my interactions with these individuals have been civil, albeit superficial. I sit through these conversations, listening intently but sceptically, sifting through their words for fragments of truth amidst the overwhelming tide of falsehoods. Yet, there are those whose blatant lies have deeply irked me. Their overt and unapologetic dishonesty shows a blatant disregard for both my intelligence and time.

However, it's a complicated dance of discernment, as these fabricators often weave a delicate tapestry of lies and truths. Over the years, I've honed my ability to extract the few strands of verifiable information hidden within their complex labyrinths of deception.

But among all the storytellers I've encountered, an Iraqi man named Junaid Alawash stands out as the most blatant and unashamed liar of them all.

'So, are you going to meet him again?' Diya enquired. She leaned back languidly in her wrought iron chair, the smoke from her cigarette curling up into the air like a lazy serpent in the damp cold night air. She was referring to Junaid, a man we had encountered over lunch at a restaurant in Neukölln in Berlin earlier in the day.

Diya had been conducting an interview for The Taz in the area, and we had decided to grab lunch together.

Carrying our trays from the counter, we had settled ourselves at a table for four on the sidewalk where a stocky man, perhaps in his late fifties, was eating bread and curried meat.

Barely a spoon or two into our lunch, the man interjected, 'Not like that.'

He was addressing me, and unsolicited advice was about to pour forth.

'You take this,' he said, pointing to the tabbouleh, 'and that,' he gestured towards the hummus, 'Mix! Mix! And then eat.'

It wasn't my first encounter with tabbouleh or hummus. Far from it. Besides, I was already combining them before eating—just not on my plate as my fellow diner instructed, but on my spoon.

'Really?' I asked, more out of politeness than interest. The man, Junaid Alawash, seemed to have taken it upon himself to enlighten what he assumed were two naive Indian tourists.

Diya, a seasoned food writer, paid him no heed, focusing solely on her meat stew and bread. She was someone who often ended up educating others about the culinary traditions of their own countries. And Junaid wasn't the first overzealous 'educator' we had encountered in our travels.

'Yes!' Junaid exclaimed, oblivious to my sarcasm and Diya's silent disapproval. 'This is the Iraqi way. This restaurant serves the best Iraqi food in Germany!'

I responded with a non-committal smile, not bothering to mix the tabbouleh and hummus as he suggested. Tabbouleh and hummus aren't exclusive to Iraqi culinary traditions, and I wasn't particularly interested in adhering to traditional methods.

Junaid, however, was undeterred. 'Eating correctly shows respect for one's family and culture,' he continued, his pride in Iraqi culinary traditions evident. 'This place used to have those who knew good food. But now, it's not the same.'

Intrigued, I asked, 'Why? Has the quality of the food declined?'

He shook his head, his spoon leaving a gravy trail on the table, as he pointed behind me.

'No, the food is still good. The problem lies with them . . .' he said, nodding his head to point behind my back, his tone taking on a note of disdain.

Turning around, I saw a group of young college boys dressed in casual shorts and tees gathered around the takeaway counter. They were engaged in a lively debate over their orders, pooling together notes and coins.

'The crowding, you mean?' I ventured.

Junaid's expression hardened. 'No, not just the crowding. It's these men,' he said, his forehead furrowed in disappointment and voice laced with contempt.

Confused, I pondered over what he meant. What was so significant about these men?

'Roma,' he proffered, without me asking, and shrugged as if that one word explained everything. 'They're everywhere, ruining everything.'

Ah . . . now I understood. Junaid's problem wasn't the dilution of culinary purity but of racial ones. It was the age-old Roma hate that's been around for centuries now, stretching from Europe to the Levant, uniting Semites, anti-semites, and everyone in between.

I had no interest in engaging in a conversation laced with casual bigotry. So I shifted focus, turned to Diya, and asked about her plans for the rest of the day. In fact, I switched to Bangla to indicate our disinterest in further conversation with Junaid.

Her replies were short, her attention seemingly elsewhere as we finished our meal. Meanwhile, Junaid, who had been served mint tea, lit a cigarette.

'You are tourists? First time in Germany?' Junaid asked yet again, not registering our disinterest.

'Journalists,' I replied.

'Both journalists?'

'Yes.'

'Oh . . . interesting. So what kind of journalist?'

'Political.'

I was done with this man and my meal and began wiping my hands and mouth on the second tissue paper. But Diya had lit her cigarette, so I would have to wait a while.

'You are Indian, no?' Junaid asked. 'Then what political news for you in Berlin?'

'Global politics.'

'Global politics, eh? Then you must interview me!'

'Why would I do that?'

'Because I was Saddam Hussein's bodyguard.'

The man held my shocked gaze and, with a grin on his face, savoured the moment as much as he did his mint tea.

'So, Mr Roy, are you going to meet him?' Diya asked again, her voice breaking the night's silence—or at least the silence outside my head. Diya and I had gone out for post-work drinks and, as it usually did, the merriment had gone on into the wee hours.

Her question hung in the air, unanswered, along side the serpentine smoke she was breathing out for several long moments. I avoided her gaze and stared down at the black iron top table, at the only watering hole that was open all night. The table's surface was speckled with droplets from an earlier drizzle. Each of the droplets reflected the glowing crimson tip of her cigarette like the mosaic of a fly's eyes. The dead silence of Berlin's Anton-Saefkow-Platz at 2 a.m. made it impossible not to hear the soft crackle of ash from her cigarette. In my mind's eye, I could see her drag the smoke into her chest in a way only she did.

By this time, we had drained several beers, the empty bottles standing as silent witnesses to the night's progression. She had asked me other questions before this one too. They'd all just hung in the night air, unanswered.

I was lost in the darkness of Berlin's night, not caring to remember, barely listening, and even less willing to respond to her small talk or questions. I was struggling to calm the whirlpools of exhaustion and resignation churning through my mind. The alcohol sloshing in my veins did little to numb the acute sense of impending failure—failure in my professional pursuits in Germany and, even more distressingly, failure to avoid the train wreck of a love story unfolding before me.

Before I had got to know Diya during our fellowship, I had browsed her profile on the group page and dismissed her work. Besides my ego, which said that what I did was real journalism and that hers wasn't, the derision came from jealousy. She was a lifestyle journalist doing soft stories and getting love for writing hyperboles about some pork thigh she ate in Lyon or a cardamom coffee she had in Egypt, while I was rushing into all manner of trouble. Yet, little fame and even less fortune came my way. Some just have it so sweet in life.

But then I fell in love with her. What was I to do?

Far from a flaky lifestyle journalist, Diya spoke of food with a political nuance that was right up my street. The very first time we sat down for a meal together at an eatery in Stuttgart—barely three days into meeting her—she said, 'Tell me more about your Bangladesh investigation. Things you haven't written down.'

She'd read my Roads & Kingdoms piece called 'Cricket in the Caliphate' and had sensed that I had more to tell than I'd written.

Once, on camera, she was asked by our cohort's chaperone, 'How can you possibly discuss something as politically serious as the Syrian refugee crisis in Germany with something as simple as food?'

'Food is neither simple nor apolitical,' Diya had tersely shut down the condescending woman. 'When people leave their homes in wars, the only things they can carry are the memories of their homeland. Cooking their food is central to recreating that lost homeland in a place which isn't their home.'

Then there was the fact that she, like me, had accepted caffeine, nicotine and alcohol as the three primary food groups.

When the other journalists in our contingent would tire out with the day's itinerary, she would sit me down—over beer and endless cigarettes—and ask me all about my time in the company of terrorists.

That one time, drunkenly roaming around St Pauli—the infamous red-light district of Hamburg we'd been asked to avoid like the plague—she had laughed and laughed when I told her, 'Naah . . . I don't really like weed. The herbal smell gives me nausea. But the last time I had it was when I shared a joint with a wannabe suicide bomber.'

What had started with lovely company, peppered with flirting, turned into a glowing crush. It was as if I was a teen again. The trouble began when I fell in love. The nearly ten-year-old ring on her finger glared its golden guilt at me and her.

She made no promises. But I dreamt of things that weren't.

Each drag she took from her cigarette that night in Anton-Saefkow-Platz, every look she cast at me from her kohl-smudged eyes, reminded me that she was the strong one. Anything but floozy. She could love me for all the reasons

I wanted to be loved, letting that love play out for a brief period of time, knowing fully well that nothing other than an accident of time had made us cross paths. And then she was equally capable of walking away from it all, back to her life in India.

I hated that she, the flaky reporter who wrote about spice and all things nice, was strong. While I, the so-called hardened journalist who had infiltrated terrorist cells, was just a teenager throwing a tantrum at fate, asking, 'Why can't she be mine?'

The lack of progress in my jihadi hunting in Germany was only adding to my woes.

***

Emerging from the Rohingya camps in the sweltering mid-summer of 2018, I had landed in Germany on an exchange fellowship sponsored by the Bosch Foundation that sent Indian journalists to Germany and vice versa.

I knew nothing about the fellowship or the organization running it when I applied. It was during a boring graveyard shift in my newsroom at Noida's Film City, where I had a job I hated, that I typed 'Germany', 'investigative', 'journalism' and 'job.' This fellowship appeared two pages into Google's search results, and I applied. A month later, the fellowship judges called me for an interview at The Claridges in New Delhi. Another month or so from then, I was at the airport smoking lounge, waiting for a red-eye economy flight to Frankfurt.

When I had googled 'Germany', 'investigative', 'journalism' and 'job', it wasn't under some delusion that the Germans would offer me a job. Having been a nameless fixer for *Der Spiegel* several times, I knew how that world operated. The beacons of liberal inclusivity in the German press would happily have brown people like me write complete reports, but the byline would be that of a German who didn't know the first thing about the place or the people about whom the story was reported.

This wasn't specific to me or other Indian journalists like me. Bangladeshi, Pakistani, Afghani, Iranian, Kenyan—I knew hordes of others from my profession who were treated like this by White reporters who parachuted into one crisis from another and hired professional, sometimes veteran, journalists for cash-in-hand verbal contracts. Given that we third-world reporters didn't have much cash in our brown hands, we had no choice but to agree.

One such 'fixer' was a young man from Syria. If memory serves me right, he was called Mir and was the principal on-ground person who reported, translated, guided and arranged all logistics in and out of the Islamic State-occupied lands. He worked for the same foreign correspondent I worked for at *Der Spiegel*.

The Islamic State killed Mir on one such drive to the occupied areas. He had gone to 'prep the route' before the German reporter landed. Mir and his sacrifice weren't even acknowledged, while the reporter we worked for won press awards for her 'brave' reporting from Mosul.

So no, I wasn't looking for a German job. I just wanted to get to Germany by some means because I had a hypothesis to test. The hypothesis was that the Islamic State would regroup, reinvent and rearm itself in Germany, following the Syrian refugee crisis. But it would be the Indian subcontinent, and not Europe which would be the new theatre, because the new foot soldiers would be subcontinental and not Middle Eastern.

My understanding of the Islamic State had evolved significantly between 2016 and 2018. I wanted to observe how the large Muslim diaspora from the Indian subcontinent would react to active Islamic State operatives entering

Germany in the guise of refugees. This wasn't just a fleeting curiosity; my tryst with studying the Islamic State had grown into a deep-seated fascination bordering on obsession, one that I believed—perhaps wrongly and egotistically—was far more informed and nuanced than the understanding of the general public.

By 2018, the Islamic State had become a household name, capturing headlines and dominating discussions in newsrooms across the globe, particularly in the United States and Europe. Journalists and political analysts were grappling with this group's rapid changes and unprecedented tactics. From the bombing of the Radisson in Jordan to establishing a Caliphate in the war-torn city of Mosul in Iraq and then forging alliances with anti-Assad groups in Syria, the Islamic State was not just challenging, but completely dismantling, the framework of global jihad as it had existed under Osama Bin Laden's Al-Qaeda. They weren't just rewriting the rules—they were obliterating them. They were replacing long held principles, strategies and moral high grounds taken by jihadists with a remorseless doctrine where brutal means were justified in pursuit of the absolute end of establishing a global Caliphate.

Their approach was merciless, disregarding the established norms of warfare and humanitarian ethics. The members of the Islamic State weren't just some garden-variety war-dogs. They were a mad, rabid, frothing-at-the-mouth pack. Breaking free from any semblance of political restraint, this pack would, every now and then, snap with their drooling fangs at the very hands that had fed and nurtured them. They displayed a level of defiance and independence that both shocked and terrified their creators.

The ringmasters of the West and the gamekeepers of the Middle East who had let the beasts of the Islamic State loose on the world had thought they'd be an alternative to Osama's lot and the Afghan Taliban who had outgrown their puppet roles and were now seeking their own sovereignty. Moreover, they would keep the circus of fearmongering news cycles going, while these international players drained foreign lands of their oil and natural gas.

But both ringmasters and gamekeepers found themselves in a complex state of emotions thanks to the antics their pets were pulling. In fact, among the highest echelons of clandestine circles in the West, there was an element of awe at what the Islamic State was doing. Even the most hardened hawks of the West and its allies' deep states hadn't fully anticipated the sheer enormity and barbarity that the Islamic State would come to embody.

Simultaneously, there was an underlying current of fear, a dread that this beast, unleashed and uncontrolled, could potentially turn and ravage the very homes of those who had once held its leash. The Islamic State was nothing like anything postmodern jihad had seen.

While I knew all this as much as any other journalist or analyst following the Islamic State did, my perspective diverged significantly from the mainstream narrative.

Western pundits had said the Islamic State would change global jihad forever. The old days of the Al-Qaeda style was over. No more the strict hierarchy of Bin Laden's time; the new era of global jihad that had dawned in Mosul would now be all about lone wolf attacks and it would spread across the globe in no time.

For a while, it seemed they were correct. Holey Artisan, in fact, was proof.

But my experience, particularly following my reporting assignments in Bangladesh, Pakistan, Kashmir and the Maldives, led me to a different hypothesis. I believed that the Islamic State, with its particular brand of extremism and flat hierarchy, was destined to falter in the Indian subcontinent. The reason for their inevitable downfall, I theorized, wouldn't be the military might of their adversaries but rather the unique complexities of the Indian subcontinent. The sandcastles that the Islamic State was building in Mosul would either be just blown away or, at best, become an ineffective heap of failures once they met the tides and undercurrents of my part of the world.

Firstly, the fighters of the Islamic State, hardened in the harsh deserts of Arabia, would be overwhelmed by the varying geography and plurality of languages and cultures in the Indian subcontinent. The bickering syncretic lands that lay between the Indus and the Ganges would become a major hurdle for their one-size-fits-all plan for the global caliphate. The marshes of the Indus–Ganges–Padma–Brahmaputra would, in time, swallow the zeal of zealots as they had done so many times in history.

Secondly, Al-Qaeda in the Indian subcontinent had, under the direct commandeering of the Pakistani military and intelligence, been trained as a paramilitary unit with a well-defined military hierarchy. It was a structure that had done quite well and optimized itself for over half a century. This structure and, more importantly, Pakistan wouldn't just sit back and let the mavericks of Mosul overwhelm and undo their work. In fact, during my investigation of the Easter Sunday bombings, I had seen a clear, new pattern emerge. A pattern where the subcontinent would see a neo-jihadist tendency that was a mix and match of the Al-Qaeda in the Indian subcontinent and the Islamic State.

The millennial mujahideen weren't the ignorant village idiot stereotype of the Afghan mujahideen that the American pundits have continued using as blueprints for what an ideal jihadist looks like. This new lot, like youth everywhere, wasn't going to take orders from the boomers, unquestioning and obeisant. They'd take what they like from what existed and fill the rest of their bowl with what they didn't.

Thirdly, the Middle East was a saturated market for the business of jihad. Jihadist outfits in the Middle East had changed their branding and team colours many times. The degree of reluctance and acceptance of being handmaidens of Western imperialism had varied as well. But the hard reality was the Middle Eastern jihadist market was saturated. So any jihadist 'start-up' that wanted to grow would have no option but to look farther East.

Europe already had a vast subcontinental Muslim diaspora that was now going to meet and mix with those coming from Syria and Iraq. I needed to see what happened when the delta Muslims met the desert Muslims. Would cultural history and linguistic differences be strong enough to keep them apart? Or would the sands of the dreams of a unified global Caliphate blow across geographies and flow alongside the rivers of the East?

My hypothesis was that a lot was going to change. As much as the Islamic State would change jihad in the Indian subcontinent, the subcontinent would also change the Islamic State. And I needed to go to Berlin to get evidence for my hypothesis.

Moreover, post the unleashing of the Islamic State on Bashar Al Assad's Syria and the Syrian refugee crisis that flooded the streets of Germany, Berlin had become what Paris had been in the 1960s—the city of many cloaks and even more daggers. I needed to know from spymasters, both past and present, what they were hearing, seeing and thinking.

Besides, like all wars, jihad also runs on money. The fighters have a lot of faith and grit, no doubt. But guns, bullets and explosives aren't sold in exchange for piety and goodwill. They demand cash—hard cash.

The lawmakers of the Indian subcontinent were well versed with the old hawala money routes from the Arab world to their lands. Large chunks moving in would sound off way too many alarms for the jihadists to do their work in peace.

The flawed, leaky and over-surveilled American banking system wasn't much of an option for direct fund transfers, unless sanctioned by the American Deep State itself. Besides American aid, notorious as it is, it was unlikely to find its way into the pockets of the insolent upstarts of the Islamic State in the Indian subcontinent. This was because the two big recipients of American aid who have active jihadist contingents—Pakistan and Bangladesh—have states with well-established channels for using American aid money. While some of it may go towards fulfilling American foreign policy, aka trouble making objectives, neither the Pakistani government nor the Bangladeshi one was going to give a paisa to the non-compliant youngsters who made up the rank and file of the Islamic State.

Who did that leave, if not the Europeans and their infamous private banking establishments?

A chance meeting with a Bengali gentleman at a hotel lobby in Zurich many years before had left a lasting impression on me. It was breakfast time, and I was speaking in Bangla with my mother. Mamma Roy is the stuff of nightmares when it comes to being a fussy eater. And I had taken way too many trips to the buffet spreads and back to get her something to eat.

A well-dressed man with greying hair wished me good morning and complimented me for being a patient son. A warm smile curled up under his ashen moustache as he enquired in Bangla, '*Apnara India theke aschhen?* [Are you two from India?]'

Breakfast done, Mamma Roy back in the room, I sat down for a round of coffee with this man. He introduced himself as a private wealth banker based in Sweden. Like all Bengali conversations, our talk went from food to politics. In the flow of the conversation, he revealed his acute disdain for the [Sheikh] Hasina government in Bangladesh.

'This [Sheikh] Hasina government will be the end of us,' he said, one and a half black coffees in.

I had been nodding and hemming at the gent's proclamations. What I'd meant as 'I hear you,' he'd understood as 'I fully agree with you.'

'We—you know, the European Bengalis—we are working at building a resistance. A resistance to the wayward ways of the Hasina government and her party. This time, no offence meant to you personally, but this time, we won't let the Indians come in the way.'

No, I wasn't offended. Intrigued? Yes. Was this man saying what I think he was? About funding a coup or something? Or something along the lines of the 2004 grenade attack on Sheikh Hasina?

My life as an investigative journalist was still in the future. So I didn't ask the man for more details. Besides, back then, I wasn't trained enough to make people say more than what they said. So the conversation pretty much ended there, save for a few polite farewells.

But the thought stayed with me. As someone who worked in banking before journalism, I had heard about European reserves going to fund conflicts, thanks to the immunity they enjoyed from a private banking cover. In 2018, with everything happening in Germany, the conversation with the Bengali private banker returned to my mind.

By the time I made my way to New York and Columbia in 2016, I had seen increasing volumes of radical online chatter in Bengali-speaking groups from Europe. Bolstered by the successes of the Islamic State in Syria and Iraq, anonymous Bengali handles were calling for the blood of anyone they deemed anti-Islamic and pledging bitcoins to those who would do the bloodletting.

This online chatter wasn't just empty talk. Far from it. Social media and messaging groups were full of calls to live, serve and die for the Islamist utopia being built by the new prophet and head of the Islamic State, Abu Bakr al-Baghdadi. As someone who followed these things, I can attest that these calls were strong enough to tug at younger men's and women's heartstrings.

With the fall of the Soviet Union, nearly two generations have since come of age in a world fundamentally transformed by finance capitalism. Capitalists cheered its unchallenged dominance, proclaiming through self-serving intellectuals that both history and the pursuit of grand ideals was dead. Those deeply motivated by the dream of a more just world found themselves adrift, their guiding principles dismissed as naive. Instead, society ruthlessly instilled a new motto: profit as the sole yardstick to measure success and the only motivator worth considering.

Social media emerged as a beacon of hope. It provided young people with a space to dream under the cover of anonymous and pseudonymous handles. It once again allowed for dreams of an alternate world, where success, fame and a part in changing the world were within the reach of even those not born into the 1 per cent.

Sure, this wasn't an exact rerun of Lenin's Soviet—or, for that matter, Sheikh Mujib's—dream. After all, Bush's Global War on Terror was a pathetic euphemism for a war on Muslims. It is common knowledge that this was a war started on the back of the deadliest piece of fake news ever—the claim that Iraq had weapons of mass destruction. Subsequently, the same American news corporations that were banging the tom-toms of fact-checking and diversity and inclusivity in 2016 were the ones who were outright Islamophobic and cheering on a bloodbath in the Islamic world.

Little wonder then that this new variant of the dream of a better world held a green banner with a crescent, not a red one with a sickle and hammer. But it was an intense dream, nevertheless.

A dream strong enough for a Bengali Hindu boy from a sleepy borough in London—Siddhartha Dhar—to convert to Islam, become Abu Rumaysah al-Britani, and write a travelogue called 'A Brief Guide to Islamic State.'

In the language of his peers and on platforms they frequented, Siddhartha, now Abu, eloquently wrote, 'If you thought London or New York was cosmopolitan, then wait until you step foot in the Islamic State because it screams diversity . . .'

Innumerable young Bengalis had flocked to Europe in search of college degrees and work. Many among them harboured dreams of a better, more Islamic world. Thus far, they were a weak minority in Christian White Europe and hadn't been able to do anything. But the Islamic State's successes in Iraq, and the refugee crisis from Syria, were changing that.

The question that took me to Berlin was, would these Bengali and Pakistani Muslims be able to make common cause with the Syrians, Iraqis and other Muslims of the Middle East and build a larger movement for an Islamic State? Would their renewed vigour and proximity to European banking be able to breach traditional cultural boundaries and bring the sands of Arabia into the delta of the subcontinent? Would Europe really become the new base camp for the Islamic State that took their bloody jihad to the Indian subcontinent?

Before landing in Germany, I had contacted over a dozen potential interviewees, hoping to gain their insights upon arrival. However, a month into my stay, these planned interactions had failed to materialize, leaving me with a series of unfulfilled interview commitments and unanswered queries.

Among those who had backtracked were two officers from the German intelligence agency, Bundesnachrichtendienst (BND)—one currently serving and another recently retired.

Initially, they had responded enthusiastically and confirmed interviews, only to ghost me later, ignoring my texts and calls.

During this period of letting Syrian refugees in, Germany was keen to broadcast this act of humanitarianism to the world. So, no official statement could be made that mentioned any 'Islamist radicalism'. Admitting to the possibility of Islamic State operatives having come to Germany would not only unsettle the image Germany had crafted but also show their shabby vetting process.

Yet, my interactions with several Green Party leaders and ministers—the most profusely bleeding of hearts among the throngs of bleeding hearts in Germany—revealed a barely hidden resentment towards the Muslim population they had admitted into the country—especially Muslim men.

During a press meeting with Indian reporters, which I was part of, Boris Palmer, the Green Party mayor of Tubingen, unreservedly expressed his displeasure.

'They're ruining our culture,' he bluntly stated, his words laden with a barely concealed animosity.

Intrigued and seeking clarity, I asked, 'Who are?'

His response was immediate and pointed, 'These non-German men, of course.'

Palmer's words skirted around explicitly saying 'Muslim' or 'non-White', yet the implication was crystal clear. He continued with a tone of unyielding disapproval, 'They're misbehaving with our women. They don't fit into our culture.'

I pressed further, enquiring if he was implying an increase in serious criminal offences. 'You mean to say cases of rape or molestation have increased in Tubingen after the refugees came in?'

'No, no . . . not rape,' Palmer hastily clarified. 'But the other day, a woman was riding a bicycle, and a black man catcalled her.' His attempt to mask his racial profiling as a cultural critique did little to hide his racism.

The response from the Indian reporters was a collective groan. Palmer's casual racism, disguised as cultural analysis, was stark and unsettling. Our coordinator, an Indian woman who was then pursuing her PhD at Tubingen University and desperately trying to change her passport from Indian to German, quickly diverted the conversation to more trivial matters, trying to ease the tension.

In short, it was quite well known that active Islamic State operatives had come in among the refugees and were potentially setting up sleeper cells. Off the record, it was relatively easy to find voices expressing this fear. In fact, in Tubingen itself, a refugee was arrested for allegedly communicating with the Islamic State and discussing plans to establish a cell in the town.

But try as I might, I couldn't find anyone willing to engage in an on-the-record discussion about the nuanced issue of security, particularly in differentiating between ordinary Muslims seeking refuge and potential terrorists.

So, to answer Diya's question that drunk, cold, wet Berlin night about whether I intended to meet Junaid Alawash or not, I said, 'Yes.'

The meeting was scheduled for the following day at an upscale Moroccan eatery. And I was hoping really hard that this encounter would finally hand me a strand of the web I was trying to unravel.

Smuggler, Soldier, Traitor, Lie

'Mint tea?' Junaid asked me as we sat down on the plush white leather sofas of the expensive eatery he'd called me to.

'Sure.'

'Two mint teas, darling,' he ordered the East-European-looking waitress and leaned back. The waitress nodded, gave a pallid smile of acknowledgement and walked away.

Junaid took his time checking out the waitress's derrière and then, turning to me, asked, 'So tell me, Roy . . . what you want to know?'

'Why don't you start by telling me your story . . . about your time with Saddam Hussein, what happened when his government fell and how you landed up in Berlin,' I said, taking my phone out to type notes.

'We are his family,' Junaid began. 'Saddam Hussain's family. Cousins. And Saddam was a man who only trusted his family with his security. That's how it works in Iraq. I was in the Iraqi special forces, posted in North Iraq, when my elder brother called me and asked me to come to Baghdad. He was an adviser to Saddam—part of his inner circle of trusted people.

'I asked him what it was all about. I couldn't just get leave without notice.

'"Your leave will be taken care of," my brother assured me. "You just come down as soon as you can."

'And so I did. In fact, my commander called me right after my brother's phone call and said I had been given leave.

'I knew it was something big—but it wasn't until my brother took me to Saddam personally that I understood what I had been called in for. I was going to join his elite group of bodyguards. The ones who are always with him. Twenty-four hours.

'And so I worked as part of his team until a month before the Americans came.

'My brothers called for a meeting of our family's elders in our native village. And there he said, Saddam's days are numbered. We needed to make a choice.

'The Americans promised us money and resettlement in Europe if we betrayed Saddam. And we took that offer.'

Junaid paused. The waitress had come with the mint tea.

'Not this way, you idiot,' he barked at the girl.

'Always get it covered!' he said, taking the saucer from under the cup and putting it over the light ochre broth with a sprig of fresh mint. 'You keep the flavours in this way!'

'Stupid . . . completely stupid and untrained,' he grumbled, even after the girl had apologized and left.

The serving of the tea, Junaid's outburst and the girl going back with a sullen face had brought a pause to the tale I was being told.

Still muttering, Junaid fished out a steel case from his jacket's breast pocket. 'Cigarette?' he offered.

'No thanks . . . I have mine,' I said, bringing out my Gauloise.

'This is better—Marlboro,' Junaid said, his eyebrows raised in surprise as to why I wouldn't take his 'better' smoke over my cheap ones.

I ignored him and, taking a sip from the mint tea and a drag from my cigarette, resumed the interview.

'So, which year did you join Saddam as a bodyguard?'

'2002.'

'And which month was this?'

'Ah . . . I don't remember now. Why do you want to know?'

'I'm just trying to figure out how long you worked for him. Never mind. You said you were in the special forces. What was the name of your unit?'

'Unit?' Junaid asked, scrunching his nose and eyebrows. Clutching his fists and raising his arms like a bodybuilder showing off his biceps, he said, 'Special forces, we were called. The best fighters. That's all.'

'So you went from the special forces to Saddam Hussein directly? Didn't you have to train with the Republican Guard to become part of Saddam's entourage?'

'Republican Guard?' Junaid's nose and eyebrows scrunched up again. He said with exasperation, 'Special forces, special forces . . . I said, no? And we were family . . . Qusay [Hussein, Saddam's son and the commander of the Republican Guard] was always at our home. Saddam trusted us. We handled all his security and intelligence.'

The first doubt crept into my mind. Was this interview actually heading anywhere? If he didn't know about the Iraqi Republican Guard, whose last commander was Uday Hussein—Qusay's brother—he sure as hell was no part of any force, special or otherwise.

The thing with liars and fakers in my line of work, and the reason I am patient with them, is their habit of throwing in some truths in the barrage of bluffs they spout. If appropriately sifted, the little kernels of truth become leads, even if most of the verbiage is worthless chaff.

Besides, as I said before, Germany had offered me nothing thus far, and I was desperate for something to come my way. So, I continued calmly and professionally.

'Tell me about your shift to the American side,' I changed tracks. 'If, as you say, Saddam was family to you—and you're clearly proud of it—why would you betray him?'

'Money, my dear,' Junaid said, lighting another Marlboro and smiling theatrically like a comic villain. 'Everything runs on money. The Americans promised us money and resettlement in Europe. I was given Italy. I live in Milan—not Berlin. I'm only visiting for work.'

'What work is that?'

'Sculptures . . . antiques . . . you know antiques?'

'Yes, I know what antiques and sculptures are, you bumbling buffoon,' I said, in my head. But aloud, I chose to ask, 'What kind of antiques?'

He bent to his side where a leather sling-bag was sitting and, reaching into it, brought out a catalogue and handed it to me.

I didn't know enough about old sculptures to tell if what he was showing me was of any value. But the photos caught my eye.

I knew that after the defeat of Saddam, NATO-backed looters had actively pilfered truckloads of Mesopotamian and Assyrian artefacts from Iraq and Syria, to sell to private collectors in Europe and America. Some of the photos in the catalogue looked like things I'd seen in online reports of that loot.

'Can I take a photo?' I asked.

'Oh . . . no, no . . . no photo', Junaid replied, with uncharacteristic urgency. 'This is for clients only. Very authentic, very valuable.'

'Where do you source your materials from?'

'Iraq, of course,' he replied, shrugging.

'Which parts of Iraq?' I unlocked my phone and started taking notes. Finally, I might be getting somewhere, I thought. If not terrorists, a story about looters, at least!

But Junaid didn't answer.

'Where in Iraq do you get your goods from?' I asked again.

'You are on your phone . . . you finish, and only then I talk,' he said gruffly. And mimicking typing on a phone with his fingers, he added, 'I don't talk when people go . . . tip tip tap tap, you know?'

'I'm not on my phone!' I showed him. 'I'm taking notes of what you're saying. Reporter's notes? You have a problem with that?'

This time, I didn't hide the irritation in my voice, nor did Junaid miss it. Special forces or whatever, he wasn't going to bully me in an interview. My voice had risen a measured notch to tell him that.

'No, no . . . it's okay,' he said in a conciliatory tone. He added, 'I thought you were texting or something. Young people like you . . . ha ha ha ha . . .'

'So, as I was asking, where do you source your sculptures?'

'Secret places, my friend. Secret places in the desert!' Junaid said, in the style of a grandpa telling his grandkids a story. 'The deserts are full of many secrets you don't know about. You will think this is all stories, but there is a place in West Iraq with a cave. And you know who guards that cave? A djinn! A fire and sand djinn! You will walk there thinking there's nothing. But just as you get to the mouth of the cave, suddenly, you'll see fire and hot sand rising up! And the face of a djinn will appear! If you know the secret words, the djinn will let you pass, and you can get things from the cave.'

'I believe you,' I said, chuckling. 'You're Alibaba, and the words are Open Sim Sim, right?'

'You make fun of me?' Junaid was offended yet again. 'Listen . . . you are a journalist, you say? You report on terrorists and all, no?' he asked, with his cigarette pointed accusingly at me. 'Do you know who was sitting two houses from the restaurant we were eating in the other day?'

'No.'

'The intelligence chief of Hezbollah!'

'And you know that, how?'

'Well . . . I know many things, my friend. The Hezbollah chief and I go back a long way,' Junaid leaned back again with a smug smile plastered on his face.

'Then get me an interview with him.'

'An interview with the Hezbollah chief? Are you mad? He'll kill you right there and then!'

'Why will he kill a small reporter like me?'

'This is a very complex world, my friend . . . full of powerful and secret people. You write these secrets in your reports, and they will kill you. In fact, if you write in your report that I know the Hezbollah chief, I will come to Bombay and kill you.'

'You will come to Bombay and kill me?' I asked, standing up and putting my phone and cigarettes in my pant pocket.

'Only if you tell this in your report. You can't . . .'

'Don't worry—you won't have to go through the trouble of coming to Bombay,' I cut him short. 'I don't plan to write the life story of Alibaba and his forty-first thief. You have a good day!'

I'm not sure if Junaid understood my parting remark. By then, I didn't care. Germany had disappointed me yet again.

Junaid texted me a few times while I was in Germany, trying to sell me cock and bull stories about some impending coup in Baghdad he had come to know about or some secret UFO research facility the Americans have discovered in Iraq.

The last I heard from him was when I was back in India a few months later. Eid was around the corner, and he had shot a selfie video of himself praying. Arabic hymns were playing as background music, and a caption attached to the clip said, 'Honesty and bravery are the true hallmarks of a good Muslim.'

I blocked his number that day.

The Man Who Knew Too Much

If Junaid was the top-shelf material in the rack of bluffers I had in my stock, Zakir Kibira has to be the closest second.

In December 2016, I had stopped over in Kolkata for a day, en route to Dhaka from New York. And there, I met Dr Garga Chatterjee.

Garga was still mostly writing op-eds and working his day job at the Indian Statistical Institute. His political career as the head of a Bengali nativist political party called Bangla Pokkho (Bengal Party) hadn't entirely begun, but he had built some bridges with Bangladesh's political and thinker circles because of his Bengali linguistic pride utterances on social media.

It was Garga who referred me to Zakir. I don't exactly recall now, but Garga and Zakir were either in a business partnership or planning to get into one. The business being an app targeting Bengali Muslims who wanted to keep a score of their daily halal–haram balance.

'You get points for doing good things like offering namaz, and points are subtracted for doing things that are proscribed by the Muslim faith. So you have a personal ready reckoner of your sins and piety.' Garga had described his app while we sipped lemon tea and smoked cigarettes in the backyard of his institute. 'Essentially, Siddhartho, my investments won't leave the Delta!'

Like Garga, I met Zakir, too, over a hot cup, this time coffee. While I was jet-lagged and sleep deprived and only had time for a quick shower, putting on a T-shirt and jeans, Zakir came looking rather fresh and dapper, dressed in a crisp suit.

'I was a consultant for the World Bank,' he said, by way of introduction, in a weird accent that did an awful job of mimicking an American one. He then proceeded to narrate a long list of some very important international bodies he'd worked for.

It all added up. Garga had said the same. Zakir was a permanent fixture in Dhaka's political talking heads' circles, especially the after-parties. Garga had met him during one of his jaunts in Dhaka and found him very well connected.

Clearly, Zakir was a great guy to know for a journalist like me, and I was much obliged to Garga for this lead.

As a coffee connoisseur, Zakir had strongly recommended the coffee shop we met in. Right after the first handshake, when we sat down, he had confidently taken the baton from the waiter into his own hands and run me through the different beans, roasts, grinds and their nuances.

'I'm investing in a coffee estate in the Hill Tracts,' he told me after placing the orders. 'Hill Tracts . . . in Chittagong, you know?'

'Mmm hmm—mmm hmm', I hemmed an enthusiastic yes.

'The Chittagong hills have this unique climate for growing good coffee. Absolutely unique blends can be made. And I'm setting up some estates. Organic, green . . .' Zakir held forth for almost the full ten-odd minutes it took our barista to make our coffee, the waiter to serve it at the table and for us to start sipping.

I listened with genuine interest.

Though I was no connoisseur, I liked—actually needed as a necessity—good coffee. Good meaning a few notches above instant Nescafé. Though, if fate commanded, I'd take Nescafé over no coffee. Even now, several good dark cups are still what I need to wake up and get through my day. So, it was a pleasure to meet someone who knew his coffee and was kind enough to tell me its nuances.

But half a cup of a double shot dark roast Americano down, I had to stop the Caffeine Chronicles masthead from fluttering and turn the conversation to the news—albeit not as fun—I was there to report.

'What do you know about the Holey Artisan case?' I asked, with my phone recording our conversation for notes.

'Well, I only know what everyone else does,' Zakir said, shrugging and smirking. It was a strange smirk—like he was telling me some kid's riddle I wasn't getting.

What? That's not what I was there for.

'But our friend Garga had said that you had an insider's view of the foreign intelligence circles in Dhaka. And you could tell me more specifics than what is already on the public record,' I objected. 'I need to know things that haven't already been reported.'

'What do you want me to say?' Zakir's smirk was still plastered to his face.

I put it down to the usual game a lot of people in power play. They want to know how much you know before they tell you things you don't.

Bangladesh is a country where foreign-aided NGOs rule the roost in almost all aspects of public life. If Zakir was a consultant to powerful agencies like the World Bank and the list of global corporate NGOs he'd named, he would likely be powerful in his access to information.

'Whatever you know and know to be correct,' I replied, submitting to his power. I wasn't going to play any cards I didn't have.

'Well,' Zakir continued, the smirk still intact. 'You know one can't always say the things they know, can they?'

'Of course, I understand. Tell me what you can, please. Assume I know nothing and tell me.'

He dropped the smirk, paused, looked into his coffee pensively for a minute and then began telling me what he knew and could tell.

'Well, Holey was shocking . . . absolutely shocking for everyone. I was a regular there. And I often met with foreign dignitaries—you know, diplomats and all—over there. You could say I was like family to the staff there!'

The smirk had now been replaced with a gentle smile that said, 'I'm an overachiever but also humble, you know?'

For the next ten-odd minutes, he took me through a very intent and detailed telling of what had happened that night. It was a vivid narration of the takeover by the youngsters owing allegiance to the Islamic State, the shrieks and confusion of the patrons and staff, the slow murder of the hostages one after another, the explosive charge by the Rapid Action Battalion and all such details till the sulphur laden bloody dawn.

Only, he wasn't at Holey the night the Islamic State had attacked, and he said nothing anyone wouldn't find in a news report.

'Another one, please,' I mouthed at the barista, raising a hand to get his attention. Zakir continued speaking, but I didn't register much or say anything till the coffee was served.

'Listen, Zakir Bhai,' I finally said when he'd allowed for a pause to take a sip from his now cold cup. I repeated my request from ten minutes back, 'I need to know more than what's already known. Do you have any idea who the masterminds were? Where the money and the weapons may have come from? Something more concrete.'

'I might,' Zakir said—that irritating smirk had returned. 'But you have to stop your recording if you want to hear it.'

'This is only for notes,' I clarified. 'I will never quote you without getting your okay on the quotes I use.'

I wasn't lying. This replaying of quotes remains a protocol I follow till date.

Interviews can often get long. More often than not, we need less than five per cent of an interviewee's words for a report. I'd learnt from my *Der Spiegel* days that some people follow a protocol of running the fractional quotes by the interviewee before publishing them. That way, the interviewee can't turn around and say s/he was misquoted or quoted out of context.

But Zakir wasn't going to budge.

'I'll give you the inside news, absolute inside news. But only if you turn that off.'

I relented and pressed the big red button on the screen, and the waveform flatlined.

Zakir took a dramatic pause and said with deep gravitas, 'It was the Chinese who did it!'

'What?' I exclaimed, louder than politeness permitted in that otherwise empty cafe. 'My God! What are you saying?'

My mind was blown. If this were true, the very prize, not just the grant the Pulitzer Centre had given me, would be mine.

'How do you know this?' I asked Zakir, excitedly.

'I'm telling you!' Zakir's teasing smirk was now a triumphant grin.

'You mean to say you have proof that can prove the Chinese did this? That would be explosive!'

'Oh come on, Sid . . . these aren't things of which there is proof . . . like a paper. But you can write this in your report with full confidence. The innermost circles in Dhaka have told me this. I have it from the topmost investigators.'

'But I will need proof to write this, no?'

'Simple logic, Sid. If it wasn't the Chinese, why else would India and America rush in and help the investigations? Just join the dots!'

Zakir had punctured my balloon of excitement within moments of pumping it up. I heard my Pulitzer dreams go bust with the bursting of the said balloon.

'You see the Chinese, just like the . . .' He continued with gusto.

Zakir spoke with intense vim and vigour while I sat there sipping my coffee and joining the dots. Just like I had done in my paint-by-number books from kindergarten. The dots were adding up to the drawing of an ass whose face had a grin just like Zakir's.

'Now that I have told you the real thing . . . you can restart the recording if you like.' Zakir's grin was now a full-toothed version, sparking some intrusive thoughts in my mind about connecting the white of my coffee cup with his pearly whites.

Instead of switching the recording on, I put the phone in my pocket, said, 'I need a smoke,' and stepped outside the shop.

Zakir hadn't registered my annoyance, so he continued his chatter.

'Parliaments?' he remarked, seeing my cigarette packet. 'One of my friends at the US embassy smokes this too. They love me at the US embassy, honestly! Sometimes, I think I get along much better with foreigners than with Bangladeshis [*snigger snigger*].'

'Yeah? Is it because of your access to such highly classified information?'

'Ha ha ha,' he laughed aloud, taking my remark as a compliment. 'No, no . . . I'm just a friendly person, I guess!'

'By the way, can you do me a favour?' he asked when I was done with my smoke. 'You have a foreign passport, no?'

'Indian,' I said. 'Not Chinese or American.'

'No, no . . . ha ha ha,' he laughed again—this time with even more vigour. And then, dropping his voice to almost a whisper, he said, 'New Year's Eve is round the corner . . . and people keep calling me up to get them a bottle. Can you buy some for me from the duty-free shops for foreigners, using your passport?'

A few days later, I discovered that his coffee business was yet to start. After all, one first has to gather the money to lease tracts in the hills of Chittagong for sowing coffee. Meanwhile, Zakir ran a different beverage business.

He'd get his 'friends' at the foreign NGOs and diplomatic missions to buy him bottles, which he sold to Bangladeshis with a markup. I don't know how brisk that business was since I didn't bother to meet or ask him anything again.

I had ended the interview after the cigarette, saying, 'Thank you for your time, Zakir, I have someone else to meet.'

He promptly asked me who, and I avoided answering. But then he offered to drop me to wherever I was going for my next meeting. And while I wasn't going to be rude enough to ask him to leave me—he was, after all, a friend of a friend—I stayed completely silent while we walked to the next spot.

'So, remember to keep your promise of running your quotes by me before you publish them,' he reminded me.

'Listen, man, I won't publish anything you told me. I don't publish things I haven't seen proof of. And I'm not going to say the Chinese did Holey when I have no proof to make me believe they did.'

I had to be blunt at this point.

Zakir wasn't smiling any more. His face darkened. I had hurt his ego by flat-out refusing to publish his conspiracy theories.

'This is the problem with Indians,' he said, obviously trying to insult me. 'They're always interfering in Bangladesh. From the very beginning. They got our founding father, Sheikh Mujibur Rahman, killed and then pretended to be our saviours.'

'Listen, man, I'm not going to get provoked if that's what you're trying to do,' I said, restraining my voice as much as possible. If I had gotten provoked by every verbal attack that interviewees and readers threw at me, I wouldn't have made it this far in journalism. 'But what on earth are you saying?

Why would India kill Sheikh Mujibur when their army was fighting the Pakistani army in your Liberation War?'

'Oh, are you blind to the Hindi supremacist regime in India that has always wanted to keep Bengalis down? They didn't want a Bengali nationalist to lead Bangladesh! Simple!'

'Okay, Zakir—that's enough,' I stopped on the footpath and, holding up my hands in exasperation, hit back at his bullshit. No journalism was possible with this man, so my restraint wasn't necessary. 'This is getting beyond ridiculous. The Chinese, the Americans, the Indians, the Pakistanis, everyone did everything other than the citizens of this country. And you know everything without being able to prove anything. The interview was over in the cafe, and we need to stop talking about politics.'

Though we continue to have some friends in common, I never met Zakir again. But two years after meeting him for the first and last time, I heard yet another conspiracy from one such common friend.

A year after our meeting in the cafe, Zakir took that friend, and a foreigner, to some exclusive New Year's Eve party at a farmhouse some hours' drive from Dhaka.

As per the friend's narration, Zakir had gotten very drunk and had pulled off some shenanigans that were more cringeworthy than cute. Chief among them was a run-in with a cop who was more annoyed with a very Bengali man talking to him in an indecipherable, inebriated-and-accented English than with his drunk driving.

But among other things, he had warned the common friend to stay away from me for good.

'Don't talk to Sid . . . he's CIA,' Zakir had said. '*Pucca* CIA . . . I know it!'

Big Fat Lies

I remember reading somewhere that a top American spymaster who left his CIA job and started one of the largest private intelligence groups in the world once said: 'If it's all true, then it's not intelligence!'

Though I'm paraphrasing here and not quoting verbatim, the truism being spouted by this cloak-and-daggers gent is in line with what I've said before: liars and charlatans are a dime a dozen in the world of espionage and all things clandestine. If one wants to be a productive journalist in this line of work, one shouldn't be so thin-skinned as to react in anger or hold grudges.

It is a rule I've more or less stuck to.

But I had once deviated from this stoic oath of mine. Oddly enough, it was with a journalist and not a full-time spy. Let's call him SB—short for Serial Bluffer.

This 'veteran' reporter, SB, once pitched me a story where he claimed to have a sensational insider report of a daring operation done by the Intelligence Bureau of India. I was then heading the South Asia bureau of a news wire start-up that served big American news corporation names.

According to this veteran, the Intelligence Bureau had planted an undercover operative in the Raja Bazar area of Kolkata. A young Muslim lady officer, she had gone in, pretending to be a believer wanting to join the Islamic State or Al-Qaeda or something. She had gained the confidence of a sleeper cell being run by a couple of men from Bangladesh—men who had fled in the wake of the War Crimes Tribunal set up by Sheikh Hasina and were now living in Kolkata with fake papers. She finally busted the cell by leading a contingent of armed sleuths to the sleeper cell. SB said he and he alone had all the exclusives of the operation.

My company had a strict 'no anonymous sources' policy.

'This is a killer story, but I don't think it'll pass muster for us because we can't quote anonymous sources,' I told him honestly.

'Come on, Sid . . . as if you don't know that active agents in India will never speak on the record,' SB reasoned.

He was right.

Being a proper reporter on the national security beat in India who wants to write stories of spycraft and operations is all but impossible if you care to report with on record sources. Unlike the US, which has a declassification cycle, press offices attached to various agencies and a history of deep, verifiable leaks, Indian spooks are on a lifelong non-disclosure agreement. The main body of work is all he-said-she-said, and national security reporting becomes indistinguishable from plants and propaganda or even fiction a la Le Carré and Fleming.

To work around this, several outlets in the West have a policy of limited disclosure. Meaning, if I spoke to someone who couldn't be named in the final report, I could keep voice notes (with the interviewee's permission), and should my immediate editor ask for the details, s/he'd have them as the publication's internal confidential record.

Going a step further, I followed the rule of getting clearance in writing. This meant that whenever anyone did an interview with me, I'd run the final quotes by them before putting them in my report. This way, I wouldn't be charged with quoting out of context or breaking the trust of the source.

This new wire service I was working with was very tech-forward. They had yet another layer of verification, where voice files would not only be auto-transcribed, but all image, audio and video files would be checked for metadata and geolocation to make sure they hadn't been edited or faked.

Truth be told, SB had been a useful source for me in the past. He had a solid network in India's intelligence community and was drinking buddies with many spooks across intelligence agencies—internal, external and military.

But I was wary of his reporting credentials. In fact, everyone who knew him or worked with him was, including the aforementioned drinking buddies. The very man who introduced me to SB—a former Af-Pak analyst for India's external intelligence agency, the Research and Analysis Wing—had, over a whiskey and wasabi-coated chickpeas, guffawed about the sheer number of bluffers in Indian national security reporters in general, and SB in particular.

'Sixty-forty—just like this drink you made,' the retired officer had said, jibing at my habit of diluting my alcohol a lot. 'That's how you take what people like SB say is the truth.'

'Question, sir, is sixty the water or forty?' I asked, laughing.

'You're a smart young chap . . . you'll figure it out soon!'

The analyst's warning had proven right. Only the proportion of water was closer to ninety than sixty.

SB had been thrown out of his job at the BBC for faking information. He had never really managed to salvage his journalistic career after that. He had, as he told me, also worked for the agencies, and claimed he played a crucial role in getting Assamese secessionist leader Anup Chetia to the negotiation table. 'You can ask Ajit Doval himself how X (an IB operative) and I once blew out the brains of Y (a close aide of Chetia). That sent shivers down Chetia's spine.'

What I did know was that all wasn't well with SB's work. Stories floated around about how he'd grown too clever by half and had become a sort of double agent. He'd take information from the anti-State people in the garb of being a journalist and sell them to intel agencies. Then, he'd leak little bits of operational intel to the anti-State bunch to stay in their good books.

This had pissed off some officers, and a team had even set up a trap to nab him with cash in hand, during one of his information exchange meetings with some anti-State people. Moreover, he masqueraded as a sex workers' rights proponent. Rumours in the intelligence circles said he was taking money and services in exchange for clearing papers and taking off cases lodged against brothel operators using his connections with the local police.

Maybe he was faking it, maybe he wasn't. Maybe he had crossed a line and was now in the cross hairs of the State. But neither the story of him being 007 incarnate nor his personal ethics, or the lack of them, mattered to anything I was reporting or had any bearing on what I spoke to him about. So, I never bothered diving deeper or seeking any independent corroboration about anything he said or anything that was said of him.

By the time we spoke about this particular report from Kolkata, he was writing a personal blog filled with nothing but fantastic cock and bull stories. So, he was of little use to me as a journalist. He was a useful node for me to get in touch with real sources, and that was it.

'Okay, let me try and talk to my seniors in [Washington] DC,' I said without prejudice. 'I'll need you to interview the agent in person. Record the interview on your phone and upload the file to our system. Make sure the file is unedited and the geotags are intact so they can verify the tape. Otherwise, it'll be rejected right off the bat.'

SB went silent for a few moments. Then he burst out in a slew of abuses, calling me everything from a two-bit pathetic wannabe to an ingrate to asking who the fuck I thought I was questioning his sources and merit. He even gave me a tally of the several thousand dollars he made a year, which a pathetic low life like me could only dream of ever making.

I was completely caught off guard by the verbal barrage.

I tried to pacify him, calling him 'Dada' [Elder brother] and shifting to Bangla from English. But far from being pacified, he hollered, 'YOU DON'T KNOW WHO YOU'RE DEALING WITH! I'M NOT JUST SOME PANSY JOURNALIST . . . I'VE BUMPED OFF [that militant's aide in India's North-east]. YOU WATCH YOUR BACK NOW! YOU WATCH YOUR BACK, YOU BASTARD!'

I cut the phone and was left feeling like I'd been punched in the stomach.

True, I didn't always believe everything he said. I didn't do that with anyone. But I'd always been cordial with him. Just as I have always been with all sources, and all of a sudden, this man was threatening to have me bumped off? All I'd told him was the editorial protocol of a publication I worked for!

I did the deep breathing everyone on social media keeps talking about. Counted to ten and back. And then wrote a quick two lines to my CEO and executive editor informing them that I'd just been threatened by a source.

The company I worked for had security and legal insurance in place—meant to fund any security snarls like kidnapping, attacks, ransom calls, etc., and pay for legal fees thereafter. One of the insurance conditions was that you had to record a threat or the possibility of a threat as soon as it happened. Otherwise, the insurance was null and void.

The CEO immediately called back and said I should get myself some personal security. There was an allowance for it, but one I hadn't used.

This calmed me down a bit. But only for a bit.

The initial feeling in my stomach started rolling around, morphing from insult and shock to anger. Soon it was unrestrained anger. I needed to give it back.

What SB didn't know was that I had several hundred megabytes of his voice records. The boisterous loudmouth that he was, in those tapes, he'd abused the prime minister, the home minister, the national security adviser, calling them everything from motherfuckers to incompetent assholes for not listening to stalwart thinkers like him. Not stopping at that, he'd named names in the highest echelons of the Deep State and bragged about the dirt he had on them.

So, let alone getting his so-called friends in high places to come after me for something as little as asking him to follow editorial rules, he'd be in serious trouble should those tapes be made public.

I called him back.

'Etiquette be damned,' I growled to myself while the phone rang. 'No way-past-expiry blob of lard is going to threaten me and get away with it.'

I called him back and said things in words I hadn't used since my college days and in a tongue I got very little opportunity to use any more—crass, thuggish Marathi—the kind that best lets my own violence be spoken to its purest intent, harking back to a time when I wouldn't let go off of half an opportunity to pick a meaningless street fight. One that has made me live with a stab wound in my left arm and a bump of stitch marks in my skull.

Prefacing with unprintable words that referred to SB's late mother and to his derrière, I said something along the lines of: 'Try it, you fatso! Try getting a hit on me, you pathetic unfuckable bag of lard. Before you move your so-called big guns, first practice getting off the couch in your living room! As for your gun, I'm sure a whole bunch of underage hookers in Sonagachi can attest to exactly how big your gun is under those layers of lard!'

After disconnecting the call, I sat at my desk for a long time expecting his number to show up in a text—if not a call from some unknown number giving me the threats he'd promised. But nothing came. Not until almost a week later, when I received a text from SB. He had shared a LinkedIn post about a job opening at the Washington Post with a comment saying, 'You should apply. Much better fit for you than your current job.'

I didn't respond to his text. I've never spoken to him since. Nor do I ever intend to in the future.

There are many things I regret doing in my personal life and a few in my work life. The company of the violent men that I have kept for all these years comes with a side of such regrets.

But talking the way I did with SB that day—or for that matter, even knowing him and using an unscrupulous wheeler-dealer of a man like him as a source of information—ranks among the highest of those regrets.

Middlemen of Maoist Lands

In my years as a journalist, navigating through mazes of lies and deceit has been a recurring theme. Interviewees, interlocutors and translators everywhere weave these webs of half-truths and fabrications. Fetching the real, usable information out of that tangled, messy web is *the* most demanding part of my work.

Yet, without a shred of doubt, the single biggest embodiment of this deceptive tapestry I have encountered has been in Chhattisgarh. Liars and damned liars are stacked among all groups in the state—officers, rebels, guides, translators, professional journalists and bureaucrats.

Here, amidst the half-a-century-old armed stand-off between Maoist rebels and the Indian State, truth isn't just elusive—it is the first and biggest casualty. The only unchanging truth in Chhattisgarh's conflict is that every party with a stake or a say in the conflict systematically smothers, reshapes and creates lies that suit their agenda for the day.

My first foray into the forests of Chhattisgarh took place in 2018 with the feisty Hindi language journalist, Kamal Shukla. I'd met him two years ago in New York when he'd accompanied Malini Subramaniam to Columbia University.

Malini had been a dogged and fierce anti-State voice from Chhattisgarh. Angered by her relentless reporting and immunity to the police establishment's strong-arm tactics, pro-state goons had attacked her on the night of 7 February 2016 at her home in Jagdalpur.

As a result, Malini was awarded the International Press Freedom Award by the Committee to Protect Journalists that year.

'Hi, Malini,' I held out my hand after the award ceremony was done. 'I'm Siddharthya. Many congratulations for the award. I've followed your work very closely for such a long time.'

She smiled a soft, lovely smile and held out her hand in an equally soft handshake. And then she introduced me to a kurta pyjama-clad, stocky, bearded man with the trademark Indian left-wing favourite side sling-bag, standing beside her. The man was Kamal, her principal guide to the rebel-held areas.

He shook my hand and grunted a greeting. But we didn't speak any more.

'How long are you going to be in NYC?' I asked Malini. 'I'd love to talk more when you have some time.'

Malini told me about a programme organized by a group of Indian–American expat activists called Friends of South Asia, where she had been invited to speak. I was more than happy to go.

At the sparsely attended event, decorated with an old poster that said 'Decolonize the Discourse', Malini presented photos of her time with the rebels and spoke of the fallout of the mining and forest looting lobbies that were wreaking havoc in the lives of indigenous and tribal people. Malini spoke in English. But when she asked Kamal to add to what she was saying, he shifted to Hindi.

During the tea break, Kamal joined me for a smoke, and I asked him about his access to the rebel-held areas.

'*Dono taraf hai!* [I have access to both sides]' Kamal offered immediately. 'When do you want to come?'

I didn't have a specific time in mind at the time. I would only finish my studies in 2017, and then my schedule would depend on where I worked and what work that would be. I knew very well that by the time Columbia ended, my purse would be running on fumes, and I wouldn't really be able to pick and choose every story I did.

What I did know for sure, though, is that someday I would report on the Maoist–State conflict. Moreover, I also knew that I wouldn't report it like Malini or Kamal did. Because, while I genuinely liked Malini's reportage and her bravery in standing up to the State machinery, I also had my differences with her approach.

Ever since I had entered professional journalism five years ago, I had consciously kept my activist shoes outside the newsroom. Not that I wanted to be one of those neutral reporters who keep spouting a holier-than-thou 'Both sides are bad' stance. Hell no! There were many things happening around the world where the good and bad sides were distinct and beyond reasonable doubt.

But I was going to be objective. Neutrality and objectivity are two very different things in journalism.

Neutrality comes from either not caring about what's happening and reporting headline-driven news like an unfeeling robot or from participating in the pretence that news anchors enact to be in the good books of the powers that be and keep their career prospects unharmed.

Objectivity, on the other hand, is when you aren't insular to the crimes of a powerful entity or the plight of the powerless. But you acknowledge that there can be more than one powers that be, and that you aren't going to ignore the ills of your preferred power centre while exposing the other side.

That's where Malini, and many activist journalists like her, and I differ and disagree.

I disagree with their moral absolutism that presupposes a 'State-bad, rebel-good' hypothesis, irrespective of the facts of different episodes in a conflict and showing a blindness to the trajectory that conflicting parties take over time. They only select facts that fit this absolutist hypothesis and stay wilfully blind to everything that doesn't, and then their reporting becomes the spouting of false truisms and they become political pawns of one ideology or another.

After all, even a cursory reading of the history of long-standing political conflicts shows very clearly that rebels become who they claim to fight. In political science jargon, they become proto-states, fighting a legacy State. And as with anything proto, the rebel-held proto-states aren't evolved products. For example, rebel-held areas don't have an evolved justice system or a democratic polity. They are, more often than not, more totalitarian than the States whose injustices they've picked up arms against.

The Kashmiri rebels' dream of handing over Indian Kashmir to Pakistan and calling it a fight for freedom is full of cut-throat Sharia fundamentalists who will maul anyone who dares peep outside the veil of what they call morality. The Islamic State's proclamations of building an Islamist utopia in opposition to barbaric Western imperialism notwithstanding, they're perfectly okay with slaughtering civilians, with no quarter given to the Geneva Convention or the Universal Charter of Human Rights. The Tamil Tigers of Sri Lanka had a loot-and-pillage system that they called taxation. Their camps were run on the backs of unpaid labour, and Prabhakaran's regime was held together by a ruthless militia network that would put the German Gestapo to shame.

The protracted people's war of the Communist Party of India (Maoist) is no different. To date, they remain perfectly okay running kangaroo courts that sentence tribals to death based on nothing but allegations and suspicions of being police informants, while their overground supporters call themselves human rights defenders and write pamphlets decrying the Indian government as cruel.

Objectivity, as opposed to neutrality, is knowing and saying yes, Kashmir needs to be demilitarized by India; yes, Western imperialism is a barbaric war machine; yes, the Tamils of Sri Lanka deserve their land and their rights and yes, the tribals have the first right to the forest. But it is also saying that the Kashmiri freedom struggle is little more than a proxy war by Pakistan's political and military elites with a side of harsh Sharia. It is saying the Islamic State is a pack of mad war-dogs high on drugs, killing and raping their way through Iraq and Syria. It is saying the rebels in Chhattisgarh are responsible for several crimes.

Given my approach to reporting, Kamal's response—an access to both sides—was exactly what I hoped for. Professional and forthright, for a fee, he was willing to guide me through the forest and facilitate unfiltered interviews with fighters from both sides—no partisan or ideological strings attached.

It was only when Kamal accompanied me on my maiden trip to Abujhmad that I realized that he was anything but professional. And little in him was forthright.

It wasn't until I was back from Germany in 2018 that I had the opportunity to connect with Kamal. The Chhattisgarh state elections were around the corner and soon the Maoists would declare their usual fatwa against participating in them.

Since their inception in the 1969 Naxalbari uprising, the Maoists, aka Naxals, of India have this theory that says that the Indian bourgeoisie are compradors—meaning, puppets of the big bourgeois of the West—and don't have any real roots in this land. The bourgeois State, that is, the government of India, is only held together by the force of the Indian police and the military and not the support of the masses. Therefore, should the military might of the Indian State be attacked, the State would come crumbling down.

This is what I wanted to report on. Not the mining or forests rights issues, not the human rights issue and most certainly not the traitors versus nationalist debate that had swamped every political discourse since the rise of Narendra Modi.

Not that I thought these other issues were trivial. Of course not. But Malini and her activist journalists on one side and the pro-State big corporate news on the other had done enough reporting about these.

I simply wanted to go in and ask the Maoists, the State officials and, most importantly, the indigenous people—the tribals, whose greater common good both sides claimed to represent—how they saw the great Indian election jamboree. Did the tribals want to vote and bring change through electoral democracy? Or did they willingly buy into the Maoist diktat that the electoral democracy be boycotted?

'*Bilkul aa jaiye* [By all means, come over],' Kamal assured me over the phone. 'I've spoken to the Maoists and the villagers, and you will get to speak to them. We'll drop our luggage off in Narayanpur town and go right in.'

'Hundred per cent,' he added, for good measure, and proceeded to tell me about car and hotel bookings, the route we'd take and the translators, drivers and guides we'd book for entering the forests.

When I asked him about his fee, he avoided mentioning a figure and humbly said, 'Let's first get the story done—we'll talk about money afterwards.'

Accompanied by a cameraman, I landed in Raipur soon after and took a cab to Narayanpur in Bastar. We were to pick Kamal up from his hometown, Kanker, and, using Narayanpur as the base, enter the Abujhmad forests, which were completely under the control of the Maoists.

We reached Narayanpur late in the evening. There was only one hotel in the squalid little town square. Stepping into my room, I realized that the squalor didn't end at the hotel's threshold. Au contraire, it flowed right in!

The beds had ochre stains from previous lodgers' bloody conflicts with bedbugs. The bathroom wall tiles were smeared in brown stains and I prayed to the high heavens they were algae or mud and not the first thing that came to mind.

But even if this was one of the worst lodgings I had had to put up in, I had been in a lot of less-than-hospitable lodgings enough number of times to resign myself to fate and accept the stains and bedbugs.

It was only after checking in that Kamal pulled the first in what would be a series of many surprises.

'This is Metam sir,' he introduced me to a dark man in his late thirties or early forties, wearing a tucked-in off-white shirt and brown trousers, who sported a large, humble grin on his face that showed off his bright pink gums against his dark complexion. 'He's a schoolteacher, speaks Gondi and is on very good terms with them.'

From this point on, for Metam and all the villagers we met, 'them' was the shorthand for Maoists.

'Great! So what time are we going in?'

Metam's gummy smile turned into a confused half grin. He looked from me to Kamal, Kamal to the cameraman, and back to me.

'No . . . I mean . . .' He cleared his throat, ' . . . we have to make the arrangements first . . . no?'

'Arrangements?' I asked Kamal. 'What arrangements are pending?'

Instead of replying to me, Kamal raised his voice in a mix of surprise and enquiry and said to Metam, 'Tell us what arrangements . . . we'll do it . . . yeah?'

'*Nahi matlab, gadi wadi* . . . [I mean, car and all] . . .' Metam responded, his voice trailing off.

'We already have a car,' I said.

Something about this conversation wasn't right. I didn't quite know what—but something wasn't what it should be.

'No, no . . . the car has to be different, you see,' Kamal said, as if explaining something very unique. 'Drivers have their areas, you know. Local drivers won't allow a Raipur car to go in. Lobbies, you know . . . ha ha ha . . .'

'Fine, let's get a local car,' I shrugged. This wasn't a big deal. In fact, it would be better if a local car was hired as the driver would know the forest routes.

With uncharacteristic hurry, Metam and Kamal proceeded to call a driver. Yet again, I knew something was off. But I went with the drill.

We waited for the car guy. Kamal and Metam, meanwhile, started discussing dinner and drinks. With grins on their faces, they asked if I partook of alcohol.

I said, no, thanks. Taking the cue, evidently against his will, the cameraman said no as well.

'Where exactly do you want to go?' the car owner asked. Metam told him the name of a village and, waving his hands, explained some routes and shortcuts.

'*Dada log se baat ho gayi?* [Have you spoken to the Big Brothers?]' the car owner asked.

'Dada log?' I asked, confused.

'Ha ha . . .' Kamal laughed again. 'These people call 'them' Dada. Out of respect, you know. Ha ha ha.'

Metam laughed too and, replying to the car chap, said, '*Us ki chinta mat karo . . . ho jayega* [Don't worry about that . . . that'll be taken care of]'.

'Ek minute ek minute . . .' I interjected. 'What do you mean it'll be done? It hasn't been done yet? What's happening, Kamal?'

I was getting a little hot behind the ears. I wasn't insensitive to the nuances and difficulties of such places and was not acting like a boss, but I had only three days to wrap up this reporting and had informed Kamal about it. Only after he had confirmed that everything was set and three days were enough to wrap up the shoot, had my editors given me an advance and permission to do the reporting.

'Arey, Metam (Kamal had dropped the sir and raised his voice) . . . you said you'd made all the arrangements, no?' Kamal berated Metam.

'I don't even know which leaders you want to meet, Kamal Bhaiyya! You just told me some American journalist was coming, and we'll discuss the details when we meet.'

Metam looked less like the 'sir' he was and more like a sullen kid from his classroom, upset he'd been unfairly scolded by the teacher when he'd failed to answer an out-of-syllabus question.

'*AREY* . . .' Kamal started yelling at Metam again.

'Okay, okay . . . calm down, guys,' I intervened. 'This is probably some misunderstanding . . . let's sort this out.'

I wasn't trying to be a better man. I was being selfish about my work. It was clear that Kamal hadn't made 'all the arrangements', but shouting about what wasn't done wasn't going to get my reporting done or write my story. Besides, I had no backup plan if Kamal failed.

We entered the forest the next day. But barely beyond the last Indian government check-post, the mud road was broken by rain. On cue, Kamal, Metam and the driver declared their surprise and promptly suggested that we return to Narayanpur and replan the entry point.

I refused.

'We're going in even if we have to walk it,' I said. I was desperate. My hardy Marathi cameraman said he would follow wherever I went. Kamal hemmed and hawed a bit but then agreed.

Metam refused to walk. The very guy hired to be our local guide because he knew the forests, the tribals, their tongue and the Maoists straight up refused to go into the forest!

'I'll go back and establish phone contact with the Dadas. So by the time you're at the Abujhmad hills, they'll be ready to meet you,' he said before leaving. The stupid grin was back on his face.

We trekked for three whole days in the forest. The brief was simple—start at dawn and shelter by dusk in whichever village you're in. Else, if not the forgotten mines and booby traps, the bears will get you.

No meeting with Maoists happened on that trip. Metam didn't make any calls and Kamal didn't manage to pull any strings or wield any influence.

To be fair, it wasn't entirely in his control. Some eight hundred-odd paramilitary forces had entered the forests in a combing operation, and the Maoists had gone into hiding amid a defensive formation.

What was irritating, though, was seeing that Kamal felt no remorse about leading me on about having 'arranged everything' and his false promises that I would meet the Maoist leadership and get my interviews.

On our way back, we were caught by the paramilitary, handed over to the police and detained and interrogated for over eight hours. Instead of reporting the news, I became the news.

While most of the forest had no mobile signal, one small network line appeared on a basic model phone we had carried at the first check-post where we were detained. I managed to send an SOS to several journalists in Delhi.

They, in turn, broadcast it to social media and the news gained traction. Journalists and journalist bodies alike—even big names like Reporters Sans Frontiers—rang the alarm bell, and calls started coming in from all over the country to the office of the district police chief.

To date, I'm certain that we weren't shot by the cops and passed off as Maoists' victims only because of that furore. In fact, there was another reason why that assignment could have been my last.

A team of two reporters from the Indian State television channel Doordarshan had gone into the forest at the same time I had. Instead of going alone and doing the trek like we were doing, they rode with the police and paramilitary contingent.

During an exchange of fire right after they entered, the reporters were killed because the Maoists mistook them to be part of the police.

Because we'd been through some really hard days in the forest together and the detention and harassment thereafter, by the time we were allowed to go back to the hotel in Narayanpur by the cops, I genuinely forgave and forgot Kamal's irresponsible acts. Besides, in the tribal villages we sheltered in, I thought I saw him for who he really was—a happy-go-lucky gonzo who would throw his punches at life, take some hits, lie, be lied to and then drown it all in whatever cheap liquor was at hand.

This is how he lived his life as a reporter and an activist. And he fit right into Bastar and its life, culture, politics and political reporting. The misfit in Bastar was I and my journalism.

Despite our abortive reporting mission, we parted as friends. I even paid Kamal the price he had asked for before leaving Raipur—a kill fee, as they call it in this line of work. Not all stories can happen at the times we want them to. Given my arrest and the ensuing brouhaha, my editors would understand as well.

Metam, however, turned out to be a pathetic vermin.

When we were brought to the Narayanpur police chief's office, the cops first confiscated our cameras and memory cards and made copies of them. Since there was nothing for us to hide, and no recourse to law at that point, we handed them over.

The police chief thundered and threatened. But I didn't take it personally and I wasn't going to get provoked and make it any worse. When he realized this, he rang a bell on his table and ordered his assistant, '*Unko leke aao* [Bring them in].'

In walked Metam and the driver.

'*Chalo . . . bolo tum log* [Speak up, you two],' the chief barked at them.

'Sir . . . I had told them not to do such things . . . not to go into the forest. Especially without permission from you, sir,' Metam began, crying. His right eye was bloodied from the hard slaps the cops had landed on his face. The driver's cheek showed similar marks.

In fact, I felt really sorry for them. I thought he was speaking out of fear. But after a week or so, a Narayanpur-based journalist, J, who was witness to the entire police fracas, called me up.

'*Siddharth bhaiyya, kaise hain?* [Sid brother, how are you doing?]' He started off, jovial and warm.

'All good brother . . . what's up with you?' I reciprocated.

'When is your next trip here? Your story remained unfinished, no?'

Clearly, this bloke was offering to replace Kamal and offer his services instead. But I didn't respond to his offer and instead said, 'Not anytime soon, I think. Besides, from what I saw the cops do to Metam, I'm not sure I want to put a non-journalist in trouble.'

'*Arey, Bhaiyya* . . . you have it all wrong,' he said. 'After he left you at the forest's edge, Metam went straight to the last police check-post and ratted you out! This is how it works around these parts . . . you can't trust anyone.'

'But then, why was he beaten?' I asked, puzzled.

'That was just an overreaction. The commanding officer at the check-post was angry that he wasn't informed *before* you entered. And with Metam returning, you were basically left without a chaperone. But it was just a few slaps, *bhaiyya*. And they [the cops] made it up to him with a bottle.'

'Also . . .' he said after a few moments of awkward silence, 'You made the wrong decision by choosing Kamal Bhaiyya. He's a trouble magnet. If you'd gone in with someone else, you wouldn't have attracted so much attention.'

I didn't respond to this last line. Because when J had met us in Narayanpur, he had played a yes-man to both sides. He shook his head heavily when the police were threatening and lecturing us. But right after we were released, over dinner, he couldn't stop praising his 'Kamal bhaiyya' for being the brave inspiration he was.

To J's credit, though, after the saga of my detention had played out in Delhi's press circles, an old journalist friend called up and reiterated what J had said about Kamal being a trouble magnet. He'd been at the Delhi Press Club the previous night, sharing a table with some old hands of the trade when the conversation of my misadventure came up at the table alongside chicken tandoori and subsidized whiskey soda.

'This senior editor who had worked in Raipur for a long time said if you had just gone with someone else and not Kamal, you would've been saved from all this trouble. He's constantly picking fights with the cops over every little thing.'

But as I said, I put the 2018 Chhattisgarh episode behind me pretty fast and wrote it off as happenstance. Besides, I had other stories to report, and my editors understood that one can't report every story. Nor should one expect to.

However, my last interaction with Malini remains the most bitter aftertaste of 2018.

She sent me a very angry message for having called Kamal a fixer. I was guilty of having done that. It's a term that I have suffered under, and I regret using it for Kamal.

But when I had said it, it hadn't come from a place of imperiousness. In the desperation of sending a quick SMS using that one tiny twig of signal and to save time and space,

I'd written, 'Myself, cameraman, and fixer detained at XYZ police outpost'. I sent the text—or at least tried—to almost every Indian journalist I knew.

As always, before leaving for the assignment, I had sent the names of Kamal Shukla and my cameraman to my editors in the US. At least one of the Indian journalists would post my text to social media, I knew. And if an SOS ever reached my editors via social media, I knew they would declare the names and seek safety for us.

But Malini took umbrage at my use of the word 'fixer' for Kamal and wouldn't accept my explanation for doing so.

A few days after the last text with Malini, her rebuke festered inside me, and my apology turned to anger. She may be someone whose reporting I'd read and liked. But I wasn't a child who needed her lecture, nor was my expression of appreciation of her work an admission of thrall.

I wanted to hit back at her, saying, 'You are a hypocrite and in no position to lecture me. If you are so just, equitable and respectful of those who help you report, how come I never saw Kamal's name or him standing next to you when you took your award in New York? And I paid Kamal in full despite not delivering the story. How much of your award money did you give him?'

But one can't win every argument. Nor should one want to.

***

The last time I went back to Chhattisgarh was in May 2023. Many things had changed. And many had not—especially the litany of lies, back-stabbing and misdirections.

The objective of this trip was way more hardcore than the previous one. The lead came from two very senior operatives in the Indian intelligence community. Since they are active agents, let's call them S and P.

It was a warm March evening when S met me at a hotel. I'd known S for a while; he had been a source for me before. S brought P along for a cup of tea. This was a pleasant surprise. For well over a decade, P has been a name to reckon with in the Indian security establishment—an absolute New Delhi loyalist and a soldier to the core.

'You know Madvi Hidma?' they asked.

Of course, I knew who Madvi Hidma was.

A Bastar tribal, Hidma had seen a meteoric rise through the ranks of the Communist Party of India (Maoist), and had gone on to become one of the fiercest fighters and military strategists for the Central Military Committee—the military counterpart of the political Central Committee of the Maoist Party.

Born and brought up in the forests of Bastar, he knew the land far better than the officers and fighters the State was sending in. He was the mastermind of several major ambushes and slaughters of the paramilitaries.

'What about him?' I asked P.

'We have information that he's dead.'

'Like the dozen times he's died before? Or the two dozen times the government's pet news channels have broken the news of his surrender?'

'No, no . . . we intercepted wireless chatter that he's either dead or seriously injured.'

'From one of your drone bomb attacks?'

'Sid . . . this is unfair of you. We haven't been bombing anyone. Whatever you may say of the Indian government, they won't sanction the bombing of their own civilians!'

'But the Maoists have said that's been happening. Not once, but several times. And a fact-finding team of human rights activists went in and presented photos and testimonies of the tribals, affirming the drone bomb attacks.'

'No, there is no drone bombing.'

Both S and P stood their ground. While they had no reason to lie in an off-the-record conversation, I wasn't going to accept or reject their version without verification.

'Then was it in that helicopter ambush?' I asked, referencing an operation by the Indian State where they had attempted to land a helicopter gunship with fighters, and a crossfire had ensued.

The State's version was they were simply doing a drill and didn't know the Maoist guerillas had a camp where the helicopter was going to land. The Maoists had taken the landing as an attack and fired at the chopper. There was one confirmed casualty on the guerilla's side and several grievous injuries on the State's. That's where the news trail had stopped.

I was intrigued. I wasn't going to buy either side's story, but if India had indeed been bombing its own citizens, it was a ghastly thing. And if none other than Madvi Hidma had been killed or injured, this was a turning point in India's oldest civil war.

'What can we do to help you?' P had asked, clearing the crumbs of a chicken puff from his impeccable suit.

'Help me by staying completely away,' I replied. 'If they [the rebels] even get a sniff that I know someone in the intelligence set-up, they won't bother understanding that you're just a source. And that's how you will always be, right, S?'

We had all laughed at that and ended the evening soon after.

P was almost in his car when I called him back and said, 'Wait, there is one thing you can help me with. If not the rebels, your guys are more likely to become the troublemakers. Can you make sure none of my electronics or footage are confiscated in case I'm detained? You know how much your people are supportive of journalists like me—especially after the 2018 fiasco.'

S and P thought about this for a moment, looking at each other. Then they said, 'OK . . . let us see if anything can be done. But it'll be a very indirect thing and only to be used as a last resort.'

'Goes without saying,' I agreed. We shook hands and parted ways.

A day later, I called the reporter who had first broken the story of the drones. I won't name him because he's still working in the danger zone and runs the risk of upsetting low- and mid-level operatives of the State and rebels alike.

'Yes, yes . . . I'm more than happy to go along with you,' he said, when I told him that I wanted to do a long-form feature about the drone story. And, just like Kamal Shukla had said in 2018, he added, 'Don't worry about the money . . . we'll talk about it after the work is done.'

Unlike Kamal, though, this young reporter was far less ideologically driven and not known to pick random fights and get into brawls with officers.

'Have the drones really dropped bombs?' I asked him straight up.

'I don't think so,' he replied. 'If you ask the tribals there, they'll say yes. And sure, I've seen the drone parts myself. But I have no reason to believe they had bombs.'

'Do you know the make and model of the drones?' I asked further.

If I knew that, I could work backwards, calculate the payload capacity from materiel brochures, and tell if the drones could even carry bombs.

'I don't know how to tell that . . . but wait . . . hold on . . .' he put me on hold and walked to a drawer or cupboard. I heard the grating sound of something wooden being opened.

'Yeah . . . so I have this battery from one of the drones that the villagers downed . . .' he continued. 'And it . . .'

'Does it have a serial number? And which language are the texts in?' I interrupted him.

'Erm . . . there is something written on the battery . . . but I can't read it . . . the cover is mangled and hard to read . . .'

Again, if I could get a serial number for the battery, I could work my way backwards, get the drone's model and from there, do the payload calculation. But we agreed to do this in person when we met in Jagdalpur.

Kamal was the next person I called. Despite the mess he'd made the last time we worked together, I was desperate for a way in and decided to try my luck with him again.

We exchanged greetings like old friends, and he once again immediately agreed to accompany me.

'You let me know just two days before you land in Raipur, and I'll join you in Kanker,' he assured me.

'But we won't be entering through Narayanpur this time,' I corrected him. 'I'll be going through Jagdalpur. I need to enter the Bastar forest from that sector and go deep inside till I reach the hills near Godavari . . . you know, the Chhattisgarh–Telangana border where the drone attacks and the ambush happened.'

'That is expensive . . .' Kamal hesitated.

'I'll pay for your travel, of course. And stay in Jagdalpur.'

'*Theek hai, theek hai*,' Kamal said. We ended the call with him repeating his assurances, 'I'll start making enquiries right away.'

But a week passed, and neither Kamal nor the young journalist called back. They didn't respond to my calls either. I had a ticket to Raipur, and all stays and cabs were booked, and now, yet again, I wasn't sure if I was going to get a story!

Two days before I was scheduled to fly to Raipur, my phone and laptop rang together, and the name Kamal Shukla glowed in bright letters against the black lock screen.

'Helloooo . . . hellooooo,' Kamal's voice rang out from my computer. He was dead drunk at twelve noon.

Diya, who was now my partner and was working sitting next to me, looked at me with a mix of shock and an expression that said, 'What the fuck?'

'Hellooo . . .' Kamal continued in a high-pitched slur. He was howling his hellos like a stray dog on a cold night. His voice sounded nothing like its usual deep tones and more like a man possessed by a demon.

'Siddharth . . . Siddharth? Are you there?' he repeated several times, not registering my repeated, 'Yes, I'm here, and I can hear you.

'Yes, Kamal! I can hear you,' I replied loudly one last time, swallowing the bile welling up in my throat.

'I'm drunk . . . see . . . I'm very drunk. I saw your missed calls . . . but I'm drunk . . . very drunk. These people . . . these motherfucking people drag me into fights . . . you know. Fights? I don't want to fight . . . but then they drag me into it. They put me in the lock-up . . . you know . . . because of the fight. And I came straight from the fucking lock-up to this . . . this . . . *haath bhatti* (country liquor den). And . . . and . . . I'm drunk, you know . . . I don't know when I'll get out of here . . . I . . .'

I clicked the large red telephone icon and just sat there staring at the screen once again. The icky feelings of 2018 had come back.

'Babe,' Diya asked after a few moments. 'Is that the same Kamal Shukla?'

'Yes,' I nodded.

'How are you going to work with him if he's . . . I mean?'

'Such a wretch?' I sighed. 'Welcome to my world, Dee . . . these *are* the people I do my journalism with.'

Diya sighed too, but said nothing more and went back to her work.

Diya and I have an unwritten policy of not discussing story details or sources until well after the story is done. Even then, any references I make to how I reported and who I met are generic and watered-down conversations.

She's a lifestyle journalist, and I'm a political one. Kashmir, Araku Valley, Bastar, Berlin—we often visit the same places to do our stories. But it's almost like these places and their people exist in two parallel planes—one for her, another for me. Two planes that pretend to live in complete oblivion of each other.

I love her and her work. And I often joke about how I chose the wrong beat.

'Nobody invites me to fancy dinners and stays at resorts and restaurant launches the way they invite you,' I tell her. 'All I get is to go as your plus one . . . how annoying!'

But she just rolls her eyes and says her trademark, 'Just shut up! You wouldn't want a day of what I do . . . so just shut up.'

After Kamal and the other reporter ditched me, I shut up and sulked and cursed myself for not having learnt my lesson five years back.

I did that for two hours.

Then I went into a frenzy of running my scrapers, googling like a fiend and calling anyone who'd reported on or investigated the drone attacks, ambushes or Madvi Hidma. I even called and emailed the human rights groups. But I didn't hear back from anyone.

I used my sources to obtain the WhatsApp numbers of Maoist spokespersons who regularly issued press releases on their official party letterhead. However, just like the messages I sent to their above ground contacts (who had previously confirmed the drone bombing reports under the guise of 'fact-finding missions'), my texts to the spokespersons remained unanswered.

***

'It's a fake story,' Sunil Kumar said without hesitation, sitting behind his large desk at the office of *Daily Chhattisgarh*. Mr Kumar, a veteran of the state's reporting circles, was poised, patient and as kind as one could expect.

'But don't take my word for it,' he added, with a smile curling up his lips. 'And since you've come all this way, I'm sure you won't take my word for it. About how to get in, I'll give you two numbers.'

He put me in touch with Ranu Tiwari and another journalist whose name I can't find in my notes now. Let's call him Jaffer. Jaffer didn't respond to my call, while Ranu responded immediately. And so Jaffer became unimportant to the story I was out to get—at least until we entered the forest.

Ranu, whose real name is Ankush Tiwari, had been making waves as a news vlogger running a YouTube channel, Bastar Talkies. His work with Bastar Talkies was commendable. Completely self-taught, he'd get on his bike, take buses, hitch rides and just keep travelling all over Bastar and report anything and everything that came his way. His YouTube vlog had a following that surpassed that of many organizations far bigger and better equipped than he was.

'Hello!' He greeted me at my room doorstep in the government-run resort, Naman Bastar. Tall and well built, with a voice and demeanour to match, wearing jeans and an untucked shirt with a cotton towel-turned scarf thrown around his neck, Ranu was impressive. He looked and acted every bit the muckraking, independent journalist he was.

'This is ___,' he introduced me to a young Muslim man who'd accompanied him and sat down. I was in the middle of an evening drink and dinner, which I offered them. Both Ranu and his friend declined. The former because this wasn't his poison, and the Muslim man because he was, well, a Muslim.

Ranu asked me a lot of questions about who I was, who I worked for and so on and so forth, interspersing his questions with witticisms and sarcasm. He mocked me for being born with a silver spoon in my mouth, expressing mock surprise that someone who looked the way I did—specifically my long hair and skin tone—would be okay undertaking the strenuous trek through the hills and forests. He even joked with his friend about me being fat with all the foreign dollars I was making while journalists like him were doing the real grind and making paltry amounts.

I didn't take offence, taking the jibes with a smile. He was who he was and spoke the way he did because of who he was. Most importantly, he was my way in.

'*Haan, bilkul hua hai bombing* [Of course, the bombing has happened],' Ranu said when I broached the topic. 'I've been to the site twice before and seen it.'

'Seen what? The remains of the bomb?'

'The remains of the bomb, the bullet marks . . .'

'The bullets are from the chopper landing ambush,' I corrected him. 'I'm asking about the bombing.'

'Yes, that too. We'll go see the spot where the charge had fallen, and you'll see the hole in the ground.'

This was getting interesting. I had seen Ranu's videos from Metaguda, the village where the most recent bombing was reported. Though I didn't recall him showing the holes he was referring to, he was super confident.

'So when can we go?' I asked.

'When do you want to go?'

'Now.'

'Now?' Ranu looked puzzled. He looked from my face to that of his friend. 'You mean . . . at this hour?'

Of course, I was being a bit of a bitch. His demeanour and jibes had been getting in the way of having a serious conversation. I needed to get him back on track.

'Since you can't leave now,' I said with a dramatic pause, leaning back into my chair, ' . . . I'll repeat my question. When can we go?'

Ranu and his friend left soon after.

'I have to make a few calls and arrange for two motorbikes for us. And get a translator. So allow me until tomorrow afternoon,' he said, wishing me good night while taking his leave.

He didn't call the following afternoon. In fact, nearly two days passed between that evening and his call confirming my travel plans.

I used the two days to meet some more people who I knew would know things.

The first was a source in the Chhattisgarh police intelligence wing. Let's call him Amol.

I asked Amol to meet me at a newly opened rock music-themed café in Jagdalpur. I'd seen the coffee shop the previous evening when driving by. The reason for meeting there was simple. My soul was revolting against the Nescafé instant sachets that had become the sole source of caffeine, and the promise of an Americano was as enticing as the intel I'd get from Amol.

With woodwork panelling, old guitars, fake rock band posters, a long-haired barista and random American vehicle registration plates stuck to the walls, the cafe was clearly aiming for a low-budget variant of the many Bandra hipster spots I was familiar with.

Amol was late. I alternated between scrolling a glitchy Instagram and stepping out to smoke beside the mosquito sanctuary of an open drain that ran by the cafe.

Finally, he walked in with a big smile and a weak excuse for being over an hour late from the scheduled meeting time.

'*Aur, sir . . . kaise hain?* [How are you doing, sir?]' he held his hand out in a strong handshake.

In his late thirties, Amol had grown a slight hint of a belly and darkened several shades more since I had last met him five years ago. The patches of grey in his thinning hair and the new addition of metal framed spectacles told me his job was taking more from him than it was paying.

'*Sir nahi hoon yaar* [Don't 'sir' me, man],' I reminded him, smiling and asking what he would have.

Besides being a key figure in the Chhattisgarh police intelligence wing, Amol was a fixture in the press circles of Raipur, Bilaspur, Korba and now Jagdalpur. Like many in his profession, he had learnt early on that the press can't be obliterated or entirely controlled, and the police would always have a love–hate relationship with them. But unlike many in his profession, he'd kept his nose clean. No bribes were taken or paid.

He knew that information was the principal commodity in his trade. And the press was where that commodity was traded the most. So he gave reporters leaks and leads and in exchange took off-the-record conversations for filing his intel reports.

The café's dim lighting glinted off Amol's glasses. The rock classics playing in the background provided our conversation good insulation from the few other patrons present there.

'Sir . . . Hidma's days are numbered,' Amol began, slamming the table hard as if that was how the elusive Maoist fighter was going to be quashed. 'We know for a fact that he's actively considering surrender.'

His grand opening notwithstanding, as our conversation progressed, I realized that solid information would be as hard to come by as the caffeine kick I was seeking from the innumerable cups of watery broth I was being served in the name of Americano.

'Has he [Madvi Hidma] reached out to you guys through any emissary?' I asked. 'What about his own guys? Given his seniority, what will you offer him that's good enough for a surrender? Last I checked, you guys round up small fry and get the headlines to say, "Top Maoist Leader Surrenders". That's just PR, not reality. No?'

'The State's strategy is complex, sir,' Amol said, his voice barely above a whisper. 'Unlike earlier, when the Maoists had mass appeal, now they're losing the psychological war. The new generation doesn't care about their calls for revolution and equality and all. Even the smallest of towns is full of young men and women who aspire to head to a Bombay or Dilli. Mobile phones have reached the hands of tribal villagers, too. Now they want to be influencers—not revolutionaries.'

I leaned in, my recorder capturing his every word.

'But what about the intel from the ground? Do the locals see some benefit in cooperating with the government now more than before? Are they willing to snitch on the Maoists?'

Amol sighed, pushing his glasses up his nose.

'It's not that simple. The locals are caught between the Maoists and the State. For them, it's about survival. Immediate survival. Nothing long-term. They'll side with whoever they think can protect them or harm them the least this week.'

'You're evading my question,' I corrected Amol. 'All this talk about Madvi Hidma surrendering or getting killed is outright unsubstantiated propaganda. So don't regurgitate that.'

'Honestly, sir, the press restrictions make our job harder,' Amol replied with a shrug and unfiltered frustration in his voice. 'You have no idea how strongly this government controls what gets published. No newspaper or website can step outside the press office line—one word here or there, and you will get a call from Raipur. Now we intelligence people obviously depend on information from reporters. Like any political party, the Maoists talk to them.

'This extreme control has formed a vicious information loop. Meaning, now we only see what the government has fed to the press already! So fresh and independent intel is drying up!'

I nodded, understanding the gravity of his words. In any conflict, truth is the first victim. And in a place like Chhattisgarh, where the conflict has lasted for over half a century, the truth is not only dead but has become a ghost who walks in the dark and deep shadows of lies.

The long-haired barista momentarily interrupted our conversation, enquiring if we needed a refill. I declined—my interest in the coffee long gone. Amol did the same, his focus entirely on our discussion.

'I've been here for three days,' I said, getting back to the point. 'I need something concrete that can give my readers a glimpse of the real situation here. What about the money routes? That's something you guys track yourself. Not through reporters.'

Amol leaned back, his eyes scanning the café as if to ensure our privacy. Reaching into his pocket, he brought out a tissue paper. He passed along a folded piece of paper with it.

'Don't open it now, sir,' he said, glancing around the café cautiously. 'Read it back in your room.'

'Hmm,' I nodded.

'I'm sure you will find enough in this,' he said. 'But please don't keep this paper with you after you're done reading. And unlike last time, only talk to a few people this time—you know how Chhattisgarh works.'

I nodded and hemmed again, put the paper in my pant pocket along with the tissue paper, and signalled the rock star barista of Bastar to bring us the bill.

'Anything for me, sir?' Amol grinned and asked after I'd settled the bill and we'd stepped out. Dusk was falling and the columns of mosquitoes rising from the open drain had thickened from the size of bamboo stilts to that of Greco–Roman columns.

'How much do you want?' I grinned back.

'*Arey, sir . . . chee chee,*' he bit his tongue and shook his head. 'You know I don't do such things.'

'And you know I don't have any information to give other than what you'll read if I do a story, no?'

'I have always cooperated with you because you're an honest journalist, sir. But competition is tough these days. Promotions aren't easy, you know.'

Amol, or for that matter any cop or rebel, never got any information from me. All I've ever offered is money to fixers and the promise of telling an honest, unbiased story to everyone else. So, it was a bit strange to hear Amol ask for information despite knowing that.

I left with a non-committal 'OK. Let me think it over.'

Back in my hotel room, I locked the door, sat at the small table, opened my laptop and read the paper. The skies had been growling since I stepped out of the cafe and headed back to my hotel.

But now the wind had risen, and the growls had turned to deep, throaty roars. The mango, mimosa, jamun and coconut trees in the courtyard had just joined in the raucous choir of the storm winds when the first bolt of lightning struck somewhere close.

On cue, the bulbs went off.

The moment felt like a threshold. Ranu Tiwari still hadn't called back. So, I didn't know when or if I'd be able to enter the forest. But Amol's paper was a real lead—one that would either bring me closer to the truth or push me deeper into the labyrinth of shadows and secrets that seemed to define Chhattisgarh.

Filled with tiny, handwritten notes, the paper was a chaotic yet meticulous collection of phone numbers, dates and amounts. Each detail was confined to hand-drawn boxes labelled with different sectors and towns—North Bastar, South Bastar, Raipur, Narayanpur, Bilaspur, etc.

I'd seen papers like this before. The numbers belonged to hawala agents who kept books for incoming and outgoing cash alongside some legitimate front business. They charged Rs 500 for every Rs 1 lakh they couriered. And they didn't care who was sending or taking the cash as long as they got their commission.

Opening my laptop, I launched an Excel sheet and an Android emulator. I opened up Truecaller, an app that identified names associated with phone numbers, on the emulator, and started typing in the digits, noting the number and name in two adjacent columns in the Excel sheet.

I was looking for repetitions in names and payments of similar sizes made at more or less equivalent intervals of time.

After the third or fourth name, I called room service and asked for a refill of Nescafé sachets.

'*Thoda zyada dijiye, please* [Give me some extra please],' I requested the young tribal girl who had picked up the phone.

The attentive young woman, drenched by the first flush of spring thunder-laced rain, handed me not only coffee but also a thermos flask of hot water, two candles and a matchbox.

'*Sir . . . dinner thoda jaldi bol dijiyega aaj* [Please order dinner a little early tonight],' she requested.

'Sure,' I said. But I wasn't sure how long this night would be.

Like most uninitiated people swayed by movie avatars of investigative journalists, I too had once thought that being one would mean using hidden cameras, doing sting operations, travelling undercover and similar exciting things. I was misled into believing I'd wield a camera or a recorder like secret agents wielded weapons.

The truth I had learned over the past years of work was that the laptop, an Internet connection and spreadsheets would be the most useful weapons in my arsenal.

'If you can't do basic accounting and use Excel,' Ben Lesser, a senior data and investigative reporter with Reuters and the professor who taught me the eponymous class at Columbia, had told me, 'you can kiss investigative journalism goodbye.' And within that 'follow the money' was the drill, no matter how unsexy and boring it apparently was.

Soon, I forgot all about dinner, coffee and cigarettes. The hotel, power cut and storm, all blurred out, I typed and jotted, jotted and typed.

The numbers were not only throwing up names of people but also those of companies. There were construction material suppliers, contractor companies and a lot of names that only said 'XYZ Enterprises'.

I copied and pasted the names into Google Maps and tried to match them with the sectors and town blocks they'd been put in. Most locations matched what Amol had written. The intel was good.

As the jottings and mappings increased, some strands thinned, others thickened, and the web began revealing itself. In front of me stood the real enormity of the so-called Maoist–State conflict of Chhattisgarh.

This wasn't just a black-and-white conflict between two competing powers. It was an industry. An industry where an innumerable many, small and big, on this side and that, made money off this tango the Maoists and the State had been dancing for fifty years.

The biggest hurdle to ending the conflict was neither the distance of the revolution nor the brutality of statecraft. It was the innumerable middlemen who didn't want a curtain call on the tango because they made their millions off it.

Excited as I was by the patterns revealing themselves with identifiable names and addresses, Amol's warning echoed in my mind. Chhattisgarh was a land where truths were dangerous, and those who dared to reveal them often paid a steep price. And I had had my dangerously close brush with it before.

So, my analysis would, as many a time before, stay foregrounded by an easier story that told a fraction of what I could tell.

By the time I'd run through the entire list of numbers, four hours had gone by. The peals of spring thunder were just cold dampness that settled around the concrete buildings and the manicured courtyard. The very first cup of coffee I'd made was lying half finished, and the very first cigarette I'd lit was lying unsmoked with a three-inch-long limp trail of ash.

I folded my laptop, took Mamma Roy's name, holding my aching lower back and then hit the shower.

Down in the parking lot, my driver had dressed down to his boxers and vest. One leg on the dashboard, a plastic glass of country liquor in the can holder, he held a smouldering beedi in his right hand and his mobile phone played a video in his left.

'Sir, sir . . .' he responded with a startle and hurriedly tried to find a place to make the glass and beedi disappear.

'*Kya dekh rahe ho, boss?* [What are you watching, man?]' I asked, opening the door on the other side and settling in. And without embarrassing him by demanding an answer, I added: '*Wo kuch dhaba bol rahe the na tum? Wahan chalo . . . desi murga khayenge.* [Take me to that dhaba you'd mentioned—I feel like eating some country chicken.]'

The second person I called on was Badranna. That was the following morning.

He and his wife had been gun-carrying Maoists who had surrendered, served a jail term shortened by clemency and been rehabilitated into society with a government job. He even lived in a house provided by the government he had sworn to uproot.

Badranna had become an interview celebrity. One of those people who reporters like me flock to because they're easy to reach. They tell their tales with practised elan and bespoke theatrics they know will work well with a content-hungry, short-on-time news ecosystem.

Badranna even charged money to talk. Breaking my principle of never paying for a source, I paid him Rs 5000.

The cash in his hand warmed both his smile and his vocal cords. For right after he'd put the notes in his pocket, he sat up on his bed with folded legs and let loose a volley of his life story.

The only problem was that every third thing he said was either a lie or a damned fucking lie.

'I was a poor, young boy from a landless family—not even fifteen then,' he began. 'The forest officers would come to loot our crops and treat us like dogs. But the Maoists treated us with respect and dignity. Like humans. So I left my house one day. A friend and I presented ourselves at a forest camp [of the Maoists]. We were taught Marxism, Maoism and other things there and we became committed ideological warriors.'

'Didn't they also teach you to use guns?' I asked.

'*Haan, haan* . . . that too.' Badranna nodded. 'That too.'

'But what they really taught us . . .' he relaunched into his spiel about how meeting the Maoists had saved his soul.

As he spoke, he said the most wonderful things about 'The Party'. His eyes danced and he emoted with his face and hands like a Kathakali dancer as he broke into a Telugu song he used to sing in the forests with his comrades. Then came the part about how he met his wife, fell in love and married her—'But not like a wife. As a comrade! We didn't follow the regressive Brahminical rituals—it was a revolutionary wedding! See . . .'

He brought down a picture of him and his wife clad in camouflage, holding their rifles. The picture hung beside another of him and his wife, and in that she was wearing the wedding mangalsutra.

'So much for dissing the regressive Brahminical rituals,' I thought.

I mostly let him speak without any cross-questioning. Sure, there were a few interruptions from me when I asked things like:

'If you were landless, what crops were the forest guards looting from your land?'

'You said this isn't true democracy, and the real people's democracy is where the Party runs the land. Then why did you desert your party? Why do you work for the State now?'

'Why did the party give a gun to a fourteen-year-old? Isn't using child soldiers against human rights conventions?'

But I asked those questions mostly to break the monotony of his sloppy theatre. I kept the real question for the end when his vocal cords would tire out.

Badranna's performance ended with his son, or perhaps nephew, bringing in two cups of tea. As was the norm there, it was way more sugar than tea. The sugar and the ennui of the non-interview made my mouth crave some of the nicotinic bitterness that had sat quietly in my shirt pocket for longer than usual.

'Let's step out . . . I like a cigarette with my tea,' I told Badranna.

'You can smoke here aa . . . no problem . . .' Badranna graciously offered, but I insisted we step out into the little covered parking space he had.

'What's its name?' I asked, pointing to a parrot that sat in a cage near the gate. As I lit my cigarette, I extended my packet to Badranna, but he refused with exaggerated humility.

'They were very strict in the Party about this,' he said, gesturing a sweep of finality with his right hand while he held the teacup in his left. 'No addictions were allowed!'

'Oh . . . so you guys never drank *mahua* or *salfi* or smoked the ganja that's grown in the liberated areas?'

'He he he . . . that was done sometimes—but only on special occasions. And that too only if you weren't on sentry duty. Seniors had taught us to always stay alert!'

'You know I don't pay people for interviews,' I interrupted him before the glorious tales of his party time restarted. 'And

I didn't do that with you either. You're not the one I'm here to interview.'

'*Matlab? Mai smajha nayi, saar* [I'm sorry, I don't understand you, sir],' his nose had scrunched up, and his forehead had furrowed.

'Connect me to Madvi Hidma's team. I want to interview him.'

'Madvi Hidma!' Badranna grinned, then, seeing my deadpan look, paused. The grin morphed into comical confusion.

'Yes. Madvi Hidma.' I said, returning to his living room. I sat on a chair, and he was back on the cot.

His body language had shed the theatrical fluidity, and was now awkwardly immobile. He showed something like a mix of fear, suspicion and regret.

'How will . . .'

'Badranna . . . I don't work for the police or the government. Here . . . see my work . . .' I handed him my phone with links to my reporting portfolio. 'I've been told your surrender is a farce, and you are the Party's principal overground person in Jagdalpur. Your much publicized surrender protects you from the law, and you do what your comrades in the forests can't do—things like managing the distribution of pamphlets in the city. In fact, they trust you so much, you also handle donations made to the Party by people who come as NGO workers and tourists. Then you hand the cash over to a gentleman who runs a homestay at the edge of the forest. The cadres go and collect it from him. They trust you more than they do the hawala guys in the city because the police have tightened the noose around them.'

Like him, his teacup sat cold and unmoving on the cot. Badranna had clammed up. I had said what I had based on inputs I had from deep sources whom I will never publicly identify.

'I don't work for the government,' I repeated myself. 'I don't even write for Indian news. So the government can't censor what I write. I just need an interview with Hidma. He's a one-in-a-generation fighter, and the world outside India is curious about him.'

Badranna looked away, scratched and inspected an imaginary scab on the back of his right forearm.

'Listen, Badranna,' I said again. 'All I'm asking you to do is send in a word to the team that a journalist wants to interview him. I know he doesn't want to get photographed, and I won't use my phone. Just written notes. They can vet me and see if I'm a genuine guy or not. And if you can connect me, I'll pay you another Rs 5000. It's a fixer's fee . . . you know fixers, right?'

Badranna nodded but didn't meet my eye. Of course, he knew what fixers were. He had dealt with them when they brought Delhi reporters to his house.

'When are you going in? And which side will you be going in from?' Badranna asked.

I gave him the details of where I'd be going and told him it might happen as early as the next day.

'Okay, saar . . . I will send them a message,' he said, as I got in my car and closed the door, waving a half-hearted goodbye with a weak excuse of a smile.

The third man I was to meet in Bastar before going into the forest was the homestay chap that Badranna worked with.

'Hey, Sid!' he responded in crisp and jolly English the first time we spoke. His homestay catered to well heeled poverty- and simplicity-craving tourists from big Indian cities and abroad. I had called him from Jagdalpur right after I landed. 'You're most welcome to the homestay! What are your exact dates?'

I told him my dates. His calendar was free.

His homestay was my Plan B. If I couldn't make it into the forest, I'd stay at his place and wait for the Maoists to come. Then I'd directly ask them for an interview. This area was, after all, under Madvi Hidma's control.

But something had changed by the time I went from Jagdalpur to Bastar. Instead of asking me to come to his homestay, he said: 'Let's meet in Jagdalpur first, shall we? I'm visiting a friend, and we can get a coffee or something.'

If he was who I had been told he was, he would've been smart enough to look me up on the internet. And if he had looked me up on the internet, this meeting over 'a coffee or something' meant he was vetting me.

The coffee was to happen right after my meeting with Badranna. Unsurprisingly, it didn't.

I called his number when the time of the meeting had passed. The phone rang a few times and was dismissed. When I dialled again after a bit, my phone went: 'Beep-beep-beep . . . Sorry, the number you have dialled is unreachable.'

The Forest of Lies

'It's done,' Ranu Tiwari called two days after he said he would. We were to travel to Sukma in my car, park there and enter the forests on two motorbikes. Two more people, Devashish and Deepak, were to travel with us. Deepak was a tribal boy who would be our translator and guide through the forest trail, and Devashish was a local politician's sidekick and the one handling the logistics of the bikes, the parking of the car and the stay for the driver while we were in the forest.

'Metaguda is at least an hour and a half away from Minpa. It's deep inside the forest. The big roads end at Minpa, and it's all forest trails from there on,' Ranu was explaining on the ride to Sukma from Jagdalpur when his phone rang.

'*Haan, bhaiyya* . . . [Yes brother],' Ranu answered. I don't know what was said by the caller, but Ranu's voice changed from an eager smiling hello to worried 'Hmms' as the call proceeded.

'*Theek hai* . . . *theek hai* . . .' he kept saying in response to whatever the other person on the phone was saying, and then, 'Hello . . . hello . . .' as the network died.

The man who'd called him was Jaffer—the other journalist that Sunil Kumar had recommended, the one who hadn't responded to my call. He had called Ranu to inform him that the state intelligence had sent out an alert about journalists going into the forest.

What this meant was that even if we did get into the forest, we wouldn't come out without being stopped, detained or worse, interrogated and our cameras and memory cards taken and backed up.

'Did you talk to Jaffer about this?' Ranu asked with a frown on his forehead.

'I had called him, yes. Sunil Kumar gave me both of your numbers. He didn't respond, and you did.'

Ranu's frown remained. I knew what it meant. He suspected Jaffer was sticking it to Ranu for getting this gig. What Ranu didn't know was that, in all likelihood, Amol—the state intelligence officer—was sticking it to me for not giving him anything in return for the intel he'd given me.

Nothing boosts work focus like phones going dead. The same thing happened with Ranu. Forgetting Jaffer's call, we soon started discussing his work, the conflict, the political scenario in the state and the state of journalism.

I ventured to tell him my understanding of Badranna, and he agreed. He spoke a lot. And the things he said I liked hearing. He showed no overt sympathy for the Maoists even though he was critical of the State and its politicians. His anti-establishment stance wove in beautifully with his keen awareness of the poverty and plight of the tribals caught in the fight.

What resonated the most was his struggling journalist persona. And the fact that, like me, he was anti-all-establishments—rebels, State, polity and even his own profession, journalism.

'Don't call anyone or go away until at least three days have passed,' I instructed the driver. Not only mobile networks but timelines also vanish in the forests. These places are so far from what we call civilization that even something unspectacular, like a small tyre puncture, could easily add a day or two.

I rode pillion with the tribal boy, Deepak, while Ranu joined the politician's aide, Devashish. The ride was far worse than I'd thought it would be.

By the time we alighted at Minpa, my legs were numb with pain, and my mouth full of curses at my body and lifestyle. My fat paunch and complete lack of a butt had ensured that every one of the gazillion bumps on the unfinished road that got past the motorbike's shock absorbers had been absorbed by my tailbone.

The sciatica pain had hummed as loud in my head as the motorbikes did, and I heard very little of the guides running commentary, saying, 'This is where the Sukma massacre of the CRPF had taken place', 'This is where the ambush had happened four years back', 'That was where roadside thugs would stand to loot travellers up until recently.'

But this was only the beginning of what was to be nearly three days of non-stop curses—mostly in my head, but a few that slipped past aloud.

The very first one was for Ranu.

'Money? What money?' he asked after a quick lunch at Deepak's house in Minpa. Along that painful road trip, Ranu's anti-establishment, angry young man persona had blown away with the dust-laden summer winds that swept the sparse, poverty-smeared Minpa. Here he had become the establishment. He ordered people to fetch a charpoy, water, etc., with a thuggish imperiousness.

Given the number of times he'd come to these parts, at first, I thought he was just being a mock bully. But after lunch, he burped and said, 'You can pay them something if you like. I never pay them for food and all. They should be paying me to report about them!'

As I said, I cursed. But inaudibly, only slightly shaking my head in disgust as I paid Rs 500 to our hosts for the unpolished lentils and rice they'd given us. And I gave some mints to the kids who'd been hanging around us since we stepped in.

Until a year before, Minpa had been part of Maoist territory. Like us journalists, they would come and have themselves hosted by the same people who'd fed us lentils and rice. But that changed with the huge and fortified paramilitary base set up by the Central Reserve Police Force (CRPF) barely a kilometre outside the village.

The battalion in charge was called the 241 Bastariya Battalion. The Indian State had learnt from its past mistakes of being the outsiders and occupiers, and the CRPF had raised this unit not with outsiders but with several fighters from Bastar. Besides the regular CRPF jawans, this was also a base for the dreaded COBRA commandos who had been raised specifically to hunt Maoists down while fighting solo and surviving in the forests with no supplies or support.

With the Minpa Camp standing guard, a big concrete road was now being laid. The camp had also become a centre for regular medical check-ups and odd jobs employment for the tribals. The camp was also overseeing the building of a primary healthcare centre, a new day care and a playschool for children whose parents worked in the fields and forests.

In short, with the Minpa Camp and the Bastariya Battalion, the Indian State was saying a big fuck-you-we're-here-and-going-nowhere to the Maoists.

In fact, when we reached Minpa, the usual curiosity and anxiety visitors like us generally bring out were hardly visible. The villagers were busy threshing and milling their paddy in a mobile husking machine. Thanks to the road, tractors were now lugging these diesel-powered machines to villages during the harvest season.

To a city-bred person who only sees rice in packets on a shop shelf this might seem like no great shakes. But access to a threshing machine that came to their doorstep was life-changing for the tribals.

Back in 2018, sitting in Kutul village in Abujhmad, the locals had told me that the lack of roads was the biggest hurdle they faced.

'Gunfire happens once in a while. The lack of roads kills us every day. It makes being alive the biggest pain,' the head of the Jantana Sarkar (People's Government—the Maoist equivalent of the Gram Panchayat local self-governments) had told me, sitting in the *ghotul*.

'Except for this weekly market,' he had said, pointing to the cluster of vendors outside the Ramakrishna Mission, 'there's not one shop until we trek all the way outside the forest to Narayanpur.'

'But these places never had roads, and your previous generations had lived well enough,' I'd asked. This was the second question I had asked the chief to see how much they bought into the Maoist rhetoric of forest life being a utopia ruined by the capitalism of the cities. The first one was when I had pointed to a wall painting written in Hindi praising the Russian Revolution and asked, 'Do you read Hindi? Can you tell me why the Russian Revolution is so important?'

'*Wo to dada log likhke gaya hai* [the Maoist brothers have written that],' he replied with no affectation. And grinning through his betel-laden bloody gums, he added: 'You think I can write all that? I'm illiterate . . . most of my generation are. It's only the kids who are now reading and writing [at the playschool run by the Ramakrishna Mission].'

'So . . .' the chief continued, in response to my second question. 'The forest is ours, and we're of the forest. This is our home and will always be. There is no doubt about that. But we have to go to the city too, don't we? To get medicines for us, the pigs, cattle and hens. Doctors and vets don't come this far. The other day, Suku's mother fell ill. You remember? (This to his fellow villagers, who hemmed and nodded in agreement). So, sir, Suku's mother got diarrhoea some years back after *Nava Khai*. She started vomiting and, at first, we thought it was because she'd drunk too much the previous night.

'But when her vomiting and motions didn't stop by the following evening, we got worried. The ashram people have some basic medicines, but her condition was getting worse. We had to take her to Narayanpur. There were very few bicycles here, let alone motorbikes. So we just put her in a wicker basket and hung it between a bamboo pole, and four men left, carrying her on their shoulders. It was a journey of three days. Suku's mother died on the way, the night after they left.'

The chief's account was a jarring contrast to the romanticized narratives I had often encountered online. I'd read countless pieces from activist writers glorifying the untouched beauty of forest life, castigating growth and development as a cancer, they painted the forests of Bastar as an Eden untouched by modern woes.

The city dwelling activists writing these pieces were all non-resident Edenites. They posted and defended their theses using the high-speed Internet connections in their big city homes, knowing they could order food on an app when they got hungry and if the food made them ill, they had insurance that would get them treated in a hospital. To them, the only evil worth fighting were roads and electricity. Diarrhoea was nothing.

But sitting in that ghotul, listening to the chief, the reality was refreshingly different. The villagers weren't asking for some grand four-lane highway. A basic four-foot road would mean life over death—a weekly bazaar selling rice, dal, salt and kerosene would mean sustenance over perpetual hunger.

In Orchha—where we had halted the night before Kutul—conversations and complaints about roads, electricity, jobs and hospitals were what I had heard most.

When Metam and the driver had abandoned Kamal, the cameraman and me at the edge of the forest, his only parting advice was: 'Get to a village before sundown. And stay on the main road.'

Of course, we would stay on the main road. Any trails outside that were likely mined or had lethal booby traps. The Maoists, who had laid them for ensnaring State troops, are said to have made maps of these lethal spots. But neither did we have access to those maps, nor was it possible to tell such a spot apart from any other in the forest trails. Like everything else that's left untouched for a while in these parts, nature had reclaimed the deadly spots where these lethal devices lay awake, waiting for a human or animal to tread on them and meet agony and death.

In fact, a couple of hours into our long walk through the forest, we came across both, an old mine and a trap with steel spikes.

'Sir . . . I need a minute,' the cameraman had said and held up his right pinky, indicating he needed to take a leak. And with that, he set his equipment down, and turned to go into the thickets next to the road.

'OY . . . RUK RUK!' I hollered.

I'd seen something I'd heard about from a former Maoist. Since maps don't work very well in the forest, a standard way to mark a mine is to place a different rock near it. Different meaning one that doesn't belong in the nearby geography of where it is placed. And in the direction where the cameraman was headed to relieve himself sat an oval watermelon-sized basalt.

My worried holler had put the urinating on low priority, and the three of us cautiously took a look at the ground around the rock.

Sure enough, a metal connector went from the rock to a spot in the thickets. It was meant to be hidden by a layer of earth, but the layering was thin, and the earth had moved, showing the rod in parts.

We left nature's call unanswered and beat a hasty, comical retreat, running on tiptoes like a Tom and Jerry cartoon.

Some hours after the landmine sighting, it was time for me to answer nature's call. And this one was a variant more serious than the cameraman's. So I walked a bit faster, hoping to come across a stream. The wet tissues in my backpack were scarce.

The sun was beating down hard, and Kamal and the cameraman had no reason or energy to keep up with my hastened pace.

The forest gods were kind enough to place a stream barely a kilometre away from where I'd started my hurried pace. Finding a spot with privacy wasn't much trouble. I beat the bushes around with a fallen branch to make sure I didn't get any serpentine kisses on my derrière and squatted down to business.

In the midst of that business, with no phone network and therefore nothing to scroll, I looked around. Some twenty-odd feet from me was the remnant of a trail that left the main road and meandered parallel to the stream. My team was still catching up. So having done with my business and made good use of the stream, I buckled up and went to check it out.

I'd barely stepped onto the trail when I found a rectangular hole cut into the earth. Four or five rusting spikes looked up from the three-feet depth.

We had been in Maoist territory for many hours now. A wooden arch with a red banner welcoming visitors to the free land had announced it a long time ago. So, this spike pit shouldn't have been a surprise. Yet, my mind conjured up a film reel where I was running at night, and my left foot slammed into these spikes. My mind—my morbid mind—even ran a slow-motion replay of the spikes going through my shin and calf, mangling the bones and sinew.

'Oh . . . Siddharth . . . you a-hole,' I cursed and walked away as I heard my teammates chatting and walking up.

The first part of Metam's parting words—'Get to a village before sundown'—had nothing to do with Maoists, the State or the revolutionary conflict that's been playing out for half a century. This was a much older conflict that the tribes had been fighting—one with bears and wild boars.

'*Bhaalu to bohot hai* [bears are aplenty],' a young Madhiya man had said in Orchha when we were sitting around, talking and sipping mahua with salt and red chilli powder on the side. 'But the real pain in the ass are the boars. They eat our crops and then fight us. Fight us like demons even when they're half-dead!'

'A . . . MONU!' he called and beckoned this other young man who was helping our host cook our dinner of pork and rice. 'Show your back to sir.'

Monu smiled, drunk and shy. But he took his shirt off and showed us the long scars that ran from his back to the side of his chest.

'We had sown some corn in our land, and the harvest was due in a day or two,' the narrator continued. 'I took Monu with me to the field to stand guard for the night. But the drunkard that Monu is, he came with two bottles of mahua. Just before dawn, the rustling began. Monu had drunk almost all of the two bottles and was sleeping. I tried waking him up, but when he didn't, I took my spear and threw it into the bush. I couldn't see well—but I took a chance. Sure enough, one beast squealed and started struggling while the smaller ones grunted and scattered. Hearing the sound, Monu woke up with a start and, like a Salman Khan, ran to fight the pierced boar. The boar gave him what he deserved. Look at him now!'

We all laughed at what surely mustn't have been a laughing matter when it happened.

'See this one, sir . . . see this one,' an enthusiastic young lad dragged a man in his thirties from the ghotul to our quieter gathering in the host's yard. The man who had been dragged in was rather miffed and cursed his comrade.

It was Nava Khai day, and the ghotul at Orchha was a raucous party. Abuses, slurs, flirting and curses were flowing as hard as the mahua and salfi. No Madhiya man would want to leave that and attend to city-bred blokes who had just crashed at their place unannounced. As for the Madhiya women, they didn't even bother looking our way. The ghotul was where they would be for that day and night.

The man who was brought in had a gruesome visage. The left half of his face looked like it had melted, and the flesh and skin were trying to reach his shoulder.

'This rascal got some love from a bear!' the lad announced, laughing. 'Tell us . . . tell us what happened . . .'

The man grunted something in Madhiya before plonking down beside us. We needed no translation for the universal grunt that said, 'Oh, fuck you.'

Reeking of sweat, burping mahua and frothing at the mouth, he told his tale among howls of laughter. The lad who had dragged the bear attack victim in spoke some Hindi and translated thus:

'I was a bit drunk that evening and had a fight with my wife. She was complaining that I'd spent too much of the money she'd given me to buy stuff from the city. I swear I hadn't. It was just some change. I'd only eaten two vadas and drunk some English. But that wench wouldn't stop cursing me. And her anger kept rising and rising. When she gave the kids some rice, I also asked for some. Instead of dinner, she threw the plates at me and said take these and eat some pig shit.

'So I went off to the forest to cool off. Sometime early evening it was. I walked for a bit, but it started drizzling, so I took shelter beneath a mahua tree.

'The shower cooled the air, and I dozed off.

'I don't know how long I was out, but I woke up to the smell of an animal and something big moving around where I was. It was dark and at first, I couldn't even see the animal.

'It was a bear!

'It was mahua season at that time, and the flowers had fallen to the ground with the rain. The bear had come to eat them. You know how bears eat a lot of mahua and get drunk. They can be very violent when that happens.

'I stiffened and waited for a chance to get away quietly. But just as I tried to crawl, the damn beast noticed me, roared and brought his paw down on me!

'Perhaps it was my shouting, or the bear was already a bit drunk, but there was a bit of a pause between the first blow and the raising of the paw for the next one. I managed to get away in that little pause and ran for my life. I'm lucky to be alive. That goddamned beast would have torn me apart that day.'

'You're lucky your wife didn't leave you with that face, you lout!' the Hindi-speaking lad quipped. 'You're such a drunkard you keep picking fights with everyone in the village. You got your lesson the day you thought you were big enough to pick a fight with a bear!'

More laughter ensued, and the mauled man demanded mahua for his storytelling. I poured him some from my glass and clinked my steel glass with his, saying: 'From one drunk to another! Cheers!'

'And how did you get those?' I asked, turning to another quiet young man. This man was our host and hadn't been drinking because he wanted to cook and attend to us. 'Those look like burns.'

'Electric line, sir,' the man replied.

'Electric line?'

'Yes, sir. They were setting up high-voltage lines to supply electricity to the villages. I signed up as a labourer for the contractor. One day, when I was up on the tower, joining the wires with a technician from the city, someone turned the line on.'

'WHAT? How can they do that without clearance from the ground staff?' I asked, bewildered.

'That's how it's supposed to be, sir. But who knows why? Someone turned on the supply, and I was flung from the tower. Luckily, I didn't break my neck or back, but the skin on my palms and forearm were all burnt.'

'Were you compensated by the contractor?'

'No,' the boy smiled and shook his head.

'What compensation, sir?' the narrator of Monu's tales took over. 'That bastard [contractor] didn't even pay our dues for a month-and-a-half; he just vanished. The towers are still lying unfinished.'

We ate very well that night. There was pork cooked with nothing more than a bit of oil, lots of green chillies and garlic, and a little onion. The only dry spices used were salt and turmeric. With that, there was rice: white, government-given, ration rice, cooked into a mud-like thickness. A scraggy dog appeared from the direction of the ghotul and joined us for the meal.

Around 11 or 12 p.m., when the darkness and cold came down hard and snuffed out our mahua-laced mirth, we left the bonfire to the dog and slept in the covered barn. It only had a mud-tiled roof held up with bamboo, so the cold night wind blew all around and chilled us. But it was the best we could have gotten.

The ghotul was mostly quiet except for the loud proclamations of a woman who had outdrunk every man there and was berating and teasing them in words I didn't understand but in tones that needed no translation.

The night passed mostly sleepless and uneventful. Except for the one time my cameraman shrieked and woke us all up, shouting, 'Snake! Snake! A snake went over me!'

In the light of our mobile phones, the snake turned out to be a piece of wild boar that had fallen from a basket above us. Madhiyas like curing and drying their pork, and that's what our hosts were doing in the covered barn. One smelly, fatty and delicious chunk had mysteriously grown wings in the dark, cold night and, jumping over the edges of the wicker basket, had landed on the tummy of the cameraman.

So yes, bears, State police and Maoists were all very real fears in Bastar. But snakes were another. It would join my list five years later when I made my way from Minpa to Metaguda.

Ranu, Devashish, Deepak and I left the highway and turned sharply into the forests where no real roads existed. We were headed to a place where nobody from the State—not even doctors or forest officials, let alone troops—had dared enter in over seven years. The best the State could do was send drones.

The State said the drones were for surveillance. But the Maoists said they were being used to drop bombs. And that's what I had gone to investigate and report.

At any rate, all semblance of roads ends at Minpa. Thereafter, it's just forest trails.

Riding a motorbike through the trails is possible but not for those who aren't familiar with the terrain or not very good at handling bikes. Most certainly not for those who aren't okay with pushing, lifting and struggling with unsticking their bikes from the thick mud and deep ruts every so often. For there isn't even a mile-long stretch where one doesn't have to get down to get around a thorny overgrowth, wade through streams with muddy banks or climb over clusters of loose boulders.

Right after Minpa, we stopped at a village in the middle of the forest. I forget the name of the village now, but I remember why we halted.

Unlike the winter days of 2018, my 2023 meet-the-Maoists was a peak summer affair. On the one hand, the sun bore down hard on our heads; on the other, the dust laden winds we were breathing and the huffing and puffing from dragging our motorbikes made us very thirsty. This village was much cleaner than Minpa and had a tube well with a very clean concrete basin around it.

'Time to refill our bellies and bottles with water!' We all agreed.

I splashed my face with the cold water, scooped out from the dark belly of burning hot earth, and lit a cigarette while the others took their turn.

A little ahead of us, along the path we were to take, was a teak glade. If one wished away the shit smeared pigs running around in the background and ignored the smell of cow dung and pig droppings, the glade was picture perfect. Sturdy old teak trees stood, defiantly staring back at the searing sun. Piles of large fallen teak leaves in different stages of ochre decay played around in the summer wind with whispering little rustles.

I wrote this line down on my phone right then and there. Such poetry! I patted my back.

Then my mind whispered, 'Rustles . . . like Russell's . . . the viper. Remember what Dad said? Always assume there is a snake in a pile of fallen leaves.'

Within moments of that thought, I actually ran into the biggest, fattest, scariest Russell's viper I've ever seen!

After filling water, we got on our bikes and started off.

'Watch out for snakes,' I told Deepak, with whom I was riding pillion.

'Aaa,' Deepak replied, nasalizing the As. That was his standard reply to nearly everything I said on that trip.

Just as we entered the glade, I shouted, 'SNAKE!'

Our front wheel had barely missed the tail of a rather healthy specimen of snake. Brown skin, leopard-like print, and a little over four feet long, I estimated as it slid away from one clump of leaves to another.

Evolutionary biologists say that we humans are hardwired with the ability to see snakes even when they are well camouflaged. 'Snake Detection Theory', they call it. It may well be science, but when I saw this one just in time to avoid it and the fact that one had appeared right after I'd thought of it, my atheism notwithstanding, I simply put it all down to manifestation and miracles.

For one, in the pile of leaves, the colours of the snake were so well camouflaged with its surroundings that it was nearly impossible to find the serpent. Especially with the degree of myopia I've had since childhood. Two, if our bike had reached the spot a few moments earlier, either Deepak or I—most probably both—would be writhing in pain from a bite from one of the most poisonous snakes in the world.

Third, and most annoyingly, why was it I who saw the damned snake? Deepak—the 'local' boy—expert of tongues and terrains, was the one who should have known these things, not I!

This wasn't the first time I had seen a Russell's viper. I'd read they can grow up to five feet in length. But I'd only ever seen smaller specimens in Bengal. Much smaller. Maximum two, two and a half feet, nose to tail. And not this healthy by far.

The terror that the snake sighting struck in me can be gauged by the fact that after all these months, I still feel shivers and quivers go up and down my spine even as I write these lines sitting in my fourteenth-floor apartment. This despite knowing there is next to no chance a Russell's viper—or, for that matter, any non-human serpent—will pay me a visit.

I scolded Deepak a bit for being careless when I'd specifically told him to be careful. But given how scared we both were and how we had a long ride through the forests ahead of us, we let the matter slide—nearly as quickly as the snake had. I ended the talk with 'Keep your eyes open, man!'

To which he said—but of course—'Aaa aaa'.

Just like Kutul in 2016, Metaguda in 2023, too, was in Maoist territory where the Indian State had no dominion. But the two places were very different. Whatever sixth sense or gut feeling I'd developed in all these years of reporting—every fibre in me was telling me that Metaguda was the real deal.

Unlike Kutul and Orchha, where we were greeted with 'Namaste', the cluster of villagers gathered under a massive tamarind tree in Metaguda greeted us with a 'Laal Salaam'—the revolutionary greeting that communists exchanged in the Indian subcontinent.

More importantly, Orccha, Kutul and even Minpa were places where people were cautious about talking about their political affiliations, Metaguda was wearing its politics on its sleeve. This village made no bones about declaring who held power here and whose word was the law of the land. A large red concrete martyr's column stood on the common ground, topped by a steel flag pole that ended in a sickle and hammer.

I told the villagers who I was, showed them my most recent article in the *New York Post* and declared that I was there to report about the drone bombings. They barely reacted. As if they knew what we'd come to do the moment they saw us.

'So, has your village been bombed?' I asked straight up.

'Yes . . . yes,' they said in unison.

'Did you see the drones?'

'Yes,' they said again. 'We see them regularly,' some added. 'It's been happening for three years now.'

'The bombing, you mean?'

'Yes, yes . . . the bombing. This is the third time it's happened.'

This was a reporter's dream. Straight answers to straight questions. No beating around bushes, no deflection. Just dishing out the bytes.

The kind of reporting I do, I rarely get such straight answers. People say whatever they want to, twist the truth to suit their agenda and meld generous amounts of lies in their truths. And then it's up to me to slog for days and weeks, sorting through interviews, cross-checking dates, places and numbers to find maybe one out of ten interviews that has something that's usable, starch-free reality.

Here, away from the crossfire because the State wasn't around, was I really going to be so lucky as to do my reporting, pack up and leave? My heart danced at the prospect.

But then, with the very next question, the dance of joy and gratitude to Lady Luck started fading.

'Can you show me the site of the bombing?' I asked eagerly, camera ready.

'Erm . . . erm . . .' the villagers who had just greeted me, their 'journalist comrade', with Red Salutes, started looking at each other's faces. They spoke in their tongue, and nobody bothered to translate.

'What are they saying, Ranu?' I asked. 'Where's Deepak? Oy Deepak!'

The moment we entered the village, Ranu, Devashish and I had gone straight to the men gathered under the tamarind tree, while Deepak made a beeline to a hut. He was now sitting on a charpoy, grinning, chatting and giving high fives to some bloke.

'Ask them where the bombing site is and tell them I want to see it,' I instructed Deepak.

Deepak spoke to the men for a while, then turned to us and said, 'Won't happen.'

'Why not?'

'They're saying no.'

'Ranu? What's happening?'

'*Nahi matlab dikhane mein koi problem hai?*' Ranu asked the villagers directly, and in Hindi, if they had a problem taking us to the bombing site.

'*Nahi matlab . . .*' they had shifted back to Hindi. Clearly, they understood and spoke the tongue. 'We have to inform the people inside before we take anyone,' the oldest man in the group said. He gesticulated to the forests that rose up a hillock.

The people inside were the Maoists. And they had a camp in the direction in which this man had pointed. In all likelihood, it was a platoon or two led by Kamal Akka, a female fighter who reported to Madvi Hidma. Without Kamal Akka giving the nod, the villagers wouldn't dare do anything.

So much for the revolutionary freedom the Communist Party of India (Maoist) promises to the tribals!

Those who belong to the anti-establishment ranks of a polity often think that anyone who opposes the State is automatically a better option. And they have good reason to think so. No State, certainly not the Indian one, is kind to the weak or at least as kind as it is to those in power. But that doesn't automatically mean that rebels are the promised alternative and that the so-called liberated areas are the promised land.

In fact, most rebel-held areas—not just Maoists—are harsh, hegemonic and arbitrary and not even a semblance of civil rights is maintained.

'Fine,' I said aloud. I even smiled and threw up my hands in a gesture of submitting to the will of the people and the people's guerilla army. 'We'll wait to get a go-ahead and only then go see the site.'

The men smiled and asked us to sit down, and the old man ordered no one in particular to bring us some tea.

Ranu and Devashish slumped down on the charpoy while I asked a young man for a notebook and pen. I wrote a small handwritten note for the guerillas telling them who I was and what I had come to report about and requesting an interview.

I handed the note to the old man. Their group dynamics had told me he was the boss.

'Send this inside, please.'

'Hmm,' he grunted a yes and walked off to his house.

'You said you saw the hole caused by the bombing,' I asked Ranu when tea was over, and we had lit a cigarette each.

'Erm . . . yes, I did see what they showed me,' he said. His voice was missing the confidence with which he had told me this in the hotel room in Jagdalpur, 'Yes! The villages are being bombed!'

This yes was far weaker and full of doubt.

'So where was it?'

'In the forest,' his face had become innocent and confused now. The witty gonzo turned Minpa celebrity had given way to a scared mouse.

'Yes, obviously in the forest. But where? You were here in this village. Which direction did you go from here?'

'That I don't really remember. I had come with a group of other reporters, and the villagers had taken us to the spot.'

I sighed.

'You aren't thinking of going to the spot without getting an OK from them, are you?' Ranu checked with me.

No, I wasn't. I knew the protocol of working with armed groups: state or non-state. But I didn't reply to Ranu.

Perhaps sensing my thoughts or trying to divert my attention from his changing of the story about the bombing site, Ranu brought his mouth close to my ear and said in a whisper, 'That old chap? Who took your note? He's the head of the people's militia. Do you know the militia? It's not the same as the People's Liberation Guerrilla Army, which is their armed front.'

Yes! For fuck's sake, I knew the people's militia!

The PLGA was the army, the PM was the police. The Jantana Sarkar was their local self-government, and the People's Court was the kangaroo equivalent of a court of law. I have known the Maoist party and its systems for many years now, and lessons on that are not what I had brought Ranu along for.

'How big and deep was the hole?' I asked instead.

'*Itna hoga,*' Ranu gestured with his hand.

'A little over six inches in diameter?'

'About eight or ten.'

'And how deep was it?'

'About a foot, I guess.'

That didn't sound like a hole left by a bomb. But I said nothing.

'So that old guy,' Ranu took my silence as a cue to continue his tale. 'He's a militia leader. And he has a pistol in his house, I think. I saw him with it once. He'd covered it in plastic.'

'Then it's probably a single-shot country pistol.'

'Munger *katta*? Like they showed in *Mirzapur*?'

Ranu was referencing a popular web series called *Mirzapur*, with several episodes dedicated to the poor quality and cheap guns once made in Munger, Bihar. Though production has now moved well beyond Munger, they retain the name and are the most common illegal firearm in India. One common problem with these weapons is the poor quality of pipes used to make the barrels. Often, they aren't made from cold-drawn seamless pipes like proper gun barrels should be. Instead, scrap pipes with welded seams are used. As a result, the seam often comes apart when the cartridge ignites on a hammer strike, and the shooter ends up injured instead of the mark. The other common problem is the cocking and trigger mechanism getting rusted and jamming up.

So if a gunman is out in the rain, low-cost protection for the low-cost gun is to put a cheap plastic bag over it.

But I told Ranu none of this. Instead, I asked, 'So what do you know of Hidma? Do you think they'll take us to him if we ask? This is his zone, after all.'

'Arey, sir . . .' Ranu's eyes had widened and for the first and last time, he'd said 'sir' instead of *bhaiyya*. 'Don't even say such things. They will kill all of us. Hidma never meets anyone from the press. Ever. He moves around with some hundred and fifty fighters and nobody can reach him.'

'Then how do people know he even exists? What if he's just a lie like Ganapathy was for over a decade? Or Ramakrishna was, for years after his death?'

'*Haan, ye baat* . . .' Ranu was cut short by the reappearance of the old man—Comrade People's Militia Leader.

He'd come back with a young man on a motorbike and some heavy liquor on his breath.

'Guruji will take the message inside,' he said, swaying and pointing to the young man. And with a silly grin, he sat down beside us on the charpoy.

'Why did you call this young man a Guruji?' I enquired.

'He's a government-appointed informal teacher.'

'Jantana government?'

'No, no . . . state government.'

Given the inability to build schools in Maoist areas, the Chhattisgarh government had started a scheme where they named the most educated resident of a village as a teacher to teach basic literacy and numeracy. He or she—mostly he—offered informal tuitions and was paid a stipend by the government. This person was called a 'Guruji.'

Metaguda's 'Guruji' was a lanky twenty-something who had barely touched tenth grade. But he was a guruji nevertheless. Given the general baseline of widespread illiteracy in these areas, coming anywhere near the tenth grade was a big deal. Guruji could read and write, making him useful not only to the villagers but also to the Maoists, whose ranks were largely uneducated.

'So nobody from your village ever went to college or studied in the city beyond school?' I asked.

The drink was hitting Comrade Old Man, and his already broken Hindi was slurring beyond my comprehension. I looked around for Deepak. He was nowhere in sight.

Ranu stood up and called out for Deepak. Devashish came out of a hut saying, '*Kya hua bhaiyaa?* [What happened?]'

'Arey, where's Deepak?'

'He's . . . he's . . .' Devashish looked around.

A young kid from the village, clad in an unbuttoned school shirt and oversized shorts, understood what we were saying. He'd been hanging around us since we had come there, partly because he was curious about all our phones and cameras but mainly because I'd given him mints.

He said something and pointed in the direction of one of the two roads that led out of the village into the forest.

Was he pointing to the bombing site?

'Ranu, get Deepak, please,' I said in a hushed and excited whisper.

Ranu went and fetched Deepak. He had been busy rizzing up a young girl.

'Translate what this boy is saying,' I instructed Deepak, and we all sat down again. But before the boy could say anything, the old man scolded him, told him to beat a hasty retreat, and took over the storytelling upon himself.

For the next three minutes, Deepak nodded his head a lot and said a lot of 'Aaa aaas' with the old man, completely ignoring the rest of us.

'Hello!' I intervened, quite irritated now. 'I need you to translate for me! Don't have a conversation by yourself!'

'Aaa aaa,' Deepak said to me as if he'd understood his job after all this time.

'Ask him who the most educated chap is in this village. Other than the Guruji.'

'Madvi Hidma,' the old man replied.

'Wait, what? Did he just say Hidma?'

'Aaa Hidma,' Deepak confirmed.

But this wasn't the Madvi Hidma—famed and feared leader of the People's Liberation Guerrilla Army. This was some other young man. And they proceeded to tell me his story.

Nineteen-year-old Hidma of Metaguda had gone to Sukma to study. He stayed there with some relatives. Far more ambitious and meritorious than his folks in the village, he did well in his studies. He'd only ever come back on holidays and festivals—but that too for short periods. He'd really started liking Sukma town. He was even planning to go to Jagdalpur or Raipur once his eleventh and twelfth grades were over.

'But he was executed last year,' the old man said.

'Executed? By the police?'

'No. The people's court. It happened right here (the man pointed to a salfi tree not far from where we were sitting).'

'See, we were seeing the drones come repeatedly to this area. And the Party comrades got wary of insiders passing on information about locations to surveil and drop bombs. This Hidma used to stay in the city, so obviously, he was the most likely to have become an informant.

'Besides, he'd gotten addicted to city life. Whenever he came, he complained about phones not working in the village, the food, the life—he had started hating his home and his people. He could've become the guruji here, but he spat at the idea and said he was going to build a life in the city. He didn't want to marry here; he didn't want to work with his family. He wanted to have nothing to do with his homeland. He wanted to become a city man.

'Most importantly, he was always stuck to his phone. The last time he came, their suspicion was proven right!

'Akka (Kamal Akka) was coming with her team to get rations. *Dada-log* had made a big camp over the hills, and they needed food for a few days. We had rice and potatoes from the [government] mid-day meals, which we would give them, but we also decided to tap some salfi. This Hidma boy was a good climber, so we told him. He agreed. But once on top of the tree, he pulled his phone out of his pocket and started moving it around.

'"What are you doing, you idiot?" we asked him. "Looking for network," he said.

'The very next day, the helicopters came and fired at the big camp. One girl was killed, but Akka's team and the big group managed to escape.

'In a day or two, Akka returned with her team and a people's court was set up. Hidma was put on trial. It can't be just a coincidence that he went up on the salfi palm and pulled his phone out right before the attacks. He was obviously giving them GPS coordinates!

'So the trial was held, and he was charged guilty of being an informant and sentenced to death.'

My jaw had dropped hearing the old man's story about the killing of a nineteen-year-old.

'So the people's court checked his phone and found him sending GPS coordinates?' I asked.

'That we don't know . . . but then it's simple. Why would you go up a tree and pull your phone out if not to capture GPS coordinates?'

'So are you telling me you executed a boy based on suspicion and no concrete . . .' My words were cut short by Ranu's fingers tightening in a pinch on my leg. Nearly imperceptible, he was moving his head in a 'Please stop . . . you're going into very dangerous territory.'

I stopped. Ranu was right. This wasn't a place for questioning. If they could label a young man an informant who deserved to die on the basis of his search for a phone network, they could do the same to us.

It was a fear that came close to coming true the very next morning when Old Man Militia leader suggested I be taken hostage and interrogated.

As a young Marxist, I have rent the air shouting slogans against the unjust bourgeoisie and its collaborator, the State. During the many anti-fee hike, anti-privatization, anti-war and anti-capitalist protests where I've been beaten, arrested and locked up by the police, I firmly believed that ideology was the sole indicator of right and wrong.

I still am a Marxist and still call the project of building an equal world, where people come before profits, my own. But journalism has changed one significant aspect of my understanding of ideology and power.

Through the actions of states, Islamists, Communists, Hindu supremacists, Tamil liberationists and secessionists in Kashmir and India's northeast, I've come to realize that not only is ideology a source of power, but that power when accrued in sufficient amounts becomes its own ideology.

Pet rhetoric or team colours notwithstanding, those in power will do everything they can to continue being in power. If that means mangling the very ideals they started with, then so be it. If it means trampling over the lives of those who they said they would liberate, so be it. If humans aren't saying and doing things that are right for the powers that be, the powerful have no dime to give to the rights of those humans.

So, while state power may jail me and make my life hell for being too inquisitive or not toeing the line, the anti-state powers, who have no jailing infrastructure, will simply kill me.

'This is a class war, you see,' Old Man had gone into a flow. His illiteracy notwithstanding, he knew all the keywords of the Maoist lexicon. 'There can be no tolerance for traitors. Those who collaborate with the bourgeois are unwelcome here.'

The old man paused and lit his beedi. Then, with a smirk and that lecherous twinkle back in his eyes, he looked me straight in the eye and said, 'You are *buddhijeevis* (intellectuals). You are most welcome here to tell the world how we're fighting against exploitation. You are necessary bourgeois.'

'*Bhaiyya to Communist hai* (Bro is a communist).' Ranu proffered a character certificate for me. He'd brought in his trademark pally tone to ease the tension. 'He's an old school communist . . . he was a student activist who went to jail and all . . . tell him!'

Old Man Commie didn't respond. His smirk remained while he puffed out smoke from his beedi—head tilted up, watching the curling smoke rise up at the turbid grey sky.

The group fell silent. The village was very quiet, too. The evening was setting in. A small breeze played around the yard and a hint of petrichor hung in the air. The chickens that had been scampering around all this while, pecking at dirt, perched themselves on the low-hanging branches of a clump of moringa trees near us.

Only the pigs hadn't registered any change. They were still sauntering around, grunting and looking for grub.

A young boy had just defecated some twenty metres from where we were sitting. The pigs got into a fight over who'd eat the shit even before the boy had properly stood up. The ones who didn't get a share of the shit cake went back to the unwashed dishes piled in a plastic tub near us and licked little bits of rice off them.

'When do you think Guruji will return with a reply?' I asked, breaking the silence.

The response came in a loud crack of thunder, and the inky blue evening flashed in electric blue. The first raindrops came soon after, and we carried the charpoy into what was to become our night shelter—a hut storing heaps of drying tendu prunes and tamarind and an ad hoc pigsty.

We had barely dragged the charpoy into the hut's overhang when the gentle pitter-patter of rain escalated into a relentless downpour. The wind, which had been gambolling around the yard, teasing the weak branches of the moringa, whispering playful secrets to the vines of the overgrowths, began roaring. A playful imp some minutes back, the wind morphed into a howling demon, its ferocious calls demanding the mighty mahuas and teaks dance a frenzied, possessed dance.

The chickens ran off somewhere, and the pigs huddled in our hut. Their grumbles climbed up several notches on seeing unfamiliar humans in their domain. But then, as the storm raged on outside, an unspoken truce was formed between us and them—a compromise born of necessity in the face of unconcerned reality.

The yard ran muddy streams, and the hut's roof sprang a dozen leaks, giving us a preview of what the night held in store for us. It promised to be a long, sleepless ordeal, filled with the cold dampness of the leaking hut and the heavy mix of the aroma of ripe tendu prunes and tamarinds piled at one end and soiled pigs on the other.

Ranu got onto a second charpoy next to the fruit heaps, saying he needed to stretch his legs a bit. Soon after, he was snoring loud and deep.

Deepak too had vanished into the adjacent hut, and little bits of his laughter, mixed with a girl's giggle, floated into our hut between the symphony of the storm, Ranu's snoring and the feverish grunts of the pigs every now and then.

Devashish, Old Man and I fell silent. With no phone to scroll, I amused myself with a play of words about spring thunder and being in a pigsty.

Back in 1969, the Chinese Communist Party, in its support for the Naxalbari movement—the precursor to the Maoists of today—had termed the arson in Naxalbari a 'peal of spring thunder that would set alight the prairie'. It was a metaphor for the revolutionary fervour they anticipated would ignite dead Indian politics. Disappointed with the Communist Party of India (Marxist), which had firmly embraced the democratic electoral approach circumscribed within the Indian Constitution, the Chinese communists overtly backed the renegade faction led by ousted leader Charu Majumdar and his call for direct violent action. Their hope was that this revolutionary fire would soon burn down the parliament, which they called a pigsty.

Buoyed by this backing, the Naxalites scribbled 'China's chairman is our chairman' on Kolkata's walls, pledging their loyalty to the Chinese way over the Soviet one, and started calling themselves Maoists, instead of Naxals.

Metaguda that night was an apt metaphor for how things had come to be.

The Chinese Communists, under Deng Xiaoping and later Wen Jiabao, chose remorseless pragmatism and state-controlled capitalism over ideologically and emotionally driven praxis. They'd learnt their lesson from the Soviets, who spent way more time exporting the revolution in the spirit of internationalism and doing too little to fortify their economy.

By the time I was of college-going age and a card-carrying member of a Communist student union, the Chinese had stopped calling Maoism an ism altogether. They toned it down to saying their way was the 'Mao Tse Tung Thought' applied to classical Marxism and delivered through a standard Leninist party.

They had cut off all contacts and sponsorship of the Naxalite–Maoist brand of Indian Communists and had instead built their bridges with capitalists around the world. In fact, the ranks of the Naxalites had split many times over. The largest one—the Communist Party of India (Marxist–Leninist) Liberation, CPI(ML) for short—had made a complete U-Turn on the armed path and settled for elections.

Deprived, on the one hand, of the political strength of democratic overground mass organizations like trade and student unions and, on the other, of Chinese funding and validation, the Maoists of India had left the cities and gone into hiding in the forests. Over time, they had become more brigands, struggling to hold their jungle camps, taking cuts from forest produce traders and contractors, than Bolsheviks who would take down the bourgeoisie.

Not that all memories of the spring thunder had been erased. But it remained as localized thunderstorms like the one raging outside the hut. And the storm had no option but to accept the stalemate of coexistence of the pigs and the bourgeois in the pigsty.

'Oh . . . thank you . . . thank you . . .' Devashish and I stood up to take a kerosene lamp the school shirt and oversized pants-wearing boy brought us. Unlike any of the adults around, most certainly unlike the lout of a 'local guide', Deepak, this young boy had brought us some light—guarding the flame with his little left hand while holding the base of the lamp in his right.

This broke Comrade Old Man's stupor, and he loudly summoned the people from the next hut.

'How can you leave our guests languishing in darkness?' he berated his neighbours. His voice was a mix of disappointment and command directed at the hut's owner.

Old Man's voice made Deepak abandon his romance and rush in as well. The pigs ran away, Ranu woke up and the timid face of the girl Deepak was romancing peeked in from the gaps in the split bamboo walls. 'You haven't brought them any food or drinks or started a fire. You're just shooting the shit by yourselves. They're here to meet Akka, and this is how you treat them?'

For some reason, the Old Man was speaking Hindi much better. Perhaps it was the waning liquor or a desire to announce to us that he was in charge as much as to the people he was berating.

'No, no . . . it's alright . . . we're fine,' Devashish tried to broker peace.

'It's not alright!' Old Man declared. Turning to me, bringing his signature grin back on his face, he added: 'You are *buddhijeevis*! We have been told by our leaders to always welcome buddhijeevis with open arms. And you are our guests. How about some mahua? Have you had that before?'

'Yes, I have,' I replied. And added a shrug to indicate, 'I don't particularly care for a drink or merriment.'

And it honestly was the case. I didn't really care about mahua or having a feast. All I wanted to do was get my story and get out.

'Salfi?' Old Man asked. His lips had a coat of saliva that mirrored the flicker of the kerosene lamp.

'No.'

'Then bring sir some salfi, you idiots. Sir . . . here in Metaguda, you will have the best salfi ever.'

'OK,' I nodded. This time, with some more enthusiasm and a smile—or so I thought in my head.

The hosts brought in some rain-smeared branches and got to lighting them. It made far more smoke than fire. A gourd bottle was brought in, and Old Man triumphantly announced, 'Ah! Salfi!'

A round was poured for everyone in steel glasses and teacups. Some toasted raw lentil was brought in as a snack. Ranu refused the local broth and instead opened his whiskey bottle. But we raised our glasses and cups and, wishing a round of cheers as city people do, took our swigs.

The lentils were undercooked and quite inedible. The liquor was raw and tart. Besides, it was mahua, not salfi.

The next morning, we woke up stiff and wet from the rain. New members had joined the hut next to us. Kamal Akka had sent in a team led by a young woman, her personal valet. Sacks of flour and potatoes were sent in as well. The rebel leader and two armed teams under her command were to have lunch with us.

We did our morning business in a swampy pond, then relit the branches we'd been given the previous night and made tea. The warm morning sun felt good on my cold skin. The muddy yard and the water dripping from the tamarind leaves had turned the fierce storm into the memory of sweet summer showers.

The village was yet to wake up. Kamal Akka's visit was still several hours away.

'Let's go for a walk,' I told Devashish. He agreed. I chose the forest that went up the hillock.

From the gesturing and gesticulating that the villagers had been doing the previous day, I was quite certain that's where the previous camp was. Besides, news reports had spoken of a clearing on a hill where the paramilitary had tried landing and the ambush with Madvi Hidma had ensued.

No harm in checking out the area while we waited for the official version from Kamal Akka, I reasoned. What if I found a spent cartridge or discarded magazine?

'What do you want on that side?' the young man from the neighbouring hut appeared.

'Nothing, man . . . just strolling,' I said, acting innocent. 'Maybe pick up some mahua flowers and tendu fruits? As you can see, the rains have brought them down.' I pointed to the ground.

The ground was indeed chequered with the beautiful, succulent, light, nearly neon-green mahua flowers, and ripe yellow–brown tendu fruits lay on the forest floor with specks of dirt on them.

I picked up a few of the mahua flowers and ate them. The mahua flower is one of the finest things I have tasted. It has a full-bodied starchiness like liquid barley, a floral scent and sweetness for which I don't have a simile—I've always liked mahua this way.

Devashish and the other young man politely refused when I held out my cupped hands at them. They, like everyone else around, probably liked it fermented and distilled. Even in Jharkhand and Maharashtra's southeastern forest districts, where mahua trees are common, I've at best found people willing to eat the flowers stuffed in parathas or rotis. But never the way I like them—raw and unprocessed. Moh, the Marathi name for mahua, is such an apt one. Moh means love and lust, but also affection and infatuation—a fluid definition—just like the undefined sweetness of the flower.

My little dreamy poetic escapade was cut short by a startle.

A few metres from where I was picking mahua, an angry boar was hiding in the undergrowth. It had let out a scary grunt and stuck its tusk adorned face out. Thankfully, the hog had been kind enough not to take the shoot-first-ask-questions-later motto of these parts and had simply fired warning snorts.

Throwing the mahua and poetry back into the dirt, we beat a hasty retreat before the animal withdrew its leniency.

When we walked back to the yard, we found Old Man had reappeared. His geniality from the night before and his grin were missing. But the liquor stench had gotten its early morning refill.

After some polite enquiries about whether we'd dined well the previous night, he told us we had to wait for some time before Akka and her teams came. How much time? He didn't know.

'Can we see the bombing spot while we wait?' I asked. Something was feeling a bit off about all of this.

'Erm . . . what is he asking?' he asked Deepak.

Old Man had conveniently gone back to speaking no Hindi, and I had to use Deepak for translations. As expected, Deepak doled out summaries and 'Aaa aa's'.

'He said no,' Deepak translated.

'He said a lot more than no! Translate Deepak, don't summarize!' my voice was raised now.

I wasn't paying Deepak to do a great job flirting with women or to use my phone to further his fledgling influencer career while being a half-arsed translator and pathetic guide.

'Sorry, sir . . . he's saying the hole might be filled up now due to rains . . . no point visiting it. Best to wait for Akka and her team to come.'

Nice. So damn convenient and nice. The rains had washed away not only the bomb hole in the ground but also Old

Man's veneer of welcoming politeness and garrulousness. It was back to standard stalling by the militia boss-man till the real boss woman came to town.

'Tell him to show me the bomb fragments, at least. Or the drone they brought down. The rains haven't washed away those, I'm sure.'

Of course, Old Man understood what I was saying. He'd spoken enough Hindi for his dumb act to fool no one.

He tried to bring his grin back and say, 'Relax . . . please have breakfast, and then we'll head to the forest.'

'Yes, breakfast will be good,' Ranu had appeared. He'd woken up an hour or so after the rest of us had and was just back from his morning shit. '*Waise dinner bura nahi tha, nahi? Simple tha . . . lekin achha tha, nai?* [Dinner was simple but good, no?]'

'Yes. This picnic in the forest is actually turning out to be really good fun. We went from you being sure in Jagdalpur that the bombings had happened to not being sure if it was a bomb hole you saw. Now, the hole has conveniently been filled up by the rain. How about we start planning for lunch and dinner? I've heard they have bows and arrows, and maybe we can hunt some hares and boars. Our Comrade Militia Leader here can also lend us his plastic-wrapped gun for that!'

Ranu's face soured. But I didn't care any more.

'Deepak . . . go to the Old Man's hut and insist on fetching the bomb parts. If he doesn't produce them, I'm off.'

Deepak went off, and Guruji appeared in shorts and a tee.

'Did you send the message?' I asked him eagerly.

'Yes,' he replied.

'And?'

'And nothing. They didn't say anything about what time they'll come or not. But I think they will.'

Deepak, the Old Man and his wife appeared some half an hour after I asked to see the bomb fragments.

His wife carried two pieces of mangled plastic and metal. Old Man didn't carry his grin, but his breath carried the stench of yet another round of liquor. Clearly, my presence and persistence were causing him unusual levels of distress.

Deepak, too, carried an uncharacteristically grim expression.

The 'bomb' they brought me wasn't a bomb. As was later confirmed by two munitions experts, it was a pressure mine with steel balls as shrapnel. The kind that bursts when stepped upon. Made of reinforced polymer, these mines were a made-in-China variant that the Indian forces didn't have in their armoury. Moreover, these devices were useless if dropped from the air. And also too heavy as payloads for the surveillance drones the Indian forces were using.

Clearly, the Maoists had straight out lied in their pamphlets. Their overground counterparts, masquerading as human rights activists, had put out a bogus fact-finding report, validating the lies. The villagers had been instructed to repeat those lies in front of the media.

'Sir, we should leave,' Deepak said in a hushed tone as soon as I was done taking photos and videos of the mine.

'What's wrong?' I asked. Deepak's voice, for the first time during the entire trip, sounded very serious.

'Sir, the old man is talking to the other villagers about you. He's saying he thinks you're not a real journalist. He's asking why you have come after so many months of the bombing. If you're a real journalist, you should've come when the others had come.'

'Seriously?' I wasn't sure if I was more shocked at the stupidity of this argument or upset at my credentials being questioned.

'And sir . . .' Deepak added: 'Old man is saying he's going to tell Kamal Akka to detain you and interrogate you. You may be an informant.'

We left Metaguda around four in the afternoon. Ranu and I had stopped talking by then. He had taken umbrage at me calling his bluff out, and I didn't give a fuck.

The ride back was worse than the one we'd taken to get to Metaguda.

Deepak lost his way, and we met the stream in a spot where it was far deeper and broader than we could cross. By the time we were nearing the snake grove, the sun had set, and the horizon was losing a battle against the darkening earth reaching into the last of the day's colour.

'Be careful in that grove,' I told Devashish—who I was riding pillion with this time instead of Deepak—when I spotted the snake grove some eight hundred metres ahead of us. Little did I know that two minutes after I said that, Devashish would shout, '*RANU BHAIYYA SAMHLO!*' [RANU! WATCH OUT!]

Deepak hadn't noticed a massive cobra crossing the path and had almost trampled its tail. With lightning quick reflexes, the snake had stood up with its hood flared open and swung. While it missed Deepak and Ranu's bike, the swing was taken at us, who were following close behind.

For three days after the encounter, I kept waking up from sleep in shudders. The snake's swing had been so close to my left shoulder that I'd felt the trailing wind rush past my neck and face. We almost lost our balance and fell off the bike, but thankfully didn't.

Serious kudos to Devashish's riding skills and nerves. Had he toppled over, the cobra would've done its deal. There, in the uninhabited expanse with no medical recourse, we'd be lying dead.

A split second after missing the snake's bite, I looked back from our speeding bike and found the reptile standing its ground, swaying furiously and looking straight at us, moving away. It was fuming so loud I heard it over the sound of the motorbike's engine. The golden-brown head with the spectacle mark shone in the last light of the dusk, its milky white underbody foregrounded by the darkening grassland on which it stood.

Its posture and sway embodied the defiance of a local goon, hissing a threat, 'How dare you tread in my realm, you machine-borne outsiders? Come back, and I'll show you who rules this land!'

Cloaks and Daggers

Before I actually became an investigative journalist, I imagined that my life as one would involve a lot of the proverbial cloak-and-dagger tales a la Larsson and Carré. But I got a harsh and funny reality check one early evening, as I was typing my master's thesis out at a lab in the Journalism School at Columbia.

My batchmate Somayeh Malekian, aka Somy, sat some seats away. While I was furiously typing away words from my recently concluded trip to Bangladesh, she was editing her video reel about her coming to New York from Tehran. The plan was that we'd work without any breaks till the clock struck 7.45 p.m., and then rush to a supermarket a few streets down Broadway and get in right around 8 p.m.

The end of our final semester was nigh and whatever money I'd brought in from India and she from Iran was nearly over. So we often shared our meals. One particular supermarket a few streets down Columbia University had become our default dinner place. After eight, it sold leftovers for cheap and by the pound. Sure, we generally got a box where cold salad would run into chicken and grits that nobody wanted. But if you were lucky, some of the pasta or clumped cold mac and cheese would still be available!

Around 7 p.m., a young man came in, said a brief hello, sat down in front of me and opened his laptop. I'd seen the guy around campus, but didn't know who he was. Somy, who had been holding her head tilted to one side, gently massaging her temples, looked back.

She knew the guy and they said hellos. Somy introduced me to him and I shook his hand.

'You were there at the text analysis workshop at Brown [Institute] the other day, right?' the boy asked.

'I was. You were there too? I'm so sorry I don't remember.'

'But I remember you. You're the guy who gave up an investment banker's job to become a journalist.'

'Ha ha . . . yes, we all have our stupid moments in our past,' I laughed. 'Besides, I wasn't a real investment banker. I worked as a programmer who worked at an investment bank.'

'Whatever, dude . . . that's quite something to give up! I mean I totally appreciate your bravery, but why would you do such a thing? You could've always written on the side while making much better money than writing will ever get you!'

'Well, let's just say I was bored of spending my life making super-rich people even richer while I wasted my life away in front of a computer screen,' I shrugged.

The guy made a mock inquisitive face and theatrically bringing his right hand to his chin asked, 'Wait, wait . . . you became a journalist because you wanted to get away from sitting at computer screens all day, eh? How's that going for you now?'

He was as sharp and witty as he was good-looking. We all laughed a long hearty round and went back to our work.

But it's a thought that's stayed with me till date.

Life as an investigative long-form journalist is hardly cloak-and-dagger. I have never done sting operations, and the only three times I've had to work with an assumed identity are all mentioned in this book. Twice because my editors and I felt there was clear danger in exposing my identity, and once because the host requested it. It's mostly reading unending screenfuls of text, followed closely by spreadsheets. That's how it's been for all these years now.

Which isn't to say that I never had any cloak-and-dagger encounters. Although there have been more cloaks than daggers, there have been a few daggers that have swished close enough for me to question my life choices.

Being threatened with dire consequences for doing journalism isn't something out of the ordinary anywhere. And I have a distinct honour of having gotten that for the very first article I ever wrote.

The piece I refer to was a provocative first-person essay called 'The Ambedkar Party', written for *The Hindu*. I was young and wanted to celebrate the life and ways of those I'd grown up with—the Dalits in Pune and Mumbai's slums. I wrote with a loose and carefree tongue that kind of said, 'Yes, we're crass, yes, we dance on the streets. Because we belong in the streets and the streets belong to us.'

As much as they were friends and family to me, I always held a grudge against the Pune Brahmins and the Brahmin-adjacent well heeled. They were snooty, casteist and imagined the world needed their validation to go about their lives. Well into the 2000s, they had somehow missed the memo that the Peshwas weren't in power. And this article became a vehicle for my venting.

The article went viral—albeit at a time when going viral wasn't even a thing—and my inbox started filling up with hundreds of emails telling me what a pleasant shocker of a piece I'd penned. The then Chief News Editor of *The Hindu* PKS wrote in with an appreciative note, marking Editor in Chief N Ram. The Reader's Editor S Viswanathan mentioned it in his weekly column. The Tamil Nadu Untouchability Eradication Front translated the piece into Tamil. In short, I was in a tizzy with the success of my very first professionally written piece.

But then came some emails from folks who'd taken serious umbrage. Ironically enough, these weren't upper-caste folks. They were from people who called themselves Dalit activists and thought I was demeaning Ambedkar Jayanti and the street parties by writing of it the way I had. When I tried to reason saying, 'Guys, you're getting it all wrong,' they went a notch higher. A particularly angry chap wrote on behalf of some group called Kovai Friends saying, 'Watch your back' and added they were trying to find where I lived and would beat the living daylights out of me.

After a point, threats like this became annoying. Not boring, but annoying. Threats can't be boring. But when almost everything I wrote upset someone enough to threaten to beat me or kill me, it became annoying.

As things stand today, my standard response to petty threats is, 'Get a life, you losers! Neither am I a Seymour Hersh whose reports are shaking up empires, nor are you some killer secret agent who'll hunt me down no matter where I am.'

But yes, I did meet some killers who came very close to killing me and some secret agents who were immensely impressive at what they did.

The Bengalee

'Saeed Bhai, you ask a lot more than the others,' Mohib smiled, shifting the betel nuts he was chewing to his right cheek. 'More than the usual things people ask me. Maybe because you're a Bengali and not White.'

'Or maybe because I'm a good journalist,' I said with a smile.

Given his role as a leader of the Rohingya refugees, and a well-known face who'd met high-ranking diplomats and politicians lobbying for repatriation and human rights for his people, Mohibullah always had a line of foreign reporters queuing up outside his hut. I too had been one among them the first time we met.

But something clicked between us and from the end of my very first formal interview with Mohibullah, we'd become friends. Sitting with him and his daughter Afnan for an hour or two at the end of my workday in the camps became a ritual during my time there.

These meetings were just two men talking. No interview questions.

He'd tease me by using the assumed name I used for the undercover work I did in Bangladesh. Over the lemon tea we shared, the betel leaves he chewed and the cigarettes I smoked, we'd talk about the past and speculate about the future. He'd pensively hold forth on things he thought were happening or would come to pass.

Mohib would express his anxieties and tell me his hopes and I'd ask him for advice and pointers, 'Who do you think I should meet for X question,' 'Am I understanding Y correctly?' He'd gently correct my course, or tell me to do this and not that.

This particular response about me asking more question than others had come because I had been asking to meet some of his comrades from the time they fought the Burmese junta alongside Aung San Suu Kyi's National League for Democracy (NLD). I knew some of them had escaped to Bangladesh, India and elsewhere. And I wanted to tell the world that story. Unless the story of Aung San Suu Kyi turning her back on the Rohingyas was told, the story of the Rohingya genocide would never be complete.

'I'll make a few calls tonight,' Mohib offered reluctantly. Evening was approaching. The camp had gone quiet and he'd taken off his shirt and was sitting in his favourite lungi–vest combination.

'It's a sensitive matter, you know,' he said, picking at his calloused feet. 'But let me see if I can get you the contact of this one senior leader who lives in Chittagong.'

Back at my hotel in Cox's Bazar around 11 p.m., when I'd just showered, eaten, set my data backup routine in place and gotten into bed, my phone pinged. A text from Mohib: 'You will get a call tonight or tomorrow morning.'

Almost immediately, while I was still reading Mohib's text, my phone rang.

'*Seed*?' a heavily Bengali accented baritone said from the other side.

'Hello, yes, this is Sid,' I replied, instantly alert, my fatigue from the day's work momentarily forgotten.

'Mohibullah told me about you. He says you want to talk to me,' the voice continued, its tone measured, yet warm.

I sat up straighter, my mind racing.

'Can you come to Chittagong tomorrow?' the man asked.

I agreed without hesitation. This was exactly the kind of breakthrough I had been hoping for. 'Where and when?' I asked, reaching for my notebook.

'Have you come to Chittagong before? Do you know the city well?'

'I've been to Chittagong but don't know it very well. But that won't be a problem. My driver knows the city well enough.'

'Hmm . . .' the man paused. 'Tell your driver to drop you at the Jame Masjid near the bus terminus and call me from there. I'll tell you where to meet me. Come alone, Sid—no driver.'

'OK . . . sure'

'What time will you reach Chittagong?'

'You tell me, sir. It'll take me around four hours I think . . .'

'Google Maps told you that?' The man laughed a bit. 'It will take you longer than that, Sid.'

'Actually . . . let's do this,' he said, after a pause. 'I'll call you in the morning and tell you a more convenient location. Leave after that.'

'Erm . . . OK . . .' I didn't know what else to say. 'By the way I didn't get your name . . .'

'Good night, Sid . . . I'll call tomorrow.' He disconnected the phone.

I lay back in bed, staring at the ceiling fan as it whirled around the cold AC air around my room. This was a big breakthrough—a direct line to the uncomfortable political past that India and Bangladesh were trying to bury. A past that was a crucial piece of political history and yet one, if published, could potentially be used by the Myanmar government to paint the Rohingyas as extremists.

'Would this upset the Bangla authorities enough to throw me out?' I wondered.

The Bangla government was more than happy to showcase the good work they were doing by housing the Rohingya refugees. Journalist visas were given freely to anyone who said they wanted to visit the camps.

But I was often infringing that welcome by reporting on other things that the government didn't want reported. The student protests in Dhaka and the disproportionate use of force to quell them. The drug war and its killing spree. The hunt for Islamists that had become a witch-hunt for political opponents of the Awami League government. The far less than civil and way beyond legal–ethical methods used to coax confessions out of the accused and frame cases.

This had made me both friends and foes in the Bangla political and security establishment. The well-wishers gave me leads and leaks, but also kept warning me that my reports were being read and I was being watched.

'Keep a bag packed and be prepared to leave Cox's Bazar at an hour's notice,' a source in the Bangladesh Army had told me the very day I landed in Cox's Bazar. He had coldly added, 'That is, of course, assuming I get the information before someone gets to you.'

'Oof! Baba re baba!' I said aloud, flung the door to the balcony open and stepped into the muggy, saline, night air and lit a cigarette. 'Way too much information to process for my small brain,' I repeated a line I often still use about myself.

I didn't sleep well that night. Not that I often did—but that night was one of the worst ones.

I'd forgotten to close the balcony door when I returned to bed after the smoke. I woke up much before the alarm with several red itchy mosquito bites on my arms and legs. The hot humid air outside had ruined the cooling of the air-conditioning, and my bed and pillow were damp with sweat. Though I couldn't recall my dreams exactly, I had once again dreamt of some shitty sentimental arguments—ones where I see my parents abandoning me or my ex berating me for not being good enough while I struggled to explain myself to them.

But fuck sentiments. I had a big job to do that day.

'Abu . . . get ready and come as soon as you can, please,' I called my driver. 'We're leaving for Chittagong.'

'*Theek aache, sir* [OK],' Abu replied, his voice drenched in deep sleep.

I quickly checked if all uploads had completed, cleared the local files from my camera and voice recorder, formatted my SD cards and hit the shower.

'Good morning!' The hotel's manager greeted me as I walked into the breakfast room. His smile and raised eyebrows said: 'Oh, look who's eating breakfast today?'

I'd befriended the manager as I usually do in places I stay for long. I'd asked him about good places to eat, to which he'd (sincerely, I think) offered that I try the food at the hotel itself.

'Not boasting because it's my hotel, but people come from all over the city and even Dhaka to dine with us. Even guests at other hotels come over. You'll see our restaurant full at dinner time!'

He'd even introduced me to the head chef.

'Whatever I make is special. I take up the challenge to satisfy gourmands like you, personally!' The squat smiling cook had offered with a grand laugh and a handshake when I'd ask what his specialties are.

But let alone dining on specialties, that morning was the first time I'd even stepped into their restaurant for the complimentary breakfast. Every other morning, my breakfast was chaa and unbranded doughy biscuits at a stall near Dolphin circle. Partly because I never had enough time, but mostly because I have for all my adult life, absolutely loved roadside chaa–biskoot.

I don't quite remember what I ate for breakfast or how it tasted. My mind was too full of anxious anticipation to register anything. Anxious because of the wait for the Rohingya revolutionary's call and rehearsing and rephrasing the questions I'd ask when I meet him. Anticipation because 'Ooh . . . I'm going to write a killer story that no one else has!'

But 7 a.m. slowly and painfully turned to 9 a.m., and 9 a.m. turned to a restless 10 a.m. And yet no call came. Abu, parked in the street between the hotel and the beach, had the faintest of confused frowns on his brows, wondering why, after the eager summons, we hadn't left. But the quiet man that he was, he didn't ask any questions.

'I'm waiting for a call,' I proffered—almost apologetically.

'*Theek aachey, sir*,' he replied—repeating the line he always did.

I pulled out my phone and tapped the screen a hundred times to see if the network had died and hence the silence. A couple of times I even thought of calling the number back. But I didn't because that's not how these things go. Not with people like the one I was to meet.

Without proper precautions, what would be just another interview for a journalist like me, could for an underground activist like him, turn into a bullet in the head—if lucky.

Around 11 a.m., I sat down at the small desk in my hotel room.

'Act like a grown up and use the time to transcribe interviews, you unprofessional piece of shit,' I scolded myself. 'Neither the voice files nor the reporting notes are going to write themselves. There's still no technology available to simply take your thoughts from your head and write your story out. Even if there was, a struggling two-bit journalist like you could never afford it. So yeah—sit your ass down and use the time properly.'

I tried to do the bidding of my disciplinarian alter ego. But kept failing at being able to write even a paragraph. Instead of any useful texts on the screen, only the worry about things I couldn't control and the chastising admonitions of my other self kept piling up.

Around 11.30 a.m., the phone rang.

'Good morning, *Seed*,' the voice wished me. It was still the sombre baritone but had a tinge of jolliness to it.

'Good morning, sir! Could you . . .'

'You in your room?'

'Erm . . . yes . . . I am in my hotel room . . .'

'Open the door. I'm coming up.'

He was relishing the trick he had pulled on me. The smile from under his bushy moustache showed it. It had stayed unchanged since he'd walked out of the elevator, extended his hand speaking aloud his first name, entered the room, and sat down on the chair next to the small table, holding his jute file folder close on his lap.

Le Carré was far closer to the real world of clandestine services than Fleming and his fairy tales, meant to make the MI6 look like cool dudes, and not the bungling idiots they had been during the Cold War. Despite Le Carré's best efforts, he'd done little to dent the myth created by Fleming about what spies look and act like. This man in his terrycot pants, dull chequered shirt, bulging paunch and overall 'Bengali uncle' vibe, was living proof of Carré supremacy. He was clearly as real as it got.

By telling me to come to Chittagong and instead appearing at my doorstep in Cox's Bazar, he had pulled off a classic double-blind move. He probably had someone in Cox's Bazar recce my hotel to see if I was under surveillance. Once certain I wasn't, by appearing at my doorstep, he'd ruled out any possibility of me unknowingly leading anyone to his location.

What remained the most impressive was, of course, his network. I'd never told Mohib which hotel I was staying in. And yet this man had, in no time, found that out, down to the correct room number.

'Tea or coffee,' I asked my visitor—who we'll call Mr N hereafter.

'*Chaa-i bhalo* [Tea's better],' N replied in clear Bangla and added a rhetorical question, '*Aapni to Bangali, na?* [You're a Bengali, aren't you?] Which real Bengali can ever prefer coffee over tea?'

I chuckled and nodded at him, picking up the phone and telling room service to send us a pot of tea. He was again reminding me he'd done his homework on me and, as I said, I was genuinely impressed.

'It is true Bengal consumes way more tea than coffee. But didn't your background check on me not tell you that I'm not Bengali enough? And you most certainly aren't one either.'

'I'm a Bangladeshi citizen, sir!' N declared with mock umbrage.

'Those are your papers, sir. Not your ethnicity. But having hung out with Rohingyas, I know tea still rules supreme.'

We chitchatted a bit till we finished the tea. Then the interview began.

'How do you respond to the Myanmar government's charge of being called a terrorist organization that's threatening the integrity and sovereignty of their country?' I opened.

Impressed as I was with his spycraft, he needed to know that I wasn't in thrall to him. Although my craft was much less sexy, I was as good at it as he was at his.

His smile receded momentarily but came back again and he responded with the oft repeated, 'One man's freedom fighter is another man's terrorist.'

'Are we the ones killing, raping, looting, setting people's homes alight? Or is the Tatmadaw doing that? And what they're doing to the Rohingya in the Arakan will be done to the Kachin in the North and the Shan in the East. The pattern is clear and the tactics are the same. A small bunch of elite Burmese sitting in the palatial offices of Naypyidaw funded by the narco-moguls of Yangon are out to subjugate every other identity in Myanmar.

'They claim to be protecting the nation but, in reality, they are destroying it. They're destroying the centuries of unity different peoples had. Tearing apart the very people they vow to defend.

'We Rohingya fought shoulder to shoulder with Aung San and his Anti-Fascist People's Freedom League when he led the independence struggle against the British. We fought shoulder to shoulder with his daughter Aung San Suu Kyi's National League for Democracy against General Ne Win.

'Suu Kyi was the darling of the West because of her Oxford pedigree. But the reality is that she was born with a silver spoon in her mouth and didn't know the first thing about Myanmar's common people and their struggles when she returned. And yet, we unquestioningly accepted her leadership just as we had her father's. And what did we get in return? This!

'We are patriots. And we've proven it time and again. It is the Tatmadaw which is a terrorist organization. That too has been proven time and again.'

'But Rohingyas have also wanted a separate Muslim state for a very long time. Are you going to deny that Arakan Rohingyas had offered to join Pakistan because it's a Muslim country and Myanmar would never be one? The

RSO (Rohingya Salvation Organization) was backed with arms and money by the ISI and their leaders given safe haven in Pakistan.'

'The first time Rohingyas wanted to join Pakistan was when India was partitioned. Muhammad Ali Jinnah and his dream of Pakistan was a beacon for all Muslims around the world. And yes, we Rohingyas are committed Muslims, so Pakistan seemed like a good idea to some of our leaders and thinkers at that time. The 1940s were a time of self-realization of identity-based nation states that had been colonized by the British. We dreamt the same things as Pakistan or India did. How are we an exception?

'The second time was when Pakistan—the Muslim nation that was the hope of Muslims around the world—was getting divided into two by your India . . .'

'Bangladesh was formed on the basis of the same identity-based self-realization that you just mentioned. Why are you not calling that breaking up when you don't say that about Myanmar?'

'Don't hide the fact that India armed the anti-Pakistan Bangladeshis. Had it not been for the Indian Army, Pakistan would still have been intact. India was doing illegal intervention. Simple.'

'Was it intervention when India supported Suu Kyi and sheltered the NLD activists who you say you were fighting alongside?'

'That's different, Sid.'

'How?'

'This is becoming an argument. Not an interview.'

'It need not be an argument. But you're avoiding my questions and invoking my identity as an Indian.'

'What is your question? That we are terrorists funded and armed by Pakistan? The answer is no! Don't ask me about the RSO because I don't speak for them. We (the RNO) haven't gotten a single bullet from Pakistan or anyone. If we had the guns and money, do you think we'd be the victims of a genocide? We're requesting everyone, America, Canada, Europe, China, even India, to talk to the Myanmar military and tell them to stop killing the Rohingyas. But nobody is interested.

'The real reason the Burmese are driving us out and burning our homes and fields is because we sit on one of the world's largest oil and gas reserves. Nobody wants to upset the Myanmar military—not even Suu Kyi and her Western masters who gave her the Nobel Prize—because tomorrow when the genocide is completed and all the Rohingya lands are empty, the oil drilling will begin. And India, China, Canada, US, the Saudis—everyone wants a share of that pie! Rohingyas be damned! They can always be thrown some titbits of charity and kept prisoners in refugee camps.

'And if any Rohingya speaks out against this injustice, label him a terrorist! Simple!

'The question, Sid, is who do we call a terrorist?' N added, after taking a pause from his charged spiel. 'Don't get me wrong, but if you are going to ask me if I'm a terrorist based on stereotypes developed by the West, it's unfair.'

'In fact, if stereotypes are to be followed,' he added, with a chuckle. 'You, Saeed Bhai, look way more terrorist than I do.'

I chuckled too. He'd taken a dig at my habit of keeping a beard and a trimmed moustache that often invited the 'You look like a Muslim' remark.

White airport security pulling me aside for 'random checks' basis my brown skin and 'Muslim look' had become a part of my life. Friends, family, random strangers assumed things too. I had made it a point to never correct anyone. Firstly, because my Hindu birth identity notwithstanding, being called Muslim wasn't a slur for me. Second, it actually helped my reporting. Passing off as a Saeed or any other

Muslim name I'd make up if the situation called for it was far easier than I'd imagined.

'Not stereotypes, Mr N,' I said. 'But say I was living under an assumed identity, obtained through false papers, as a citizen of Bangladesh. Using that identity, I set up a business in exporting handloom textiles to the West, marking the price up several times for specific clients. People who aren't actually clients but leaders and funders of a political movement in exile. That extra money was then used to run a political movement, buy arms and ammunition and pay fighters and operatives in my home country with the express intent of overthrowing the government. Would that qualify as terrorism?

'Don't get me wrong, Mr N, but that sounds like someone who's very close to blurring the line between freedom fighter and terrorist.'

N stayed frozen for a couple of moments with his mouth slightly open. The grin had slipped off his face. Now I grinned in his stead.

I lit a cigarette and pointed at the jute folder he had been hugging. It bore a circular, printed insignia of a convention of Bangladeshi handloom exports.

Handloom exports . . . Rohingya leaders in exile in the West . . . this man being the principal fund management guy . . . I had just strung them into a probable causal relationship and hit N with it. I had no idea it would hit as close to reality as I saw it hitting.

N looked at his folder for a few moments. Then he guffawed and extended his hand to me. I joined him in his laughter.

'Mohib was right. You are different,' N said with his trademark grin back on and proceeded to bring out a metal box with four rolled betel leaves inside it. Offering me one, he said, 'I'm impressed Sid . . . I'm impressed.'

'I can smell the zarda and fermented supari in it,' I said, politely refusing the betel leaves. 'That combination is way beyond my league.'

'Yes, yes . . . I was told you never eat paan, even at the camps. That's the only missing part. Else you would have made a good Rohingya! You have our sharpness. Full detective like, eh?'

'That's just my Bengaliness. I read a lot of Feluda at home.'

The Louts

Among the many bad things insurgencies and counter-insurgencies do, one insidious act often overlooked is how outfits on both sides of the divide become safe havens for louts. Addicts, losers, liars, perverts and all manner of men who would never find acceptance in constructive society find perfect homes in these groups. Thanks to the violent ways these groups use and the moral justifications that are offered in favour of mindless violence spouting greater causes, the inherent violence of bad men finds easy ideological camouflage in extremist organizations.

Essentially, a lot of street thugs do their run-of-the-mill thuggery and pass it off as soldiering. Their banners—whether green, red, black or stripes and stars—are just flimsy covers for acts that would've otherwise put them in prison.

In fact, among the few daggers that have swished close to my neck, it's the louts that rank the highest. Not hardened ideological warriors or soldiers—but louts and thugs.

And two of my closest brushes happened in Bangladesh.

N and I had spoken for a long two and a half hours. Seven years later, the copious voice notes sit tagged in my mind as a book—one which I may never end up writing.

He left with a word of caution, '*Seed*, ARSA is not an ideological group. They're criminals. Thugs. You should be careful.'

Mohib had told me the same.

But the ARSA—the newest outfit in the bouquet of Islamist Rohingya groups that took to the gun—had recently pledged their allegiance to the Islamic State. A low-res video showed a bunch of them at an undisclosed location, offering their loyalty to the new chief of the Islamic State and the successor of Abu Bakr al-Baghdadi, Abu Ibrahim al-Hashimi al-Qurayshi.

The video wasn't that impressive. The bloke in the centre of the frame, a scraggy man with an unkempt beard, was waving a pistol. But his lackeys didn't have any firearms. They thought they'd make up for what they lacked in materiel resources with enthusiasm. The result was more comical than terrifying.

But honestly, that's not very out of place when it comes to this part of the world.

Al-Qaeda was built as a hierarchical organization with well defined ranks, duties, departments, division of work and other things that go into building a political establishment. It had a military wing and a standard proper political party. It had ideological leaders and ambassadors—thinkers and doers.

The Islamic State, on the other hand, at least outside Iraq and Syria was, and remains, less of a political party and more of a bandwagon party. No less dangerous or violent—but far less organized or deserving of objective respectability.

And I don't say this pejoratively. The Islamic State was dreamt up by the usual suspects of the West and its allies elsewhere to be exactly what it was—a flat network that anybody could claim to be a part of without any proper investiture or training.

As with all militaries and paramilitaries, running groups like Al-Qaeda takes a lot of money and time. The Islamic State was a low-cost handmaiden better suited to late-stage capitalism and its reduced spending power.

The world will always have enough disgruntled young people who want to feel like they're worth something and that their lives have a purpose greater than just living to pay their taxes and debts. All that such people have to do is create some vile and violent nuisance and then flash the black flag of the Islamic State—and there you are! A 'lone wolf' gets his fifteen minutes of jihadist fame and the military–industrial complex another excuse to pile their coffers with moolah while taxpayers lose their homes, starve and die of no healthcare.

If Al-Qaeda was American network TV, the Islamic State is Instagram. While both are soul-sucking and mind-numbingly stupid, the former needs people to work their way up a harsh hierarchy, and the latter is where you do your silliest, most-attention-seeking thing possible and take your shot at fame.

The ARSA video was exactly that. A bunch of scraggy louts with one pistol shouting themselves hoarse praising the Islamic State's new supremo and pledging to die for him. Just like English soccer team fans whose existence the real players didn't even know of. As I said, this wasn't out of the ordinary in this part of the world.

A week after Abu Ibrahim al-Hashimi al-Qurayshi took office, a bunch of Bengali boys went into a thicket and took a video of the same pledge of loyalty. These losers didn't even have that one pistol the ARSA guys had. They just covered their faces with a keffiyeh and raised their forefingers threateningly to the sky as if saying, 'We will finger every infidel to death! [insert angry emoticon]'

Comical as the ARSA may have been, they had the potential to become something big, at least for news media. I wanted to be there when it happened.

'Yes, I went in and interviewed them,' a reporter who worked for the *Dhaka Tribune* had told me. I'd established contact with him from New York, and he was going to get us into the ARSA circles. In addition to his day job of working for the *Tribune*, he moonlighted as a fixer for White news outlets. He was telling me about how Vice had hired him to go into the Bangla–Myanmar border forests and meet the insurgents. 'They put a black cloth over my head. But I had a radio tag in my shoe that recorded my location. Vice people are very particular about fact-checking.' Eventually, his facts didn't really add up to anything, and he couldn't get me any of the long list of things he'd promised. So, I set out on my own to explore all things Islamic State in and around the Rohingya camps.

'Sorry Sid . . . I can't help you with this,' Mohib had said when I asked him if he knew any ARSA or RSO people in the camps. 'For them, I'm an enemy because I want a democratic struggle, whereas they want to go down the violent path.'

Ilyas, my translator, couldn't help me either. Besides, he'd already shown his unreliability. When I asked him about the drug trade in the camps, he suddenly became amnesiac and pretended never to have heard the word 'yaba'.

I had messaged the ARSA Twitter handle many times. But no response had come from them. That was expected as well. The Twitter handle posted photos of press releases that claimed the exact opposite of what the video showed and what was being spoken of on the ground.

The language used on the Twitter handle indicated it was run by some English-educated lot who wanted to project a holier-than-thou ideological stand. They pretended to eschew violence and said they were all for including Hindus and Buddhists in their independent Arakan while ARSA on the ground was saying they'll establish absolute Sharia and kill every infidel. In short, they had little to do with the guys on the ground.

So, I just began broadcasting my intent.

Whenever I met someone who spoke about fighting for the Rohingya cause, I asked, 'So which organization do you work for? RNO? ARSA? RSO?' Obviously, everyone denied having any truck with these proscribed outfits on record, but I knew the news would spread, and someone might reach out.

And someone did.

'Hello . . . Mr Roy?' a voice from an unknown number asked. I was strolling on the beach in Cox's Bazar that evening. I'd been tipped off about a methamphetamine drop from a fishing boat and was waiting for it.

'Yes, this is Roy,' I replied in Bangla. The man who'd called wasn't fluent in English, so I saved us the trouble.

'We want to meet you. We heard you've been asking for us.'

'Who are you?'

'I'm Sheikh Azizullah—Rohingya Army.'

'ARSA?'

'Yes, yes . . . ARSA'

'How did you get my number?'

'You have been coming to the camp, no? We heard you've been asking for us. So I called. Can you meet us tomorrow?'

'Tomorrow is difficult for me. I have some work to finish. Is the day after okay?'

'The day after is fine. You come to Himchori Beach. You know Himchori?'

'I don't. But my driver will know.'

'No driver . . . you come alone.'

'But what's the problem with the driver taking me to Himchori? It's not like he'll sit with us during the interview.'

'Take a bus.'

'What? No. That's very inconvenient.'

'Fine, then park your car at Himchori Beach and call me from there. Come by five o'clock.'

'Five in the morning?!'

'No, no! Five p.m. Evening.'

A little past 5 p.m., two days from the phone call, I dialled the number.

'I'm here. Where are you?'

'Have you left your car?'

'No, I'm still in it. But I'll leave it here. Tell me where to come.'

'Send your location . . . (I did) . . . okay, you'll see a trail to your left. Do you see it?'

'Erm . . . no . . .'

'Get out of your car and walk down a little, and you'll see a tea-stall on your left. The trail goes into the forest next to the tea-stall. Keep walking in, and you'll come to a small clearing. Wait there.'

As I left the car, Abu asked me where I was going for the first time since I had employed him. He asked me this with a clear hint of concern in his voice and furrowed eyebrows.

'I'm interviewing some people,' I replied casually, trying not to betray the gravity of the meeting.

'In the forest, sir? At this time? This area isn't good. It's better to ask them to come on the main road and talk. Or I'll come with you.'

I appreciated his concern, but this is how things work in my line.

'No, Abu, they want to talk alone,' I said, attempting to sound more confident than I felt. 'Don't worry, I'll be back soon.'

Some five hundred-odd metres down the spot on the highway where Abu had parked his car was a tea-stall. A tiny little shop, with three men sitting around sipping tea. The trail was there, too.

I wondered if I'd raise the suspicions of the tea vendor and his customers by taking the trail at this odd hour. But they paid me no heed.

Some hundred metres into the trail, there was indeed a clearing. I wasn't sure if this was the specific clearing I'd been instructed to wait at or if there was another one up ahead. But I had no way of cross-checking. The already weak mobile network had completely vanished at that spot. With daylight all but out, the thought of venturing further into the forest wasn't welcoming. If not terrorists, snakes are aplenty in these parts. Besides, the people whom I was to meet would surely come looking for me at this spot.

So I stood there and waited. Big, fat mosquitoes began their assault. I lit a cigarette in the feeble hope that even if the smoke didn't send some of these vampires away, it would at least distract me.

Half a cigarette in, three men came walking down the same path I had—the same three men who were sitting at the tea stall.

'Huh! Neat trick,' I said to myself, threw my cigarette down, and stubbed it with the heel of my shoe.

The trio included two thin men and one stout one.

The lankier one among the thin duo was wearing an untucked shirt. The other two were wearing T-shirts. The stout man was wearing a tee one size too small for his proportions, and his belly peeked out from where the tee ended, just above where his pants started.

'Mr Roy?' the lanky one asked. His voice was steady, betraying no emotion and in stark contrast to his dishevelled look. 'I'm Azizullah', he added, but didn't hold out his hand.

Before I could respond, the stout man stepped in and began patting me down without a word of warning. His brusque manner took me aback.

'Hey, what are you doing?' I protested, but he ignored my objections, his hands moving over me, pinching at the contour of the contents of my pockets.

'We need your phone and wallet,' he said curtly, his hands pausing in their search.

'Phone and wallet? Why do you need my phone and wallet?' I asked, irritation creeping into my voice.

'For security,' he replied, his open palms waiting and his eyes not meeting mine.

'There's no signal on the phone,' I said, holding up my device for them to see. 'So, I don't think I can be tracked any more if that's what worries you.'

The thin lackey muttered something to Azizullah in Chittagonian, his tone laced with suspicion. I couldn't catch the words, but the distrust was clear in his voice.

Azizullah turned to me, his expression softer than his lackey's, yet firm. 'We must take precautions,' he explained. 'It's not just about being tracked. It's also about ensuring that no information leaves this place.'

I understood their concern but was unwilling to part with my phone. 'I'll switch it off if you want,' I said and promptly powered it down in front of them. The screen went black, and I returned the phone to my pocket.

The stout man looked at Azizullah as if waiting for orders to bite. But Azizullah gave a slight sideways shake of his head and the stout man stepped back, though he still looked unsatisfied with the arrangement.

'Let's walk some more and talk,' Azizullah said, waving his hands towards the forest.

'Why can't we just talk here?' I asked. 'No one's around. We can just sit here for a bit.'

My gut wasn't feeling right about these men and this place. And I didn't want to go any further than I had come. When it came to safety matters, after all these years in this line of work, I had come to trust my gut more than my brain.

Besides, something else wasn't adding up. If these men were Rohingya, why were they speaking in Chittagonian? Though the two tongues sound very similar, and I understood neither, I'd started picking up on the differences in my time in the camps.

'We have a hut some distance in. We can sit more comfortably there and talk,' Azizullah said. He was way more patient than his lackeys, who seemed to be angry with me from the moment they'd seen me.

My gut and mind started the usual fight. Though, as I said, I trust my gut a lot, it doesn't mean I don't doubt the gut feelings, and my brain doesn't say things like: 'Be decent,'

'Don't overreact,' 'You need this interview,' etc. And my brain was telling me all of these. So I dithered a bit.

'What happened?' Azizullah asked. This time, a clear edge of irritation had crept into his voice. 'You said you wanted an interview, and now you're acting difficult. This place is full of mosquitoes and all, so we're telling you to come with us, sit in our hut and talk. Are you scared or what?'

'No, not scared . . .'

Of course, I was, but that's the first thing people say when they're asked if they're scared.

'Then come along! We don't have time to waste.'

Azizullah's voice had risen a notch, and his lackeys had taken their cue like trained attack dogs and positioned themselves on either side of me.

'Fuck!' my head screamed, and my heart sank. 'This wasn't good. No, no, not good at all. And even if that wasn't their plan earlier, now these men are pissed with me and are going to . . .'

'OY!' A booming voice broke my thoughts. 'Who the fuck are you bastards? What do you want?'

Abu had appeared. He'd come same way I, and these men, had some minutes back. He had the car's jack handle in his hand and the tea stall guy by his side.

'Sir', he barked at me. Gone was the quiet, sombre Abu who'd been my silent, polite companion all these days. Now he commanded me like a ferocious dog, 'You come here this minute! And you bastards, get the fuck away this moment, or I'll fuck your lives over.'

'Arey . . . watch your tongue! What's wrong with you?' The stout man took a step towards Abu.

'Come a step closer, and I'll show you what's wrong. This rod will crack your fat head open is what's wrong. You think I don't know what you're up to?'

Abu sneered at the three men—the grip on the car's jack curled tight in an angry fist.

'Okay, okay . . . this is some misunderstanding . . .' Azizullah stepped in, trying to calm the hotheads down.

'Misunderstanding, my ass . . . sir, come . . . and you assholes get going . . . I'm serious. After this, my hands will do the talking.'

Azizullah's lackeys grumbled, and Azizulah seared Abu with his eyes. But choosing not to escalate the matter, he goaded them away, and Abu took me out of the forest.

'You don't understand the people here, sir,' Abu said on our drive back. 'We're from these parts and know these people. This area is full of thugs. You asked me to wait, but I wasn't feeling right about what you were discussing on the phone. Why did they ask you to go into the forest at dusk when they could've just met you at the tea-stall? So I took the jack handle and walked down to the tea-stall just in case my fears came true. When I saw the tea-stall empty, I asked the tea guy which way you'd gone. He said he hadn't seen anybody. Immediately, I knew something wasn't right. No way someone is going to miss someone who looks so different from the rest of us.

'Allah's grace, sir, Allah's grace that you weren't mugged or killed by those rascals! If I had been a minute late, only He knows what would've happened.'

'But wait . . . why would the tea-stall guy lie? He came with you, right?'

'Huh . . . that rascal was also in cahoots with the three thugs. He showed me the way only because I told him I'd break his head first and then those of whoever had taken you inside.'

I don't know for sure if Azizullah and his two lackeys were actually ARSA. In fact, I don't even know if Azizullah was that man's real name. What I know for sure is I have a brother called Abu who saved my life.

Maach, Meth and Metalhead Sharia

Get paid for one, report for three, write four. That's the rule of thumb for most journalists. Meaning every time you take a trip to report one story, gather enough material to write several more. The reason for that is simple.

Unless you belong to the glitzy infinitesimally small fraction of corporate news behemoths, nobody foots your bills for every story you need. Even with the amounts paid, the sum is inversely proportional to the amount of melanin in your skin.

I too have lived, and continue to live, by this rule of preparing more than one report on one assignment. And Cox's Bazaar was no different.

I did my story on the Rohingya camps—which is what I was paid to do. But I also did stories on the meth trade and the Islamic State, which I had reason to believe was setting up neophyte bases there. In fact, I'd soon find out that the three stories weren't very distinct and flowed into one another through tenuous yet tangible little threads.

'Today after 5 p.m.,' Nazrul said. 'A little beyond Sayeman Resort, keep walking till you come to this little backwater like thing and wait there. Two fishing boats. Small stash. Ask for Bapi, reference Monu.'

'Small stash, meaning? How small?'

'Sid, that's all I know. And why do you care how small? You're there for the news, not the meth. Or at least that's what you told me!'

Nazrul worked in the intelligence wing of the Bangladesh Border Guards. We had met in Dhaka through a common contact and became friends sipping Malta Tea.

Malta Tea isn't some exotic tea, imported from Europe. It's just plain black tea served with a slice of cheap Valencia oranges aka malta, that flooded Bangladesh's markets from China or Thailand or somewhere like that. We were sipping it right outside the Dhaka University campus at a tea-stall run by a complete whacko. Whacko because he sold absolutely ridiculous things like *paneer* tea.

'If I worked for the Brits, like James Bond, I would've treated you to a martini. But a third world country like mine, and on top of that these budget cuts and all—you'll have to live with this, brother,' Nazrul had added, clinking his tea glass with mine.

Nazrul is singularly the funniest and most cynical spy I've ever met. I don't quite know how good he is at spying or crushing the drug trade and terrorism, but should he ever take to stand-up comedy, he's going to kill it.

I couldn't help but become his friend. Among the few guardian angels I had in Bangladesh, he ranks right at the top. He saved me not only from returning empty-handed without stories, but also the deathly boredom that sets in after hanging out with political talking heads.

So, at 5 p.m., I stationed myself at the far end of the Cox's Bazar beach. This spot didn't have any tourists. In fact, I wasn't sure if I was still on what is called Cox's Bazar beach, because the 'little beyond Sayeman Resort' was nearly two kilometres beyond.

Five turned to 6 p.m. and the sun turned from yellow to deep orange-red and then disappeared below the horizon. When the clock hands zeroed in on 6.45 p.m., the evening ink was pouring into the horizon thick and fast, and all traces of daylight would soon disappear.

The two couples who were canoodling near the broken barricade by the main road left as well. The only people left on the beach were myself and four young men who were busy playing an odd but noisy game.

The game was simple. They had carefully dug trenches in the sand to connect the two small pools of backwater to the Bay of Bengal. The water from the pools began flowing in a stream out to the sea. For reasons unknown to me, tiny mullet-like fish started swimming upstream into the trench. The goal of the game was to catch the little fish with one's bare hands as they swam through the trenches trying to get to the pools.

I watched them play. Wet my feet in the sand. Took some pointless photos with dead snails in my palm for Facebook. Then said fuck it and joined the four men in their game.

Though I didn't catch a single fish, it was great fun getting wet and dirty. The men were kind to the city idiot and let me hold one of their catches in the hollow of my palms and take a photo.

'Where are you from?' one of the men asked me.

'Dhaka.'

'Holiday?'

'Yes.'

'Alone? Who comes to Cox's Bazar on a holiday alone?'

'Losers like me,' I said with a shrug. They all laughed and saved me any further enquiries.

A little before 8 p.m., all except one of the mullet-catching men left. I too was about to call it a day when I saw him take his phone out and check it a couple of times. He pretended to walk off, but didn't actually do so. Most importantly, I saw him looking at me from the corner of his eye. My tummy tingled. If this man was waiting, he was waiting for something to come in. Besides, Nazrul had never been wrong.

Ignoring my tummy, which was grumbling and rumbling with hunger, I waited. A little past 8 p.m., the dark silhouettes of two boats appeared against the light darkness of the sea and the sky. Slowly—painstakingly slowly—the silhouettes turned to real boats and hauled in and anchored on the shallow sandy depths right beyond the breaking point of the waves.

The sailors shouted orders among themselves. A couple of them jumped off and moored the boats. The young man who'd pretended to leave came back and joined in the work of unloading the boats.

I waited until the work was in full swing and then approached a man who wasn't hauling any crates but just standing next to the boat, one hand on one of the thick ropes.

'Who is Bapi?' I asked the man.

He just stared back saying nothing.

'Bapi? Monu sent me.'

He stared some more. Then reluctantly called out to the other boat, 'O Bapi bhai . . . *tomare ke khujtase.* [Brother Bapi . . . someone's asking for you]'

The gaunt face of a man with a towel tied around his head looked out from the second boat. But he said nothing and just went back under the deck.

I stood there awkwardly as the men completely ignored me and went around unloading their crates of fish.

'*Bolen* (yes),' Bapi finally came down and spoke to me. He was least interested in talking to me and made no attempt to hide that.

'Monu referred me to you,' I added with a smile. Bapi remained silent and unsmiling.

'Can we sit down and talk somewhere?'

Another long painful, awkward pause ensued. He finally said, 'Please sit. Let the crates get unloaded.'

It took the men around forty-five more minutes to unload all the crates, cover the boats in tarp and gather at a nearby shack.

An old lady ran the shack. Clearly these men were regulars.

'Please sit,' Bapi pointed to one of the two rickety plastic tables with plastic chairs next to them, and proceeded to wash his legs, hands and face. His comrades did the same one by one while he sat down opposite me.

'How do you know Monu?' Bapi asked. His gaunt swarthy face glistened under the overhead bulbs at spots where his facial bones pushed against his skin.

'We have common friends.'

Bapi didn't buy it. But he said nothing.

The old lady brought out glasses and had a bottle of country liquor in her hands. She was about to put one in front of me, when Bapi said 'Mmmh' and shook his head at her. The woman looked worried at her faux pas and began mumbling some sorries.

'It's okay,' I assured the men. 'Please have your food and drinks.'

But they looked to Bapi.

'Actually, can I get some too?' I asked the lady. Bapi looked incredulous for a moment but waved his hand asking her to serve me as well.

I waited while some white liquor was poured into all our glasses.

Some small fried fishes were brought in as well. Bar snacks with the drinks. I don't know if it was the same small mullet-like fish I'd seen being caught earlier. But I was hungry and ate a few. They were leathery, oversalted and fried beyond recognition.

Bapi took a few sips and chewed on a fish before asking me, 'So you're a reporter from Dhaka?'

'Yes, and I want to ask you some questions. I'm sure Monu has assured you that I don't work for the police. If you don't want to talk, tell me and I'll walk off.'

I don't know if it was the first few swigs of alcohol or my direct talk that worked on him, but his stiffness reduced and he said, 'No, no . . . please ask me what you want to know.'

'Where are you from?'

'Teknaf.'

'And the rest of you?' I asked the team.

'They're all from Teknaf,' Bapi answered on their behalf.

I walked back to my hotel half an hour later.

I didn't know who this Monu was or what trust and/or influence he had over Bapi, but Bapi had answered everything I asked.

The only awkward moment was when I asked him to show me some of the stash. He and his team looked a little worried.

'No photos,' Bapi requested.

'No photos. Promise.'

It was nothing of note. Beneath some layers of fish and ice, sat little plastic packets covered in black duct tape. I held one in my hand and felt the familiar little pills of Yaba in them.

Walking back, I wasn't sure how I'd tell this story. It was too little and too banal to tell. Far from an exposé, Yaba being carried by Teknaf fishermen was worse than an open secret. It was a hypocrisy that benefited the elites of both Bangladesh and Myanmar.

The Naaf river, which forms the natural boundary between the two countries, is heavily guarded by border guards from both sides. Needless to say, the heaviness only sits on the shoulders of the fisherfolk of the two countries.

The two countries have a convenient agreement on allowing fishing in the Naaf. Local fishermen from both sides are allowed to get their catch. But the reality is that the fish they catch isn't what pays their bills. It's the little pills that come packed in plastic pouches and duct tape.

Of late, Yaba had wreaked such havoc in Bangladesh, that the Hasina government was under some pressure to do—or at least be seen as doing—something to break the supply chain. Besides, the Rohingya camps were forming nascent cartels and who was to say which way the profits would flow?

So the very same border guards who took cuts from the trade were now raiding and arresting a few of the fishermen.

This change of route was to mitigate some of the losses being incurred due to the raids and arrests. Instead of simply crossing the Naaf, now boatmen were being made to go down into the Bay of Bengal. They would take a sharp turn north around Dakhinpara and drop the stuff off at different locations along the coast till they reached Cox's Bazar.

'This isn't a real route as yet,' a narcotics control officer had told me. 'Smugglers are just testing this out to see if it's feasible. See, Yaba margins aren't that high to justify this added cost of the long route. So the bulk trade is still along the traditional routes—you know the overland ones through Bandarban and all. If we have to really eradicate Yaba, we have to attack these routes. That will push them to take the water routes and affect the bottom line of the trade.'

'But you guys are attacking the bottommost rung of the water routes—the fishermen—while leaving the overland routes intact,' I asked. 'How does that fit into your plan of attacking the bottom line?'

'We're all employees who have targets to fill, Roy sir,' he replied, laughing. 'Targets for the money we collect, and targets for the arrests we make. Just like you have yours. No?'

The world over, insurgencies are closely linked to drug trade. Apart from the fact that trading narcotics is a great way to make cash, when cash isn't around, the drugs become holders of value. In Kashmir, for example, after the abrogation of Article 370 and the crackdown on fake Indian currency notes being sent from Pakistan, jihadists across the border began paying their assets and couriers in brown sugar.

And then of course the influence of mind-altering substances, which turn regular humans into killers. Religion and opium are a killer concoction that dumbs the mind, numbs the soul and drives fools into a remorseless, bloodthirsty frenzy. This bit is true not just for insurgencies, but regular armies as well.

Bangladesh wasn't very different in that matter. Yaba, and fentanyl before that, became the default currency of those who held terror as their ism. It's morbid how many metalheads I met in my time investigating these young Bengali jihadists.

A young lad, nicknamed Sagor, arrested for trying to set up a repeat of Holey Artisan with the terror group, Hizb ut-Tahrir, was a case in point. He was the epitome of a lout who loved his yaba and acted macho. He was ratted out by the young wife he beat up in his yaba-induced frenzied moments.

In a voice recording I sourced, Sagor's wife talked about how it was strange to see her boyfriend turned husband become a religious zealot. 'He loved rock, partying and yaba. One fine day he gets this older man home—someone called Musa—and starts listening to Joshimuddin Rahmani's sermons. In no time, he decides to become this pious Muslim, puts me in the parda and starts planning attacks on the government through Hizb ut-Tahrir!'

Two of the leading young men who carried out the Holey Artisan massacre were big yaba and weed lovers. They even had a band!

But among all the crazies of this kind I met, no encounter was as strange as the one with Hassan.

Hassan was a neophyte wannabe jihadist at a madrasa near Cox's Bazar. I won't name the madrasa because I never ended up concluding the investigation—reasons for which come soon.

I'd zeroed in on this particular madrasa after lurking around on Telegram group chats of Bengali extremists. I took on a pseudonym to join the group and made a background story of being a Bengali–American Muslim from New York City and began profiling the members.

One morning, I just presented myself at the time of their sermons.

Truth be told, they were a warm and welcoming lot. In keeping with my American migrant backstory, I pretended to speak only pidgin Bangla and tainted it with some of the New York accent I had picked up.

The Huzoor—meaning master—of the congregation was this very handsome, fair-skinned, always smiling old man. He took the lead in welcoming me with open arms. Literally. He gave me a warmer fatherly hug than any my father has ever given.

'Let us all welcome our young brother, who has seen the folly of Western perversion, and is seeking to come back to the true path. The only path—the path of Allah!'

Huzoor preached his sermons in Arabic, translating crucial quotes from the Quran and Hadith into Bengali. Just like the others, I sat through them like a good student.

Chaa happened at the end. Minus my usual cigarette of course. I had to be on my best behaviour.

It was during chaa that Huzoor introduced me to Hassan and Hamza.

'These two men, like you, speak English,' Huzoor said smiling. 'Hassan has joined us recently and Hamza has been with us for a few years now.' Turning to them, he said, 'Hassan, Hamza, I make it your responsibility to guide our young friend who has come all the way from America to be with us.'

Hassan, with a thin and patchy beard on his face, was in his late twenties and much younger than me. Hamza, in his early forties, was a few years older than me. But with his corpulent proportions and well kept goatee, he looked much older.

The three of us exchanged numbers and I left, promising to come back in a day or two.

Hamza called me that very evening.

'Salaam walekum, brother!' His deep throaty voice was jolly and warm. 'How did you like the first day?'

'Oh, it was beautiful.'

I wasn't lying.

The Huzoor did indeed speak beautifully. His composed ease, knowledge of the texts, restrained fervour and patient telling—it was very uplifting. In fact, as time went by and I went to the congregations several times, listening to Huzoor, even to a realist like me, the vision of a utopian world based on Islamic brotherhood and equality came alive like a beautiful impressionist painting—not all clear and made of smudging, blurring bits, but yet all of it came together to make an image of a serene haven. A haven I could happily call home.

'Lovely to hear that brother . . . lovely to hear,' Hamza said, warmth oozing from his voice. 'But don't be mistaken in thinking that what Huzoor says is simple just because he says it in simple words. The lessons are complex.'

'Of course. I completely agree.'

'Why don't we do something? You meet me in the evening, and I'll take you through the notes. If there's anything that you don't understand, I can explain. Nasihat . . . we call it.'

'That would be great! But I can't do it this evening. Maybe the day after?'

'Sure brother . . . sure. Okay then, see you the day after! Allah haafiz!'

'Allah haafiz, brother.'

I returned to the madrasa the following day. It was just as it had been the last time. Huzoor sat smiling, impeccably dressed and welcoming.

Hassan met me with a handshake. But Hamza took me in a bear hug.

During the sermon, Hamza sat next to me, whispering little explanations every now and then. Friendly as he was, I really didn't want him doing that. His breath was rank. The trademark mix of bad dental hygiene meets tobacco chewing. But I had to be polite. So after the first time, every time I saw him starting to tilt his head towards mine, I held my breath.

Praise the lord and my mother for the swimming lessons that have taught me to hold my breath for well beyond a minute and a half!

The sermon was as good as the day before. Huzoor explained the need to be unfailing in cleansing the soul and mind.

'You cannot fight the good fight, if your mind and body aren't good. Goodness starts with cleansing,' Huzoor stressed. I joked in my head about Hamza needing to extend that lesson to his pie hole.

Hassan, Hamza and I hung out for a little longer after class that day. We went to a nearby tea-stall and sat ourselves down on the long bamboo bench.

'So how long have you lived in the US?' Hamza asked, pulling out a sachet of gutka from his pocket.

'I was born and brought up there,' I lied and proceeded to light a cigarette. The first sin had been committed by the senior student. So it was kosher to indulge now.

'You lived in New York all your life?'

'No, I was born in Michigan. My parents moved to New York City later.' I didn't even need to think about the stuff I was pulling out of my ass. Hamza didn't know anything about the US other than what he'd seen in movies and TV.

He asked some dozen odd questions. Hassan had signed out of our conversation and was scrolling through his phone. In fact, he looked unfocused and ill at ease.

'Everything okay with you, Hassan?'

'Huh . . .' he seemed to wake up from some deep distracting thoughts. 'Ah yes, yes . . . nothing just checking Facebook.'

'Facebook, eh? Western propaganda all, no?' I teased him.

'Fuck the West. Just because they made Facebook doesn't mean we can't use it. Can I bum a cigarette?' Whoa! This young lad was using very familiar lingo!

'Listen, if I had my way, I'd use Facebook, Twitter, whatever and bloody hell get our Revolution going. Sure, after the Revolution, we can burn them all down. What say, Hamza?'

'Of course, brother, of course!'

'Burn what down? The platforms or the West?' I asked

'Both, man! You really think the West will ever let us build our Ummah in peace?'

'I don't know,' I mimed.

'Of course, they won't! I mean, look at America's history. They use us when they need to fight Russia or China or India or whatever. Then call us terrorists and kill us. Fuck them!'

Now Hamza had signed out of this conversation. Geopolitics probably wasn't his forte.

'The only reason ISIS is winning,' Hassan continued, ' . . . is because they're using the same techniques against the West.'

'Sure. The only contradiction is that the Islamic State is armed to the teeth with Western guns, vehicles and ammo and funded by America's closest allies,' I said. In my head, of course. I had gone there to report, not win a debating competition. Besides, rants like this were a good way to wake up from the hypnosis that Huzoor's words put me in. So I egged Hassan on with nods.

'Okay, brothers, I'm off now. Duty time.' Hamza stood up. 'By the way, where are you staying?'

I told them the name of a different hotel.

'Oh . . . that's not far from my house. Why don't I come down around 7.30 p.m.? We can do some nasihat.'

'Today at seven thirty? Ah . . . I can't. I have a meeting.'

'Date?'

'No man . . . no date,' I laughed. 'Work call meeting, I meant. Not getting any dates or anything . . . ha ha . . .'

'Ooh . . . don't act all innocent, man,' Hamza said in a teasing voice, making a funny face. Suddenly, reaching out and pinching my cheek, he added, 'With your hero looks . . . you can't be running short of women.'

Whoa!

Straight as I am, I've spent a lot of time in the company of gay men and women. Friends, family, colleagues, strangers at nightclubs—I was no outsider to the rainbow world. I had developed a gaydar that was fairly functional. And this fatso had just pinged my gaydar hard. Real hard.

All the bending over and explaining, eagerness to give private lessons, meeting in the evenings made sense now. It was a zeal alright. Just not the religious kind.

'Anyway, see you soon.' Hamza tried to give me another hug but I turned sideways to give him the shoulder.

There is some acknowledgement of the fact that a lot of acts of extreme and wanton violence come from repressed sexuality. Just that there isn't enough of it. Acknowledging it would mean acknowledging how if we let people love with freedom, they wouldn't want to kill. But that doesn't help the Big War narrative.

So even if the titans of the military–industrial complex paint their bomber planes' tails with rainbow every pride week, nothing can come in the way of windfall profits.

As for groups like the Islamic State, and other religious terrorist groups, the lesser said the better of their hypocrisy of killing gays while allowing inane amounts of perversion ranging from keeping sex slaves to paedophilia, on to using mass rape and sexual assault as weapons of war.

Returning to my hotel that evening, I took a long shower, put on my RATM T-shirt, plugged my headphones in with 'Wake Up' on loop and headed out to get a drink. I was going to get a drink and then get my belly full of food from a restaurant I'd walked by several times and sniffed a superb aroma from.

This was going to be an evening of cleansing my soul. Cleansing it of the hypocrisy of zealots.

But I couldn't drink much. First the guards at Ocean Paradise Hotel ruined the evening by asking me for an ID to enter the hotel right after letting two White people in with salutes and not a squeak about identification. Of course, I picked a row with them and took the matter up with the manager. The manager gave me a half-hearted apology.

Besides, I hadn't been drinking in a while so two small whiskeys were enough to make me tipsy. And I wanted real food. Not the soggy salted peanuts they served.

'Mama!' I hailed a cycle rickshaw. 'Dolphin More.'

The slow cooked mutton, naan, masala fried fish and rice did the job. Cleansed my soul—from both the anti-Western zealotry and Western bootlicking.

I had just about finished washing my hands at the grimy sink behind the wooden partition at the back of the restaurant when I heard, 'Arey! Bhai?'

Hassan's grinning face looked up at me from a table in the corner. A snatch of the same naan and a similar meat curry was in his hand. A biryani was waiting for after.

I kicked myself mentally. Not only did I have alcohol on my breath but RATM crying for a Marxist revolution on my chest.

'Arey! What a surprise!' I grinned large and sat down with Hassan. I had no option but to play along.

'Have some biryani,' he offered.

'No man . . . tummy full. But you please eat up. The food is really good here, no?'

'Mmm . . . mmm,' Hassan nodded, his mouth stuffed with the last big piece of naan with which he had swept up the last of the greasy gravy served in the oval steel dish.

'You come here often?'

'Often enough,' Hassan said, tilting the biryani container over his dinner plate and unloading the rice and meat with a spoon.

His eyes kept going back to my T-shirt. Fuck, fuck! I panicked. God knows what this would lead to.

'So, you're an RATM fan?' he asked, chomping on his biryani and washing it down with cola.

'Not really a fan . . . just had this T-shirt for a long time. I mean I like them . . .'

I was panicking.

'I really liked them a lot. They were actually the reason I ditched pop and moved to heavier stuff.'

Wait. What did this boy say?

'Oh . . . so heavier, meaning who?'

'Everything, man . . . I listened to everything from Black Sabbath to Sepultura. But what really made me a metalhead was Meshuggah . . .'

Hassan held forth on his favourite bands, albums, even hummed specific riffs and samples, and kept cross-checking his opinions with mine. Thankfully, my knowledge of metal was marginally better than my knowledge of Islamic theology. So even though it was difficult with him rattling off names, I kept up.

But I used a lot of nods and generic exclamations like: 'Ahh . . . that's killer,' 'That's beyond comparison' and 'That's a classic, man—no questions' to manage the conversation.

The next shocker came when we stepped out of the restaurant and he asked me, 'You smoke?'

We had smoked cigarettes earlier, so he clearly wasn't asking me that. And no, I had hardly ever taken a puff of weed or hash and didn't like either. But the fix I was in, I said: 'Yeah . . . sometimes.'

'I have some stuff with me . . . let's head to the beach?'

Anthropology and psychology say, and I agree, that humans can be 'weird'—or shall we say 'different'. Polar opposite traits and cultural values can exist in a tribe, group or individual. In fact, I've met several people who are these strange mixes. Murderers who wouldn't steal a penny. Thieves who ran massive credit card frauds but wouldn't hurt a fly. Even a hitman who was a vegan because he cared about all lives.

But sitting there that night on Cox's Bazar beach, puffing out blue-grey smoke up at the starlit sky, I knew this was peak quaintness. Outright madness, in fact.

Never in my wildest imagination had I ever thought I'd be sitting and puffing ganja with a metalhead man who was training to be a jihadi and dreaming of unleashing unrelenting Sharia.

Cannibal Corpse, Korn, Morbid Angel . . . Hassan just went on and on. The higher he got, the more he spoke about the bands, their stories, backstories, rumours, predictions, conspiracies, yada yada.

I'm not sure if the 'stuff' Hassan had was unusually potent, or if I'm just not built for such stuff, but my insides were rolling and my head was spinning after four or five drags. Just when Cox's Bazar had begun turning into Saint-Paul-de-Mausole and I started seeing the stars move and collide, he asked, 'What do you think of Ohlin's death?'

'That . . . Mayhem . . . guy . . .' I slurred.

'Yeah. I'm quite sure he gave his body to Satan?'

'Wait . . . you really believe that Satan is real?'

'Why not?'

I didn't fucking know why not! What I was choking with was trying to understand why on earth was this guy looking to die for a Muslim Ummah when he was into all this Christian myth? So no, I didn't have an answer for him about the suicide of a European crazy who belonged to a group that burned churches in the name of Satan.

Thankfully Hassan was in his own flow and didn't really wait for too many answers to questions.

'Have you ever attended any metal concerts?'

'Yeah, that one time Metallica performed in Gurgaon . . .'

'Wait, are you Indian?'

Fuck fuck fucking fuck! Goddamned weed had lowered my guard and I'd blurted out something I never should have!

'No, no . . . I had gone to India for a work trip and this was happening . . . so I ended up watching it . . .'

But Hassan had gone quiet and was looking away. I was praying to all my non-existent gods, even Satan, that he had taken my excuse as a valid story. Or at least he wouldn't remember it tomorrow morning.

But Hassan just kept looking away and said nothing.

'Calm yourself, Siddharthya . . . breathe . . . shit happens . . . collect yourself and breathe . . .' I told myself. Inaudibly, I think. I'm not sure.

'Listen, man, let's head. Have work in the morning tomorrow.'

'Hmm,' Hassan grunted and stood up.

We walked back without saying anything. When we came to my hotel, I simply said: 'Okay, goodnight' and went upstairs.

Now he knew where I lived as well.

I settled the bill first thing in the morning and headed to the airport for the late morning Biman Bangla flight to Dhaka. There was no reason to think I was safe there after the events of the previous night. Hassan and Hamza's madrassa wasn't some garden variety seminary. Their Telegram chats had made it clear they were prepping for some serious violence the moment an opportunity presented itself. In fact, I and my editor had decided that I'd use a fake name and backstory after a proper threat assessment.

For the first time in a long time, all the shotgun-toting guards at the airport were a welcome sight. I was going to go far away from Cox's Bazar and throw my local SIM and the cheap android phone I'd bought for cash away the moment I landed in Dhaka.

But fate had one final quirky twist in store for me.

I'd bought myself a duty-free bottle of whiskey when I'd first landed in Dhaka. More out of habit than anything else. It sat in my suitcase, still sealed between the adhesive tapes of duty-free packaging.

When the luggage scanner saw it, the security asked me to open my suitcase up.

'It's unopened and duty-free. I'm a foreigner,' I explained, holding out my Indian passport.

The security discussed the matter and decided to call in their shift incharge to decide the legality of the matter.

Out came Hamza from the back office, belly bulging at the metal buckled belt of his uniform. He stared daggers at me and my passport. Read the name, nationality, my face, and repeat.

I stared back defiantly, not saying a word or showing any expression. We both knew we had hidden something critical about ourselves. And here in a fortified airport, if he could call someone, so could I.

'Let it through,' he growled at his men, threw my passport in my open suitcase and walked back to his office. I proceeded to the boarding queue.

The Company of Violent Men

As I said before, despite being a journalist of little consequence and even less fame, the sheer number of threats I've gotten over the years is absurdly disproportionate.

Every now and then, I'm told to go to Pakistan by the Hindu right-wing trolls. This one time when I'd merely retweeted a tweet that was sceptical of students at Delhi's Jawaharlal Nehru University holding pro-Pakistan rallies resulted in a bunch of non-resident Indians going full Gestapo on me and trying to find out where I live so they could beat me up.

Thanks to a report I wrote about student unrest in Dhaka and the excessive use of power against them, the troll armies aligned with Bangladesh's ruling party began to name me an agent of the Islamic State and call for me to be banned. This was no investigative report. It was news that was all over Bangla Internet, print and TV. And yet, not only was I trolled, but my next journalist visa was refused.

I got a Bangladeshi journalist to make discreet enquiries about the visa refusal, and he texted back, saying some detective in the Special Branch in Dhaka had done it. This was confirmed by a response from the authorities to an email sent by my editor at thediplomat.com—the officer responding (from a Gmail ID) forgot to erase his 'Special Branch' email signature.

The bottom line was that no matter what I wrote, someone or the other got upset.

What was ridiculous, though, was that on the one hand, they'd call me a 'fake journalist' and 'hack' and all sorts of pejoratives that said I'm not really a journalist, and on the other hand, they'd take time out of their lives to send me threats and slurs.

After the first few times, I learned to ignore and live with this. I rarely ever engaged with or hit back at trolls.

Headlines shift so soon these days. Professional trolls and serial hashtag outragers are a busy lot. So usually whoever takes umbrage to what I say has other things to take umbrage to within hours, if not days. And I move on to the next umbrage invoking report I will write.

***

The one time this pattern was broken was when I reported on a series of rapes and sexual assaults committed by the militants of Kashmir.

In the winter of 2021, a source from Kashmir forwarded me a video and a photo. The vlog-style video was that of a young woman speaking in a hurry, in a heavy Kashmiri-accented Hindi. The photo was a letter she'd written in Kashmiri.

The girl said that she had been wronged and wanted to tell the world her story. No name, no ID, just that. The source wouldn't tell me much, either.

'How soon can you go to Kashmir?' he asked. He wouldn't give me any further details; all he said was, 'This woman and several others like her are there. Nobody wants to tell their stories.'

I went to Kashmir soon after and reported an explosive piece called 'Rape and Silence in Kashmir's Jihad'. I started getting threats within a day or two of the story going live on thediplomat.com's website—first Twitter, then emails and finally texts.

'Take the story down, or we'll make an example out of you,' they said.

Of course, I wasn't going to take the story down, but something much bigger than anything I'd ever faced before was playing out.

This series of threats was unlike any others I'd ever gotten. Even though the first slurs started in the usual way, calling me biased and a puppet of the Indian Army and R&AW and other such boring stuff, the tone and contents soon changed and became sinister.

They sent me the coordinates of my addresses and said they knew where I lived. They had managed to get every address I have on record in India and the US. A photo of me attending the G20 in Bali was sent as well. I was being told they were watching me.

If I went from City A to City B, I'd get a tweet or a text from an anonymous handle, saying, 'Welcome to B' or 'Watch your back. We have our teams in B.'

The last straw was when they sent me the names of my estranged daughter and parents and threatened to kill them. Estranged she might be, but my twelve-year-old remains the dearest thing I have in my life. I couldn't ignore any threats to her.

Many years ago, when I was just starting out, I met Indian journalism stalwart Dileep Padgaonkar. He had retired to Pune, and I was referred to him by the then editor of *The Hindu*, Siddharth Vardarajan.

I didn't want to write the Sunday fluff columns and freelance stories I was asked to, so I asked him for advice about how to become a real political journalist.

'That's where my heart really is, sir,' I'd told him, complaining about how I just wasn't able to break into it.

'Young man,' Padgaonkar had said. 'Not just you, to anyone who asks me how to become a journalist, I say just one thing: Don't. The risk-to-reward ratio isn't worth it.'

'But I gave up my programming career to do this. This is all I want,' I insisted.

'Isn't there a way back in?' he had asked me.

'I don't want to find a way to return,' I'd said. And then felt embarrassed at having used such grand words to a man who'd built his career on words.

But Padgaonkar had only chuckled with some indulgence.

'I know you're warning me of the dangers of becoming a political journalist. But how did you do it? You were powerful yourself, but you surely upset a lot of mighty men in your time. How did you manage?'

'Well . . .' he'd said, leaning back and thinking his words over for a bit. 'The way they (the powerful) get to you is through bribes and threats. You become the real troublemaker if you're immune to bribes or have nothing to lose.'

I never got any other mentoring from Padgaonkar, the way I'd hoped to get. By the time I met him, he'd gone into retirement mode. He passed away soon after. But that statement about bribes and threats remains with me to date.

Bribes I've never taken. A look at my bank balance will prove this. Besides, my influence is too small to command a bribe. For threats, too, my insignificance ensures that I don't get significant threats. Lastly, anybody who bothers to look at my personal and professional life will know I own and possess so little, there's nothing left to take away.

The only weakness I have is my daughter. I'd consciously and carefully hidden her from social media or conversations with strangers. In fact, very few people, save the three- or four-odd friends I have—even those who've worked with me daily—know nearly nothing about my past life as a family man.

But after the Kashmir investigation, there were a bunch of people who, angered by my report, had dived deeper than the usual floating scum of social media trolling and dug things out.

On the personal advice of a senior intelligence officer in Delhi, I went to the police and, for the first time ever, registered a case.

As usual, the junior officers I met at the station were initially annoyed.

'Ay . . .' the plump, bespectacled assistant sub-inspector (ASI) in Pune's Cyber Police Station who first met me barked at the writer. 'This chap has something to say . . . take it down . . .' he said, attending to something obviously more important than a citizen getting death threats.

The writer, however, was a kindly older gentleman who meticulously took everything down. His politeness notwithstanding, he kept asking me to repeat several details over and over again, pointed out little differences in the narrative and asked me to clarify which chronology and variant were the most accurate.

The ASI came in during this back-and-forth with the writer. He was accompanied by a young, tough-looking officer who had a file in his hand and had been sent by some senior officer. The ASI's voice changed dramatically. He'd gone from the dismissive *Tu* to the formal *Tumhi* and said, 'DCP madam has called you . . . I didn't know . . .'

I still don't know what he didn't know, but something had definitely changed. The ASI's face had darkened, and the tough young cop had a stiff body language.

The deputy commissioner of police—a tough, no-nonsense lady—was in the middle of some harrowing conversation with a bunch of people sitting around with open laptops. They were discussing some blockchain analysis reports.

'You're Roy?' the DCP asked. And without waiting for me to answer, she said: 'Come this way,' and led me into some sort of unfinished room meets ad hoc file storage facility.

'Keep this door shut till I come out,' she said to a sentry. We sat at a bare table.

'Can I see your phone?' she asked, her eyes piercing me. I showed it to her because she wasn't really asking.

She went through every one of the threatening texts and emails, put it down with an unceremonious thud and called someone from her phone.

'Jai Hind, sir,' she began. 'Mr Roy is here in front of me. This is serious stuff, sir . . .' she began and walked off to the far end of the room, and then it was just Hmm, Yes, Okay and a trail of incomprehensible snatches of half-spoken words after that.

'What were you doing in Kashmir?' she asked, sitting down at the table and looking me straight in the eye. No emotion, just staring, waiting for an answer.

'Reporting . . . I just told your officer downstairs . . .'

'Tell me again,' she cut me off.

I told her. How the story had come to me, how I went to report it, who went with me. Et cetera, et cetera.

'When did you get the first threat?'

'Erm . . .' I fumbled with my phone to check. 'It was . . .'

'Xth,' she said, without taking her eyes off me.

The date was correct. The officer had memorized the dates in just the one time she'd gone through my phone.

'Between the publication on 24 February and the first threat, did you get any international calls or make any?'

'To my colleagues in the US, yes.'

'Pakistan?'

'No.'

'Do you make regular calls to Pakistan? Or get regular calls from there?'

'No! I mean, yes . . . but that's for interviews or talking to my colleagues there.' What was this officer trying to imply? Why was I getting interrogated? Exasperated, I added, 'I mean, I have to. For my work. Why are you asking me this?'

'Because the threats look like they're from Pakistan,' she said, with the same coldness that had marked our conversation since the beginning.

'Mr Roy,' she added, getting up. 'We're going to put you and your family under protection.'

'But . . . but I have very little interaction with my family . . . I mean, I'm estranged . . .' I replied in stumbling words, partly because I was taken aback and at a loss for words but mainly because I was ashamed to admit the truth about my personal life to a stranger.

'That's your personal matter, Mr Roy. It's not my job to solve your personal life—it's to follow the law. And the law demands that cross-border threats be taken seriously. Not just for your safety, but for national security.'

I left the station with the officer's words buzzing in my head. National security?

It wasn't just about me any more, was it? Was I going to become the news, instead of reporting it? Something I've detested forever. 'National security' is such a buzzword that this news would leak out in no time, and I'd have cameras in my face.

What would follow was worse. The trolls who were hell-bent on calling me a puppet of the Indian State would have a field day. My voice was too weak to declare to the world that I was not, and didn't ever want to be seen as, a member of this camp or that.

I walked back up. The sentry was about to stop me, but then waved me in.

'Excuse me, ma'am,' I walked in on her meeting with the laptop bunch a second time.

'Yes, Mr Roy?' She craned her neck.

'A moment alone, please?'

'Tell me,' she merely came out to the threshold of the meeting room but lowered her voice to a loud whisper.

'Ma'am . . . can you please keep this out of the news? I don't want this going out. It'll get me the wrong kind of attention,' I requested.

For the first time, the officer's eyes changed expression. She looked at me for a few long seconds, then held out her hand with the slightest of smiles, 'I'll do my best. See you, Mr Roy.'

I'm not privy to the internal investigations and analyses that the police conducted. But within hours of walking out of the cop house, a gunman appeared at my door and four at the home of my estranged family.

And then, I had to do what I was most reluctant to do—pick up the phone and call my father, explaining why four men with guns had come to his doorstep.

'Your mother needs a dog walker to take Newton out for her evening shit. Get her that. Not cops,' he said, when I explained what had happened.

His words were laced with the same bitterness and disappointment that had coloured our relationship for years. He had never hidden his disdain for my career choice, and nothing—not going to Columbia, not getting recognized by the Pulitzer Committee, not the appreciation I'd gotten for my work—nothing would ever convince him I was worth anything.

This situation only caused the disapproval to resurface with a vengeance.

The conversation with my ex-wife was no less strained.

She had always resented me for what she saw as a betrayal. She had married a man she thought would provide her with a life of stability and comfort, as expected of a software engineer with well-to-do parents. Instead, she found herself tethered to a struggling journalist, whose ideals often took precedence over financial security. Her frustration had simmered over the years. And now, with threats looming over us, the anger erupted with full force. She didn't give a hoot about me getting death threats and instead took to lambasting me for bringing danger into their lives. Every word was a painful reminder of the gulf between our worlds.

I tried to explain to them, to plead with them to understand that this was never my intention.

'I never wanted any of this to touch you,' I said, my voice laden with a mix of desperation and guilt. But my words were meaningless. To them, I was the architect of this chaos—a man who had willingly walked away from the conventional path and, in doing so, had exposed them first to ignominy in societal approval and now to risks they had never signed up for.

The most painful part of this unfolding drama was the thought of my daughter caught in the cross hairs of a battle she hadn't chosen. Far from a crisis like this bringing us together, she only got annoyed, wondering what this would mean for her 'social life'.

She had chosen my father over me even before she could speak clearly, drawn in by the world he offered—a world filled with the trappings of wealth and comfort. An international school with menus rivalling those of five-star hotels, the latest Apple gadgets in customized colours, foreign vacations and desserts delivered from across the city on a whim.

I could never match the material joys her grandfather provided so effortlessly. She was the living trophy that my father used to show me what it meant to be a real man who could provide. As the middle-class son of a wealthy father, I had lost the fight to win the one woman I wanted to win. I had lost squarely and resoundingly a long time ago and I had walked off, head hung in abject defeat.

It was surreal to think of how the very career that had alienated me from them was now inadvertently pulling us all into its orbit of danger.

The burden of this reality weighed heavily on me. The threats, once abstract entities relegated to the digital world of social media and emails, had taken a tangible form, manifesting in the armed guards stationed outside my family's homes.

The irony, of course, was that for my previous report published in thediplomat.com, I was called an anti-national and pro-Muslim by the Hindu right wing and a brave journalist by the other side. Yet, things had become the exact opposite with this one report!

***

Reporting from or about Kashmir was always tricky and dangerous. Not just for the obvious reasons that both the Indian State and the anti-Indian bunch were violently intolerant of anything being reported that didn't toe their line to the tee. But also due to the very nature of Kashmiri society, which is very difficult to penetrate for a non-Kashmiri.

And I say this based on not just the one reporting assignment that got me the threats. I say this based on the many times I'd been to Kashmir, both as a journalist and otherwise.

Long before I became a journalist, I'd been quite familiar in the 1990s and with Kashmiris—both Muslim and Hindu. Several Kashmiri Pandits had made Pune their home after the exodus in the 1990s, with Kashmiri students coming to Pune colleges in the early 2000s. Most importantly, though, as a young communist in college, I'd worked with a bunch of young Communist men from Kashmir.

Perhaps because I only met the political ones, I had never met a Kashmiri man who isn't an embodiment of conflicting emotions and attitudes towards 'the others'.

On the one hand, Kashmiris exhibit a remarkable degree of friendliness and hospitality. Their welcoming nature is not merely superficial; it's a deeply ingrained part of their cultural ethos. One would be hard-pressed to find a Kashmiri home where, even on a simple visit, you wouldn't be fed to your throat no matter how little time you had with them. And if it were them visiting, they'd never show up without a gift.

For example, this Kashmiri shawl seller who'd come every year to my aunt's place in a suburb of Kolkata never appeared at the doorstep without his big grin and a packet of walnuts. Trade done or not, walnuts were always gifted.

I forget his first name—Shabbir, or something—but we kids called him Mama. A Muslim by religion, he'd not only learnt some Bangla but sat around for random pujas and rituals, participating like any other family member. After the first few years, his wife and daughter also started accompanying him. They'd come and stay at any one of the houses in the society. The woman did all things homestead with the Bengali women, and her daughter did all things girlie with the neighbourhood girls.

As these things go, his daughter—several years my junior—had a crush on a Bengali boy. A boy from a family the Kashmiri shawl mama had known for many years.

'Oh, he flew into a rage,' my aunt recounted to my mother. 'I'd never seen him this angry. I never even thought he was capable of getting that angry. The third house from the community club? Their boy wrote the girl a note with some poem or something. And she was writing something back when her father caught her. The man stormed out of the house, dragging his wife and child behind him! We all tried telling him to calm down—it's just a silly little thing kids do, we told him. But he would hear none of it!

'And then he started saying things like this indulgence is what's wrong with our culture. They were proud Muslims and would never allow such nonsense.

'Then, the Bengalis reacted to that. They said you were perfectly alright staying with us and eating with us, calling yourself family for all these years, and now suddenly you are different and better than us?'

Shawl-wallah mama didn't come for a few years after the fracas. But with some time gone by, he resumed his visits. I'm not sure if his daughter ever came along again. But I know his wife did.

I know this because they hit the news headlines.

My interactions with this Kashmiri mama were all in my middle school years. Many years later, after I'd graduated from college, one day, I read a headline in a Bengali newspaper online, 'Kashmiri Man Arrested in X,' X being my aunt's town.

Sure enough, it was Shawl mama. Some overzealous police officer barged into a wedding he and his wife were attending and decided to take him in for questioning. Thankfully, Bengal had, at least until then, remained an exception to the religious–ethnic polarization that had been sweeping across the country. The Bengalis of the society—especially the women, and all of them sindoor, shankha-pola wearing, puja-doing and fast-keeping Hindus—picketed the police station and demanded that their 'brother' be released.

He was released without any charges—real or fake. But that, I think, was the last time he came.

For Kashmiri men, or at least the lot I've met, it's always a state of perpetually balancing on the edge of a cultural–political chasm—one foot in the world of amiable social interaction, the other anchored in a realm of unyielding cultural and regional supremacy. This distance is not always overt but it lingers in the background, a subtle reminder of an invisible boundary that an 'other' might inadvertently overstep.

I'm saying this not of men who are explicitly the violent types. Just regular ones doing regular jobs or studying.

In fact, I didn't meet my first Kashmiri separatist till I began my journalism in 2011. That too, quite by chance.

Sometime late in the morning, while I was sitting at my desk doing my IT work, I got an email from a Kashmiri friend. Someone I knew from college.

'Didn't know you wrote for Kashmir Monitor! Good work, man!'

I hadn't even heard of Kashmir Monitor, let alone write for them.

'Which article?' I asked. He sent me a link.

And there it was. A full-length article analysing the anti-communalism bill drafted by activist Teesta Setalvad and her comrades but also torpedoed by some of her other comrades. The story had the headline I'd written, my byline and even a stock photo.

Only I hadn't written it for Kashmir Monitor, but for a blog.

I emailed the editor asking why he'd taken a piece of mine, printed it as if I'd written it for them, and not even referenced the original publication. He didn't respond. Several days, or perhaps weeks, went by, and I called up this lawyer schoolmate of mine.

He drafted a claims letter and sent it to the Kashmir Monitor guys.

Immediately, I got a response from the editor. After the initial shock he expressed at receiving the legal notice, he proffered that he had done what he had in good faith because there it was—with my name! He had given me due credit!

It had been a while since I'd begun writing. I was so damn done with editors who paid in 'exposure' and 'credit'. In fact, by the time this exchange was happening with the Kashmir Monitor, I'd burnt a lot of past friendships with activist–editors who ran vanity projects called blogs and kept expecting me to write for free.

I was trying to be a professional journalist, meaning I intended to pay all my bills through that.

'Comrades, prestige don't pay no bills,' I'd announced, and point-blank stopped entertaining anyone who expected me to write for free.

So, even with the Kashmir Monitor, I refused to back down.

'We don't have the kind of money you're asking for,' the editor (and owner) told me. 'You know how things are with print these days.'

But then he made an excellent offer, 'How about I get you tickets to Srinagar and a hotel stay? Hang out for a few days, be our guest, and maybe we'll work something out. A contract, perhaps? You writing regularly for us or something?'

A contract sounded nice. A paid trip to Kashmir sounded even nicer.

The contract didn't happen. For an establishment that ran on unpaid interns and barely paid reporters, I don't think he ever intended to do anything beyond pacifying me with a trip. Besides, he came from an old, influential family with friends who owned hotels. I don't think putting me up cost them anything.

'You know a driver who can take me to Gulmarg?' I asked the editor the evening after our conversations were done.

'When do you want to go?'

'Now.'

'Brother, this is Kashmir . . . not Mumbai,' he chuckled. 'You can't just up and go and travel at night. Listen, I'll have this guy pick you up tomorrow morning. And I have this friend who runs a nice resort in Gulmarg. The driver and car will stay with you. You can spend a night—or two—if you like. Actually, you *will* like it.'

Gulmarg was too touristy for me. The mules and the shit-smeared earth they toddled on were there in Karjat as well. So, no thanks, I would pass.

The resort, however, was very nice. Besides, I was given seriously good treatment—way above my pay grade kind of treatment. The editor had told the owner of the property, and the property owner had called their staff, to take 'good care' of me.

I was given a suite that looked out into a conifer thicket through which a chilled stream of melting snow flowed.

They even assigned me a valet, which threw me completely off guard. What was I going to do with a valet?

'I'll be right outside, sir,' the middle-aged, elfin valet smiled and offered. 'Anything you need, I'll be right outside. I've been told you're Sahib's friend, and I was given the job to serve you because that's what I do whenever Sahib, Memsahib or their family comes over.'

'Thank you so much, but you don't really need to be waiting on me all the time,' I told the man.

I was no sahib—brown or otherwise. I didn't have a memsahib with me. And I'd be way too conscious to relax if I knew I had a durwan waiting outside my door within earshot. What if he heard me making the inane cartoon voices I often and uncontrollably do?

'All I need is a very large flask of hot water and some teabags. Maybe a packet of Marie biscuits if you have one. I'll just sit and read for a bit and write. If I want anything more, I'll call the front desk.'

'And here . . . you take some and give some to the driver and ask him to eat well,' I added, handing him a few notes.

Late afternoon brought with it a round of mild showers. The tin roof of the wood hotel rang out in a symphony of trinkets. Soon after, just like the snowmelt stream, clouds and cold air flowed down the hillside through the pine thickets. I held out my hands to the drops of water, relishing the little shivers it sent up my arm and down my body. I fell back in bed with a sigh of cosy leisure, dreaming lines and headlines instead of actually writing.

The valet and I chatted for several hours in the evening. He told me about his life as a cook and valet for the past twenty-plus years.

'I left home at twelve, sir,' the man narrated. 'We only had a little bit of land, and my father was a smart man. He said, Son—go to Bombay. The way this place is going, it'll kill both your dreams and you. And so I went to Bombay and became a dishwasher at a restaurant where my father's cousin-brother worked. After a while, I began assisting the cooks, and from there, I became a cook. Around twenty, I was married off to a girl from a nearby village. But I left my young bride and went away. Delhi, Bombay, Kolkata—I worked in many places.

'In Delhi, I met our Sahib—the owner, you know? So I came to Gulmarg with him and started working here.'

I left the following day. The beauty, quietude and luxury of the Gulmarg resort weren't germane to my writing. The opulence was distracting and unsettling. In fact, to date, I write best in spare rooms with sparer desks and nothing but a blank wall for a view.

The driver greeted me with a big smile. He probably hadn't expected an allowance of the size I'd given. He'd been quiet from Srinagar to Gulmarg. But now on the return journey, he became very chatty. That's also when things turned sour.

'So you're a journalist too?' he asked, when we left Gulmarg for Srinagar early in the morning.

'Yes. I am.'

'So, what's it like? Reporting on wars, conflicts . . . you must have a lot of exciting stories, no?' he began. Though his tone was warmly inquisitive, I knew he was looking to hold forth on his own views, rather than to hear mine.

'Not that exciting, really. At least not most of the time. A reporter's job is to capture the truth from every angle and not really go excitement hunting. That's what movies are for.'

He glanced at me briefly. 'But whose truth? I mean, everyone says they're fighting for the right cause. The Americans say they're bringing democracy. We Muslims say we're fighting for our rights.'

'That's the challenge,' I admitted. 'To sift through the narratives, to find the human element. Truth isn't just about picking sides.'

The driver seemed to ponder this for a moment. 'But in Afghanistan, Iraq, even in Kashmir, where's the question of choosing sides? It's just the Americans and their allies being aggressors on Muslim lands, no?'

'It's complex,' I replied. 'Yes, there's a clear aspect of aggression in what happened in Afghanistan. But there are also layers of political, economic and regional dynamics at play.'

He nodded slowly, then asked, 'What about us Muslims? Do you think we're portrayed fairly by the media? We fight for our homes and families, and we're called terrorists.'

'Of course, there's a lot of misrepresentation,' I answered honestly. 'Big capitalist media narratives are often skewed.'

'So, you agree that the West, especially America and Israel, has an agenda against us Muslims?' His tone was now edging towards confrontational.

'Of course, America has an obvious anti-Muslim war going on,' I acknowledged. 'But I also believe it's not purely black and white. There are multiple factors and players involved in these global issues.'

He was silent again, absorbing my words. His head was in a slightly forward tilt like a bull looking to butt someone.

'But you see, from our perspective, it's just black and white. When you have fighter planes overhead and foreign soldiers on your streets, it's hard to see the grey areas.'

'I understand that,' I said, feeling the weight of his words. 'Being on the ground, experiencing the immediate effects of these policies, it does change the perspective. The fear and anger are real and justified.'

He glanced at me again, this time with a hint of surprise. 'You think our anger is justified?'

'Anger at having your country invaded, your homes destroyed? Absolutely,' I replied. 'It's a natural human reaction. What's important is how that anger is channelled.'

'But what about reporters like you? Do you ever feel guilty? Do you ever think about the lives you've ruined with your anti-Muslim reporting?'

'Have you read anything I've written?' I asked. The skin behind my ears was warmer than before.

'Not yours specifically . . .'

'So, on what basis what did you accuse me of being anti-Muslim?'

'Not you specifically. But you're Indian, aren't you?'

The conversation had taken a turn into dangerous territory. It wasn't just curiosity that turned to debate. He was acting out some anti-Indian agenda with an Indian at hand. And he had the upper hand in the middle of nowhere.

I tried to tone the conversation down. 'Listen, I might be Indian. And a Hindu at that. But that doesn't automatically make me anti-Muslim. All I am saying is when we analyse a war or an ongoing conflict, we must look at many layers of it.'

'No. There is no nuance,' he rejected my peace offering. 'It simply comes down to Muslims versus the West and its puppets like India. Muslims versus everyone! Look at the history! Everywhere, Muslims are under attack. In Palestine, Kashmir, Iraq, Afghanistan and even Bombay, where you're from! It's like the whole world has turned against us!'

'I agree that Muslims are facing persecution in many parts of the world,' I tried the restrained approach one more time. 'Yes, these are serious issues that need addressing. But painting it as a global conspiracy against Muslims oversimplifies and ignores the complex geopolitical factors at play.'

He scoffed. 'Geopolitical factors? It's plain hatred. That's what it is. They hate us; they fear our rise.'

'This is plain uninformed.' I had lost my patience. 'Pakistan is a Muslim country whose name you left out—one of the biggest recipients of American money and arms. Saudi Arabia, the leader of the Muslim world, is America's biggest ally. You ignored that. Laos, Vietnam, Cambodia and Korea are all countries ravaged by the Americans and not one of them Muslim.

'And it's not like Muslims haven't killed each other! The Muslim world since time immemorial has seen sectarian violence, authoritarian regimes and wars that have killed an equal, if not more, Muslims than non-Muslims. Pakistan killed several million Bengali–Muslims just a couple of decades back. Don't these acts contribute to the suffering of Muslims?

'In Kashmir itself, Sunnis have corralled Shias into ghettos, haven't they?'

'That's what they want you to believe,' he retorted. 'To look at our faults and ignore our oppression. It's their way of justifying their actions. As for Shias—it's . . . how should I say it . . . they're primitive. Unclean, you know what I mean?'

I didn't want to know what he meant.

But he continued explaining. 'See . . . man to man . . . let me tell you what Shias do. They have sex with their wife and then don't shower. The filth builds up, you know? Like cattle. Like sheep who live in their own filth. And try as you might, you won't be able to teach them to be better! So they're best left to their own quarters, no?'

For lack of a better word, I was mesmerized. Mesmerized and dumbstruck at his effortless transition from being the victim to justifying locking up a community in ghettoes. The transition from holding forth on the unity of Muslims under global aggression to calling a sect of his own religion dirty cattle.

I was quiet. I had no words to respond to this man who had, just some hours back, smiled grandly and thanked me for the food I'd bought him and was now picking a needless war of words.

'You know what you should do?' he said with a strange 'Gotcha' grin on his gaunt, handsome face. 'You should come with me to Geelani Saab. He will answer all your geopolitical questions. I'm not that educated, but he will give you all the right answers.'

'Geelani? Who Geelani?' I asked, almost knowing what he was talking about.

'Syed Ali Shah Geelani, of course!' he replied, waving his left hand very matter-of-factly.

'And why would someone as big as Geelani meet me?' My frustration had a hint of incredulous laughter at this driver's bombast.

'Of course, he'll meet you if you come with me! I was his bodyguard!'

Oh—my—effing—god.

Who was I arguing with? Why, oh, why was I arguing in the first place? Of all the cabs in Srinagar that damned editor could find me, he got me someone who worked with the biggest name in Kashmir's militancy!

The man continued, saying something about his time with Geelani and how he'd served very loyally and gotten close to him. Something something, 'but then I needed work, so I started driving' . . . something something 'activism is my real calling, this is just to survive . . .'.

I wasn't listening any more. I was on the verge of mumbling prayers to the Almighty, whose existence I'd denied all my life. But on the off chance that he/she/it/they/whoever exists, I was hoping not to find myself hovering in the beautiful Kashmiri mist of the hills and pines, looking down at my mangled body on the rocks at the bottom of the ravine that ran past the road our car was on.

'*Lunch karenge na? Sir . . . lunch?*' he poked my right hand to get my attention after I don't know how many minutes.

'Haan-yes,' the morbid thoughts had settled around my throat in a web of phlegm, and I took a good three attempts to say a muted 'Yes, I'll eat lunch. But I also want to get to Srinagar before sundown. I mean . . . I was told it's not safe to be out after dark.'

'Oh no, no . . . don't worry one bit,' he said, genial and gay as the early morning version. 'Nobody will harm you while you're with me. *Aap hamare mehmaan hai!* [you're my guest of honour] Should anyone dare to even look at you wrong, my body will be between them and you!'

'Don't worry one bit,' he added after a pause. 'Now tell me what you really feel like eating.'

'Rista,' I said. My voice was barely a squeak compared to the booming baritone heard during the fervent polemics I had indulged in just a while back.

'What?' he leaned towards me, trying to hear me better.

'Rista . . .' I repeated. 'Rista and rice.'

If I was going to find myself at the bottom of a rocky ditch, I wanted to find myself with a full belly of my favourite Kashmiri food.

As is evident, I wasn't 'ditched' by the zealot warrior driver. He drove me back safe and sound. And for the record, the rista at the small little eatery he took me to was very good.

So, as I was saying, there was always this undercurrent of anger among Kashmiris, not just those who were active participants in the Indo–Pak conflict, but even among the young men my age I called comrades. A simmering rage just beneath the surface. Not the explosive anger that's always splashed on headlines—but a slow burning, deeply-seated anger laced with frustration.

The anger wasn't always directed at the political and military strife that plagues the region but also at what they perceive as the encroachment of outside influences, diluting what they see as a pristine and, in their minds, indubitably superior way of life.

'I'd go live in Srinagar in a heartbeat, comrade . . . the food is just . . . man!' I remember telling a former comrade called Arshad at a convention of communist youth activists in Bangalore.

It was the last event before I parted ways with my Party over political–ideological differences about the party line. The automatic translator machines weren't working that year, and I had been made the human equivalent of them. My job was to translate Punjabi, Nepali, Marathi, Bangla and four odd variants of Hindi aloud. Not that I spoke these tongues, but I understood them well enough to translate what was being said into English for my South Indian comrades.

Of course, this unseated me from representing my home state of Maharashtra and endeared me to a lot of the other state committees. In exchange for lending their thundering disagreements and observant submissions my voice, chai and cigarettes were given as friendly offerings. The conversations with them became much more casual than the normative formal tone in gatherings like these.

The team from Jammu and Kashmir were a particularly blustering lot that year. They lashed out at the Delhi leadership in harsh words. While hitting back at leadership inside a Communist Party (at least the democratic ones in this part of the world) isn't out of the ordinary, the tone of the Kashmiris that year was particularly caustic.

'*Hum aapke ghulam nahi hey!* [We aren't your slaves!]' Arshad, the leader of the Kashmiri contingent, had thundered from the stage. 'We fight a battle both as Communists and as Kashmiris. It's far more difficult than any of you can imagine. Instead of understanding that, you come to lecture us about how to work in our terrain? Unacceptable!'

Needless to say, the speech hadn't gone down well. The then president, Tapas-da, a honcho of the Bengal lobby, said so in as many words and warned the Kashmiris against using such unacceptable words.

I was entrusted to bring the two parties back to the table. I did that quite literally.

'Come, comrade, sit down and eat . . . you've been standing for far too long,' I told Tapas-da. And then got Arshad to join us.

There is nothing like shared food to bring warring parties together. And there, too, it worked.

We marvelled at the lovely lunch our Kannadiga comrades had put together. I spoke of how the best meal I've ever eaten at a Party conference was in Halishahar in Bengal.

'The worst is what you guys keep feeding me whenever I come to your state,' Tapas-da jibed me. True. The cash-strapped coffers we Marathis worked with ensured that we hired only the cheapest caterer. These caterers just added huge amounts of spices to make up for the pathetic vegetables they used. And yes, we always had vegetarian menus.

That's when Arshad proffered, 'If you really want good food, come to Kashmir. Tapas-da, let's call SSR (as I was often called) for the state conference as an observer. What say?'

That's when I'd said, 'I'd go live in Srinagar in a heartbeat, comrade . . . the food is just . . . man!'

'You know,' I held forth, showing off my culinary knowledge, ' . . . I love how you guys don't overload your meats with excessive onion–garlic paste and instead play on subtle flavours.'

'Yes, yes!' Both the Bengali and Kashmiri, who were at loggerheads an hour ago, agreed vehemently.

Buoyed by my success, I added, 'It's a hill thing, I think. The farther away you get from Delhi, Bombay, Kolkata, the more soulful the food gets. You can taste the vegetables and meats and not just the overload of spices. Mizoram and Nagaland, for example. No, Tapas-da?'

Tapas-da had spent a considerable time in the Northeast and, between gulping down the last spoonfuls of the wheat and jaggery Godi Kadi Payasa, he nodded and hemmed.

'Oh, come on,' Arshad clicked his tongue in disapproval, getting up to deposit his plate. 'Are you *really* comparing our fine Kashmiri cooking to tribal cooking?'

I'm not holding Arshad's statement to some politically correct standard. Political correctness of the flaky neoliberal variety be damned. Friends can, and should, talk the way they do without walking on eggshells. But what he said had the kernel of ethnic supremacist thought that I've always seen when talking to Kashmiri men. I've seen the anger in them when anyone, even lightly, suggests they aren't unique in every aspect of their history and culture.

The complexity of this sentiment—this exceptionalism—is hard to articulate. In fact, much of Kashmiri anger is not just anger at outsiders or an occupying State, but anger directed at themselves for not being able to defend their realm against the 'crass' influence of others. Their anger is inseparably mixed with a sense of loss—loss of autonomy, loss of cultural purity and perhaps even a loss of letting the world know how better they are than everyone else. It's an anger mixed with melancholy, a yearning for a past that can never be fully reclaimed because a lot of it never existed.

'When it comes to the mess in Kashmir, New Delhi loves to blame Islamabad and Islamabad, New Delhi,' Aslam Majid had said during an interview when I was asking him about the shifting loyalties of a new bunch of Kashmiri secessionists.

A former Karachi range chief of Pakistan's Inter-Services Intelligence, he had moved to the US post-retirement. He chose the name Major Aslam Majid to hide his identity and has been a source for several stories I've reported.

'Kashmir is messy because of Kashmiris themselves! They are by nature irreverent and immensely difficult to train and discipline. I know this because I did that training for many years. They just don't want to follow orders. Breaking rules is the only rule they have! Troublemakers all. In fact, had we been in control of the Kashmiris in India as much as New

Delhi says we are, Indian Kashmir would've been *azaad* (free) by now.'

'Say more, please,' I'd asked. 'You have been training and arming Kashmiris for decades now. There's no denying that, is there? They're literally doing your job in the Valley. Then why do you say they're troublemakers for you?'

'Listen, Sid, I'm not in service any more, and I don't need to deny anything. I'm making a deeper point. And the point is, Kashmiris on both sides—your Indian and our Pakistani side—are, in their hearts, unwilling to accept any other race ruling over them. In the camps, you know, they always picked fights with the Pakistani boys over this or that trivial matter. We are trained officers. We follow certain protocols of behaviour, just like Indian officers do. Drills in the morning, showers and meals at fixed times, arms training and political lessons afterwards. Early lights out and so on.

'Getting civilians to do these things is far from easy. If the civilians are Kashmiri, you've had it!'

'The story you're reporting—the one about these Ansar Ghazwat (ul Hind) boys . . .' Majid referred to my investigation about Burhan Wani and Zakir Musa, who had shifted from Lashkar-e Taiba to Al-Qaeda to the Islamic State. 'They were a pain in the neck for everyone! These boys and their lot—I mean their generation altogether—were unwilling to listen to anything we tried teaching them beyond arms training. They argued with the trainers during the political classes. They questioned the maulvis who conducted religious lessons. They constantly complained about the food that was made at the camps. Every volleyball session in the evening would become a Pakistan vs Kashmir match. They'd even get into fights with the Pakistani boys over Shahrukh Khan versus Salman Khan!'

I don't get many opportunities to laugh when reporting. But that day, talking to Majid, I was laughing hard and apologizing harder for laughing. But what was I to do? Majid sounded more like a kindergarten teacher going mad trying to herd a bunch of naughty kids, and not a uniformed officer who had headed a vital operation.

Aslam was right. At least about Burhan Wani, Zakir Musa and their gang of young Kashmiri lads who had formed the short-lived upstart of a group called the Ansar Ghazwat-ul Hind.

This particular bunch were relentless in their pursuit of rebellion. Their political rhetoric notwithstanding, it was, in its essence, youthful, anti-old generation, rebellion for rebellion's sake.

They first rebelled against Lashkar-e Taiba, the very group they'd joined. When in the Lashkar, they had called the competing Kashmiri terror group, Jaish-e Mohammed names. Then they fell out with the Lashkar for being too subservient to Pakistan and finally went on to declare Pakistan to be a sham of an Islamic country.

'We fight for Kashmir's freedom and sharia,' they had declared, announcing their new outfit, Ansar Ghazwat-ul Hind. 'We don't fight for Pakistan and their corrupt elites. Even before the Indians, their stooges in the Hurriyat Conference need to be hanged in public.'

In a very short span of time, they managed to piss off everyone in Kashmir on both sides of the conflict. After Burhan was hunted down, Zakir reached out to the Afghan Taliban for support. They didn't respond with anything concrete. He then travelled to Mosul and pledged his loyalty to the Islamic State.

Given his nature, Zakir would likely have found resonance in the disarrayed, non-hierarchical structure of the Islamic State. But he was killed by the Indian forces soon after his return for that to materialize.

Rumours persist to date that the clinical precision with which Wani, Musa and their entire gang were bumped off happened because the Indians, Pakistanis and legacy Kashmir terror outfits collaborated.

***

'The problem, sir, is that Kashmiri men are useless, and the Pakistani ones are rascals,' Abru had said, sitting in my hotel room in Srinagar. Abru was one among the very few active women militants I've met. And by far the prettiest and toughest one of those few.

She had joined the Dukhataran-e Milat—Kashmir's first and only women-run militant group—and was taken under the wing by the group's founder, Asiya Andrabi.

Asiya Andrabi had brought to the fore a novel mix of feminism and fundamentalism that had no parallel in Kashmiri history. She publicly hit back at the senior leaders of the pro-Pakistan Hurriyat Conference and shamed them for having made it a boy's club. In time, she'd outshine her husband, legendary separatist leader and founder of the Hizbul Mujahideen, Qasim Faktoo.

Little wonder that Andrabi's protégé spoke and carried herself the way she did.

Dressed in all black, she walked in with her stilettos clicking on the floor and sat down on a chair like a queen, crossing her legs and pushing her shoulders back—the glare of the window darkening her face and highlighting her svelte contour in the camera.

She'd been a gunrunner and courier for the Lashkar-e Taiba when she struck a deal with the Indian forces.

'My son (a toddler) had fallen down from the first floor of an under-construction building when playing with his friends. He needed surgery and oxygen. It was COVID time, so oxygen cylinders were in short supply. My husband and I had to compromise.

Else, it was always sharia or death for me.'

'There is nothing more difficult than being a Kashmiri woman,' Abru said, speaking of her far less-than-ordinary life. 'Sure, my husband was a card-carrying militant. But he was always in hiding. Looking after my in-laws and our son was all my responsibility. And I had my political work, too.

'To avoid getting frisked and caught, I and a few other girls were entrusted with carrying the grenades and bullets for the men. She [Asiya Andrabi] trusted very few people. And I was one of them. But unlike my husband, I couldn't stay in hiding.'

'Are you calling the Pakistanis names now that you have moved away from them and are living under the protection of the Indians?' I countered.

'No,' she said. Sharp and curt, she held my gaze for several moments before continuing.

'I'm speaking both as an activist and as a woman. From knowing both the politics and the men. On both sides.

'If we Kashmiris could've fought our fight for independence without the Pakistanis, we would have. Not all of us want to join Pakistan. What can they give us? Nothing! But they have their interests, and we have ours. And the interests converged. Islam and freedom in Kashmir. That's what we wanted. All we wanted was to walk the path of Allah and nothing else. Not look here, not look there, just the straight path of Allah.'

'And as a woman?' I asked.

'Huh . . . the less said, the better,' she smirked and waved her hand to dismiss the men on both sides of the border. 'These men just want to prey on us.'

'I have this cousin, you know,' she narrated a story from her early days of joining the Dukhtaran-e Millat. 'Late teens or early twenties. One day, at their place, I told her to come for the moral science classes we Dukhtaran organized for young women. She said, "I'll come if you get me some brown sugar".

'I slapped that shameless girl across the face. But unmoving, she said, "Fine. I'll need at least a beer if you don't have sugar".

'I was shocked, of course. But then I asked around and found out that she had been visiting the CRPF camps nearby. After sundown.'

'After sundown,' Abru repeated—chewing each syllable slowly. 'Sure, I and some other women beat her black and blue and told our aunt to keep her locked in the house until she repented. But I knew how the men had gotten to her.'

'But how's that the men's fault?'

'Whose fault is it then? They weren't giving her beer or whatever because of the kindness of their hearts, were they?' she replied. 'They took something in exchange. I don't need to spell out what that thing was, do I?' she asked, and held her pause with a slight smile and an arching eyebrow.

Her posture, her poise, her restrained yet powerful words—Abru knew she had power over men. The diffused light glinting on the subtle sequins on her black dress and the transparent heel of her stiletto, she'd been challenging me all through the interview. Challenging both my political understanding and my gender identity by constantly trying to steer the conversation to 'men do this and men do that'.

I was tempted to hit back at her at that moment by asking: 'So now you're castigating a fellow Kashmiri woman for her choice of a drug over yours. Who's to say substance intoxicants have done worse to Kashmiris than zealotry?'

But I bit my tongue. This interview had been very hard to come by. I wasn't going to ruin it by letting her provoke me. Besides, I was well acquainted with the usefulness of awkward silences in interviews. So I just sat there, staring at her the way she had been staring at me.

'Come here,' she beckoned me closer and pulled a phone out of her bosom. 'Listen to this,' she said, unlocking her phone—her long, painted fingers clicking on the glass screen like her heels had on the floor.

She played a voice file. It was the voice of her handler speaking from across the border—a Lashkar operative who figures at the top of India's most wanted list.

In the voice recording, after the initial pleasantries, Abru says, 'I really need money for the boy's treatment. You said you'd send me the money fifteen days back, and still, nothing's come by.'

'You know how things are now,' the man said. 'Sending notes has become very difficult. Nearly impossible. You know that, don't you?'

'Yes . . . but what am I to do? Watch my boy die?'

'That's unfair now. Your boy is like my boy, too. I never considered you or your boy different from me and my family.'

'What's the solution? I really need to keep buying his medicines and oxygen.'

'Hmm . . .' the man hemmed and pondered for a bit. 'Let's do this . . . I'll give you a number. His name is ___. Call him, and he'll hand you a packet.'

'Okay. How much will he give? Given the old dues, I need at least . . .'

'It's not money', the man cut Abru off. 'It's sugar. Take the package and sell it. Whatever you make, use it. You don't need to give me any account.'

'Thank you . . . thank you so much . . .'

'Oh . . . don't thank me as if I'm some stranger. You and your boy are mine, no?'

'By the way, how come you never call me on video any more?' the handler continued.

'I'm at home mostly. Or the hospital. Video is difficult.'

'Are you at home now?'

'Yes.'

'And alone?'

'Come on, switch on the video then. Let me see your face at least.'

Though I didn't see the video, the tape confirmed that Abru had switched the video on.

'How beautiful you look!' the man continues. 'You must call me more often on video.'

'I'll try. I must go now.'

'Wait . . . don't cut the call just yet. And . . . lower the camera a bit.'

Click!

Abru stopped the tape and looked directly at me. I had no reason to, but for a fraction of a second, I felt guilty for the words of a man I had nothing in common with.

I walked back to my chair opposite Abru's and sat down. Sanjeev, my cameraman, repositioned the camera to its original frame on the tripod.

'It took me time to realize,' she spoke as much to herself as to me. 'These rascals . . . they don't give a damn about Kashmir or its freedom. All they want is the land and its women.'

* * *

'*Arey, sir, wo saarey bigdey huye log hai* [They're all just louts],' Bilal from Bandipora said in an interview.

Bilal had crossed the border as a fourteen-year-old and joined the training camps of the Lashkar-e Taiba. After his training, he returned to the Indian side and became a gun-toting militant. It was a very short-lived career.

As I'd shown in my investigation on rape and jihad in Kashmir, militants used Kashmiri homes not only for shelter and food but also to satiate other kinds of carnal hungers and thirsts. Sure, some women gave themselves willingly, seeing it as their womanly duty as Kashmiri Muslims doing their bit for the holy cause of the holy fighters. Some, I suspect, did it simply because young women like macho men. But most, I knew through my investigation, needed a prodding with the militants' guns before they agreed.

Bilal messed the macho man part up.

Instead of doing what his jihadi comrades did, Bilal fell in love with a girl whose house they'd sheltered in. Instead of raping her, he gave her his heart, and the two started dreaming of a life together. He even sought her father's blessings to have her hand in marriage.

'We were almost the same age, you know,' Bilal reminisced, sitting in his small living room in Baramulla. Evening was setting in, and the chill from the snow melt in the Chenab was flowing into the house along with the twilight. Bilal, his wife, Bushra, and I were sipping tea and eating Parle-G biscuits while their two kids were bantering over something in the next room.

'We just fell in love from the word go. I knew it would distract me from my duties as a fighter, but I just couldn't help it. She looked like the prettiest girl I'd ever met or would meet in my life. I couldn't help falling in love.

Now that I think back, I know she wasn't exceptionally beautiful or something. I mean, Bushra is far prettier.'

Bushra slapped his hand, grinning and blushing.

'I've told you never to say that,' Bushra pouted at her husband. 'She's my sister. Just like the one they took away from me.'

When Bushra was twelve, her older sister was shot dead.

I'd met Bushra the last time I was in Kashmir, reporting for the Rape and Silence story. Standing in the twilight in an apple orchard, dead in winter, she'd told me how she'd lost her arm.

The sheltering terrorists at their place had started with teasing and flirting with Bushra's older sister. Bushra was twelve, and her sister was a few years older. The teasing and flirting had soon turned to molesting. Their father requested the men to stop doing what they were doing—told them to live their lives like the good Muslims they were. But he was too weak to convince a bunch of ruffians to be better.

'Frustrated with this repeated misbehaviour, she [Bushra's sister] lost it one day and snatched a militant's rifle and shouted at them. "I'll kill you rascals if you ever touch me again." Of course, she could do nothing of the sort. She didn't even know how to hold a machine gun properly, let alone fire it.

'So they snatched it back from her, beat her black and blue and then pumped twelve bullets into her in front of the whole village. In panic, I tried to shield her with my arm, and some bullets smashed through it. That's why I have only one arm.'

Bilal's commander, a more hardened Pakistani militant commander who prided himself on his skills with the axe—he preferred chopping people dead over shooting—didn't take kindly to Bilal's budding love story. He had the girl shot dead in front of Bilal and her parents' eyes to remind his troops that the weakness called love had no place in their mission.

'When she was killed, I realized I didn't want any of this so-called freedom-fighting nonsense. What kind of freedom was it that wouldn't let me love the girl I wanted? That day, I made up my mind that I'd surrender and give up my arms.

'But, sir, honestly, the killing wasn't the first time I wanted to stop working with the Pakistanis.

'Back in the camps, the Pakistanis were very different from us. We had gone to fight a holy war—for freedom, for faith and for our land. We had ideals. But their lot was just a bunch of antisocials—men who the Pakistanis themselves don't want roaming free in their society. Perverts. Crass, thuggish rascals who wouldn't spare their own mothers and sisters, let alone daughters and wives of other people. But once you cross the line, it's not easy to return. So I stuck with them till this happened.

'All this terrorism is just business, sir. Brutal business and nothing more. These militant groups are ruthless companies that mint money in the name of jihad—a company of violent men. Their business cost Bushra her sister and her arm, me my youth and my first love.'

The evening had darkened enough for the lights to be switched on. But we didn't feel like getting up and doing it. The demure white band of an LED street light filtered in from the newly installed four-foot bridge on the snow melt torrents of the Chenab. That was enough for us. Any more light and the glistening in Bilal and Bushra's eyes would've shown. Perhaps the lump in my throat as well.

All four of us just sat there listening to the rush of the water. Bushra, Bilal, I and the wispy teenage girl in the photo on the wall behind me—the one who wouldn't age past the time she met a young boy called Bilal and fell in love with him.

***

For a year since February 2022, I lived under the heavy shadow of guns. One set of guns that wanted to end me and my work. And another that was ostensibly going to save me from that dire end.

Buying vegetables, going to the dhobi, getting dinner or a drink and even getting a book delivered had to pass the scrutiny of a gun-carrying man. Whatever poor excuse of a social life I had went out the window, and my neighbours looked at me with strange, fearful eyes.

The threats continued on and off. If a friend called and asked where I was, I wouldn't tell them. Even though the pandemic had ended, cold glass screens, framed with buttons with icons for webcam and microphone, were the only place I could see them.

'I think I know what angered them [the ones threatening to kill me] about this particular report,' I remember telling Sanjeev after we'd wrapped up our Kashmir trip and were having a drink in his Delhi home. No, scratch that. It had been more than a drink or two, and I was a bit tipsy. And with the safety of being around people I trusted, I spoke more than I usually would have.

'You know, my report hit them [the militants] where it hurt them the most. Their manliness and their piety—both in one go. It's always that way. No matter the side. Most of these buggers are, in essence, just pathetic creatures doing their pathetic things with a gun on their shoulder and God's name on their lips. They are so manly, they can't woo a girl normally. They need a gun, a State and a religious diktat to get laid. You want to get laid? Get on an app and try it out, man!'

Sure, these were words of anger. But they weren't devoid of truth.

The most common thing the angry ones had written to me was that I had besmirched the name of their holy warriors—the army of the pure. Even though I hadn't mentioned religion in my report, the trolls and thugs wrote in, saying I'd besmirched their faith.

Really? Was it I who had besmirched their faith and their cause? Hadn't they done that when they raped and assaulted women and took God's name in vain, using Him as the shield for their own shame? The truth is out there in the text and on record in video where full-grown women, whose bodies and souls they broke, are sobbing like little girls and saying: 'This is *jihaal,* not *jihad*!'

The Kashmir report led the Hindu Right Wing to forget all my past sins against their partisan agendas and their talking heads went from calling me an anti-national hack to hailing me as a 'real' journalist. Of course, alongside that they coopted my reporting to suit their Islamophobia.

The other side—the liberals who claim to support women and their rights—were no better at caring for the truth. Truth notwithstanding, star opinionators of this camp had turned their backs on the issue because it didn't suit their partisan agenda on Kashmir.

An old comrade and a card-carrying feminist texted me on seeing my Kashmir report going viral on Indian right-wing Twitter. Someone with who, in our young days, I have shouted war cries against the State, rammed barricades and taken baton charges.

'But what about the Kashmiri Muslim women?' she asked. 'What about their side of the story?'

'P . . . have you even read the piece?' I asked, bewildered. 'Every single one of the victims I've interviewed is a Kashmiri Muslim woman!'

The last I heard of my official threats case is it was gathering dust in the Pune Police Cyber Cell. Meanwhile, every story I report unleashes a flurry of strongly worded emails, texts and posts. From behind fake handles and the depths of VPN tunnels, the many companies of violent men valiantly and regularly hit 'Send' on some permutation–combination of 'Don't write that!' and 'Don't go there!'

Bless their keyboard-warrior hearts, but they do their work, I do mine.

My job description doesn't include a 'don't investigate bad guys' clause. Quite the opposite, in fact. So, jihadists today, Maoists tomorrow, the State the day after and whomever my reporting offends next—the threats will continue. And my journalism? I think that will too.

Acknowledgements

The lion's share of gratitude for this book belongs to those named and unnamed who trusted me enough to let me into their lives and tell their stories. Every one of them.

A big thank you to Diya Kohli who, in the depths of the public Covid-19 lockdown and a bout of crushing personal doubt and depression, read me the riot act and told me to stop daydreaming about this book and write it.

Thank you, Milee Ashwarya and her team at Penguin Random House India, for letting me write this book with such freedom, despite being a first-time writer with a rather strange book to offer. Thank you also for allowing the many changes in the shape of this book, and the many turns it has taken from the pitch to this print.

To John B. Judis who, despite his stature and workload, basis nothing but an email from a random struggling journalism student, took time to read the text that became the basis of five years of my work as an investigative reporter.

To Dr Ali Riaz, whose works I read, whose phone I called, whose email I bombarded with questions. Questions that he always took the time to answer and thereby taught me things I didn't know, un-taught me myths that I'd set in my head about all things identity and extremism.

To Shannon Tiezzi and her team at thediplomat.com who have, for the longest time, let their magazine be home to my reporting, starting with the very first in 2016. Thank you also for never once censoring me and my reporting to suit some political agenda.

And to the Pulitzer Center on Crisis Reporting, whose generosity helped me get started on the very first leg of my investigations which this book opens with.